Revanche & Revision

Revanche & Revision

THE LIGUE DES PATRIOTES AND THE ORIGINS
OF THE RADICAL RIGHT IN FRANCE, 1882–1900

BY

Peter M. Rutkoff

OHIO UNIVERSITY PRESS / ATHENS   LONDON

Library of Congress Cataloging in Publication Data

Rutkoff, Peter M   1942-
Revanche and revision.

Bibliography: p. 169
Includes index.
1.   Ligue des patriotes—History.   2.   Déroulède,
Paul, 1846-1914.   3.   Fascism—France—History.
4.   France—Politics and government—1870-1940.
I.   Title.
HS2385.L533R87   324.24402   80-39575
ISBN 0-8214-0589-6

In memory of
Harry Rutkoff, 1910–1949

Acknowledgments

This work, a study of the origins of counterrevolution, was begun just after the revolution of 1968 in Paris. Nothing could have been farther from those events than a history of Paul Déroulède and the Ligue des Patriotes. Twelve years later it seems that the opposite is true. Yet both the subject and the circumstance of my original encounter with it are part of the larger reality that constitutes the French historical experience.

Any journey of historical reconstruction requires, of course, considerable assistance. My guides were as numerous as they were generous and included Raoul Girardet of the Foundation nationale des sciences politiques, who first staked Déroulède's claim and then graciously permitted me to take it over; Antoine Prost, now of the CNRS, then the Fulbright advisor, who first pointed the way; Mme. Helen Tulard, *archiviste*, and M. H. Coutarel, *conservateur*, both of the Archives de la Préfecture de la Police; and most profoundly Yves and Ghislaine Barbet-Massin, who not only permitted access to the Déroulède papers but also welcomed my wife and me into their home and family with extraordinary warmth and charm.

In this country there have likewise been those who have supported, criticized, and helped in the efforts to bring Déroulède and the Ligue des Patriotes to life. Alain Silvera of Bryn Mawr College and Alfred Rieber of the University of Pennsylvania supervised, encouraged, and critiqued my work from its inception. Subsequently Arno Mayer at Princeton University and Alexander Riasanovsky at the University of Pennsylvania sufficiently encouraged my written work on the one hand and my teaching on the other to persuade me to continue in both endeavors. Grants from Kenyon College in 1972, 1974, and 1976 made that work actually possible, as did the typing efforts of Patricia Bosch, Lee Wilson, and Jean Cavanaugh. Valuable editorial assistance was provided by Judy Sacks, and Matilda and Albert Komishane. Helen Gawthrop of Ohio University Press has been remarkable for her patience, kindness and help. Two colleagues at Kenyon, Will Scott and Reed Browning, not only encouraged me as they read the manuscript but helped me explore dimensions of historical reality which had been hitherto unknown to me. Finally, Robert Carlisle of St. Lawrence University, who first taught me about things French, has remained in my mind as the teacher to whom I owe a special debt of gratitude.

Worlds of teaching and personal responsibility separate the beginning of this project from its end. They have enriched, not hindered, it. The evolution from thesis to manuscript, manuscript to book, was made possible by the sustenance of my students and family. They, along with teachers, friends, and colleagues, have my deepest appreciation. Jane Rutkoff, my wife, and our children, Joshua and Rebekah, deserve yet more than words can well convey.

June 1980

Contents

Introduction

Many historians have commented on the transference of nationalism from Left to Right in the late nineteenth century. Although they have observed this *glissement* as having taken place somewhere between the generations of Gambetta and Maurras, they differ in accounting for the when and how. On the other hand they all agree that one of the key figures in this transformation was the poet-patriot Paul Déroulède.[1] Often portrayed in the history of his times as a semicomical figure of the second rank, Déroulède is nevertheless identified by his contemporaries as the personification of *revanche*, the most powerful ingredient in the rising nationalism of the Right. Similarly, historians who have emphasized the changed character of the nationalist revival after 1905 have also pointed to Paul Déroulède as an important link between the Left republicanism of 1870 and the nationalist upsurge some thirty-five years later.[2]

As an ideologue Déroulède has never enjoyed the reputation of either his friend Maurice Barrès or his rival Edouard Drumont. Yet he possessed one advantage that both these men lacked—a political organization—the Ligue des Patriotes. In considering the shift of nationalism from Left to Right and in pinpointing Déroulède as the major figure in this transformation, historians have concentrated on the content of the nationalist program at the expense of the activity and organization of the nationalist party.[3] The Ligue des Patriotes, however, was a political organization whose unprecedented actions were ultimately as important as its ideology.[4]

Founded in 1882 and drawing its strength from provincial as well as urban France, the Ligue supported Boulanger in 1888-1889 then disbanded in 1891 only to reappear in 1897 in response to the Dreyfus Affair. Between 1897 and

1

1900 the Ligue stood in the forefront of anti-Dreyfusard and nationalist forces crowding the meeting halls and streets of Paris, where it joined the familiar nationalist cry of revision with a new appeal for violent direct action. Although not alone in making this appeal, the Ligue was the most prominent and influential group on the Right. Evidence of Déroulède and the Ligue's deep imprint on French society comes from the Dreyfus Affair, surely the episode in the history of the Third Republic which most divided Frenchmen. During the affair Paul Déroulède and the Ligue des Patriotes not only acted to polarize French society but also wrenched nationalism out of its left-wing context and embedded it firmly on the Right.

As an organization utilizing the tactic of street politics, the Ligue des Patriotes reflected the style of its founder-president. Just as Déroulède traveled the path from Left to Right, the Ligue's tactics followed a parallel route. In 1888-1889, numbering a hundred thousand members, the Ligue des Patriotes was essentially a Boulangist electoral organization. Composed of solid middle-class, well-educated veterans, functionaries, teachers, and *voyageurs de commerce,*[5] the Ligue was the core of the general agitation surrounding Georges Boulanger's ill-fated electoral attempts to fulfill the expectations of those around him. Ten years later, however, while the place of operation—the street—was the same, the Ligue's emphasis had changed from electoral to direct action. Thus, although Déroulède's concept of *revanche* remained constant, he and his organization no longer accepted parliamentary institutions or means as avenues for achieving their goals.

Posterity's refusal to take both seriously, viewing them as *opéra comique* supernumeraries worthy of appearing in Charlie Chaplin's *Great Dictator*, stems from the fact that Déroulède and the Ligue have been consistently evaluated in terms of what they said rather than what they did and who they were. This approach is significant not only as it has affected interpretations of the Ligue in its immediate historical context but also as it has pertained to its role in a considerably wider question: the relationship of the French Right to fascism.[6] Historians have tended to deny the existence of an authentic fascist movement in France because of the absence of an indigenous radical right-wing tradition. Thus, the leagues of the 1930s are identified as Bonapartist, conservative, or foreign, but not as having radical inspiration. The identification of earlier groups as composing a French radical Right would do much to disarm this argument, which in general tends to pay greater attention to program and degree of success than to tactics and social characteristics. In its rebirth during the Dreyfus Affair the Ligue des Patriotes was a tightly organized, militant, antiparliamentarian, authoritarian, violent, and direct-action-oriented movement whose ideology, if not barren, viewed the world simply, almost naively. While an authentic counterrevolutionary ideology would have to wait for the genius of Maurras, the organization and membership of the Action française descend directly from the Ligue des Patriotes.[7] Dependent on the energies of the urban lower middle class, the Ligue conjured up the psychological traits most characteristic of radical movements—fear—fear of the foreigner, the Jew, the far Left, the *sans-patrie*.[8]

In addition, its leader, Paul Déroulède, was a man who combined a sense of theater with both a naive belief in the greatness of France and a surprisingly modern view of political tactics. Although ultimately a failure—and one ought not to judge significance by success—he was ideally suited to assume the role of leader. For of all the great events in the history of the Third Republic, the affair produced an emotional and political atmosphere that was taut with expectation and intense to a degree unknown by a generation of Parisians. While the Boulangist skit had been played out amidst dandyish rides on black horses and music-hall gaiety, the affair witnessed an increasingly exciting and grim series of rhetorical battles which, though they began in meeting halls, ended in the streets. The *vedette* of the era was any man who could arouse the crowd to a high pitch of excitement and enthusiasm and move it to action. In many ways Parisian indulgence created an environment for spectacle. If honor and lightness had characterized the crowds who chanted "C'est Boul-, Boul-, Boulanger qu'il nous faut,"anger and frustration came to represent the attitudes of those who cried "A bas les. . . !" The more the audience responded, the better the actor had to perform. Often it appeared that the men on stage became intoxicated with the shouts of their own voices mixing and reverberating with the response of the crowd. The succession of meetings, rallies, and torchlight parades led by Paul Déroulède during the Dreyfus Affair had their precedent in the Boulangist episode—but so much had changed.

It is this change in mood, in society, in a France emerging from the nineteenth into the twentieth century which this study seeks to explore. Although focused on the shared history of Paul Déroulède and the Ligue des Patriotes from 1882 to 1900 and concerned with the genesis of a racist French nationalism and hence the emergence of a new modern force on the Right, it is also a study of a political and social transition. The Republic that was saved in 1905 was not the ideal republic elaborated by Gambetta in 1869. The reality was quite different, and the contribution of Déroulède and the Ligue to the constitution of this new reality was considerable.

Clearly, the first generation of the Third Republic was an era of continual conflict and resolution. Born from the turmoil of the Commune, characterized by a still incomplete industrial revolution, dominated in part by, if not the aristocratic classes, then values associated with an earlier time, France from 1870 to 1900 was searching for a social and political order that might somehow balance the continually changing mixture of substances, old and new, which formed the essential features of her society. For if we are not surprised at the continuity of the rhetoric in the first thirty years of the Republic's existence, neither should we be unaware of the important forces that persisted in moving France into our epoch. The France of 1900 was the center of a colonial empire, a European alliance system, an avant-garde culture, and an industrial pattern with a significant socialist response whose existence had been alien to *la république de ducs*. Thus, whereas on one level we may characterize this era as one of naive tranquility in which France basked in the "Indian summer of European parliamentarianism," there are significant indications that those ideologies, forces, and social and political movements that would come to dominate France and Europe after the Great War were forged and shaped well before that traditional watershed.

Within this changed context Déroulède and his Ligue evolved continuously. Although both had supported the Third Republic with enthusiasm in the 1880s, by the late 1890s and subsequently into the first decade of the twentieth century the new nationalism that they represented was in constant opposition to the regime and society from which it had come. To understand the history of the emergence of the radical Right in France between 1880 and 1900, it is important to establish that the evolution of the Ligue des Patriotes was not merely a consequence of its internal development. That the Ligue and Déroulède passed through the stages of Gambettism, Boulangism, and anti-Dreyfusism is significant. That they became radical opponents of the Third Republic only in the midst of the Dreyfus Affair and subsequently embraced a racist, anti-Semitic, ideological position in the summer of 1899 shows that they changed profoundly in the context of a tumultuous era. In order to account for the how as well as the when of that change, it has been necessary to relate the history of Déroulède and the Ligue to the larger social, economic, and political forces of their times. Without some understanding of the reciprocal relationships that existed among these forces, the path that the Ligue and Déroulède followed remains unmarked.

Surely the main emphasis of this study is to depict and explain the political journey of one of the main voices of French nationalism in the last twenty years of the nineteenth century. As a result of that journey the Ligue des Patriotes emerged, if only for a short time, convinced of its counterrevolutionary mission. Déroulède remarkably remained at the head of this constantly shifting organization not so much because of his gift for the art of political opportunism but rather in spite of himself. A man of theater rather than ideology, Déroulède's political ideas were often responses to developments and forces that he understood imperfectly. In short, the Ligue became in its several stages of evolution not only what history portended but what its opposition required.

These perceptions become crucial upon examination of the evolution of the parties, personnel, and programs of those groups that merged in the late 1890s to form a new militantly nationalist, anti-Semitic organization: the Ligue des Patriotes. For notwithstanding its left-republican origins in the early 1880s, the Ligue of the Dreyfus Affair incorporated several factors that had not been present in the French political and social atmosphere a decade earlier. Neither anti-Semitism with its complex pseudo-socialist, racist, and nationalist overtones nor a vigorous socialism of the working class played a role in the Boulangist episode. Virulent anti-Semitism was a product of the decade of the 1890s, which marked the end to a twenty-year-long period of industrial recession and stagnation and witnessed the publication of Drumont's *La France juive* and the *éclats* of the Panama and Dreyfus affairs. Similarly the evolution and growth of the French socialist parties began to have an impact on French society only following the first meetings of the Second International in 1889. In fact it has been argued that a sizable segment of the Boulangists in the Chamber of Deputies continued to represent some working-class interests at least until 1893.[9]

Hence the Ligue des Patriotes, which responded to the threats that it imagined were posed by Dreyfusards, became in due time antiparliamentary, antisocialist and anti-Semitic in the name of defending the honor of the real France against those alien elements within which sought to destroy and weaken her in the face of yet other enemies without. In the course of almost twenty years then, cries for revision of the regime came to mean something quite different from the ideals of the Gambettist faction of the Republican party. The emergence of a new radical right-wing movement must be seen as having both republican origins and responding to new, modern, and unique forces more characteristic of the twentieth than the nineteenth century.

What follows then is a history of the Ligue des Patriotes from its origins as a Gambettist patriotic organization to its reincarnation as the first mass movement on the Right in modern French history. In this context several themes will emerge, implicitly and explicitly, as important. The first, inherently part of this essay's organization, is a reconsideration and contrast of the Ligue's political, social, and programmatic nature in both the Boulangist and Dreyfus affairs. The questions that must be resolved include crucial definitions of and distinctions between Gambettist republicanism and Boulangism and will inexorably involve considerations of the political labels "Right" and "Left" within the context of the evolution of the Third Republic. Second, it will be necessary to examine the theme of nationalism's transformation from its traditional Jacobin foundations into an exclusive xenophobic form of flag-waving, clarion-sounding patriotism. Paul Déroulède, whose artistic limits were considerable, was nevertheless to prove a major force in this development. Third, attention must be given to how, with the inclusion of lower-middle-class and anti-Semitic constituents, the Ligue des Patriotes emerged as a new and modern force that reflected greatly altered conditions in late nineteenth-century France. It is hoped that this study will illuminate the intricate relationship among the Third Republic's social, political, and ideological forces and will allow them to be viewed in the perspective of historical change.

Far too often, it seems, historians have been willing to discount any dynamic within French society after 1870 and have assumed, instead, the existence of a bureaucratically static and dreary regime hidden beneath constant political instability. One need not be reminded of the complex play between those clichés of continuity and change to appreciate that even the Third Republic tended to divide a great many Frenchmen along a wide variety of fascinating and complex lines. This, then, is the history of one such series of divisions. The ultimate irony is that those who became most divisive did so in the name of national—indeed racial—unity.

NOTES—INTRODUCTION

[1] René Rémond, *The Right in France: From 1815 to De Gaulle*, pp. 205-232; Raoul Girardet, *Le Nationalisme francais*, pp. 7-31; Girardet, "L'Idéologie nationaliste," pp. 423-445; Herbert Tint, *The Decline of French Patriotism, 1870-1940*.

[2] D. R. Watson, "The Nationalist Movement in Paris, 1900-1906," in *The Right in France, 1890-1919*, ed. David Shapiro, St. Anthony's Papers, no. 13 (London, 1962), shows the shift in Paris from Left to Right as early as 1902. See also Eugen Weber, *The Nationalist Revival in France*.

[3] See Zeev Sternhell, "Paul Déroulède: The Origins of Modern French Nationalism," *Journal of Contemporary History* 6 (1971): 46-70.

[4] It remained for the Action française to graft the Ligue's organization, membership, and temperament to Maurras's already well-developed synthesis of counterrevolutionary nationalism. Peter M. Rutkoff, "Revanche and Revision: Paul Déroulède and the Ligue des Patriotes, 1897-1900," Ph.D. dissertation, University of Pennsylvania, 1971.

[5] Archives de la Préfecture de Police de Paris (APP), Series B/A 1,032, report of 7 October 1898, outlining the Ligue's history from the reports over the preceding decade.

[6] Rémond, *Right in France*, pp. 203-232. See also Eugen Weber, "The French Right"; Raoul Girardet, "Pour une introduction à l'histoire du nationalisme français," pp. 502-528; and the partial refutation of Rémond by Robert Soucy, "The Nature of French Fascism," pp. 27-56; and the new work by Zeev Sternhell, *La Droit Révolutionnaire 1885-1914* (Paris, 1978).

[7] Ernest Nolte, *The Three Faces of Fascism* (New York, 1966), pp. 88-145.

[8] Cf. ibid. and *Le Drapeau*, December 1897-December 1900.

[9] C. Stewart Doty, "Parliamentary Boulangism After 1889," pp. 250-269; and Zeev Sternhell, "Barrès et la gauche; du Boulangisme à *la Cocarde*," pp. 77-130.

PART
1
—
FROM GAMBETTA
TO BOULANGER

CHAPTER

1

—

The First Decade of the Republic

THE DECADE BETWEEN the end of the Franco-Prussian War and the death of Gambetta can be seen as a period of intense political activity and reformation within the context of remarkable economic stability. In some sense the France that many strove for in that decade was one that would be a restoration; the arguments were, therefore, over the political content of that restoration. By the late 1870s with Royalist restorations no longer possible, the republicans took the field and promised to emerge with an anticlerical, parliamentary regime that was to stand on the economic shoulders of the middle classes as it set about restoring French prestige. The political failure and subsequent death of Gambetta combined with the plunge of the French economy into stagnation (if not depression) made that Jacobin-republican dream falter. In Gambetta's place there stood Paul Déroulède and his newly formed Ligue des Patriotes. The founding of the Ligue in 1882 by this minor poet of patriotic drama and verse, more than ten years after the events the Ligue was supposed to remember, reflects then the larger economic and political currents that dominated France in this era. It might be said that these ten years were but the soil in which the frustrations of French republican nationalism took root but did not yet grow.

It is important, then, to understand that the Ligue des Patriotes, whose

11

founding was not in 1871 but in 1882, represented not simply the revanchist sentiment of French nationalism but had a political content and function as well. Simply put, the continuities of the 1870s did not necessitate such an organization and commitment; the changes of the 1880s did. Déroulède during the years 1871–1880 had only to be Gambetta's "house" poet; he had only to picnic and recite his verse to the heart's content of Juliette Adam. To that extent his career was an extension of his literary life prior to the war. It is the theme of these dual continuities which must be explored in order to answer the first question regarding the manner and time of the founding of the Ligue des Patriotes as well as Déroulède's entrance into the political arena.

Gambetta's decline, coupled with Ferry's ascendance, became in the early 1880s the signal for the Ligue and Déroulède to claim the place, politically and rhetorically, of the Jacobin patriotism that they believed Gambetta had embodied. Although *revanche* and revision had been the themes that inaugurated the decade, their abandonment first by the Opportunist wing of the republican movement and then, seemingly, by Gambetta himself, were critical to the political education of Paul Déroulède. That education, essentially *plus Gambettiste que Gambetta* began in the shadow of defeat.

The aftermath of the Terrible Year of 1870-1871 witnessed more than one miracle for France. Sacré Coeur and the ministrations of Monsieur Dupanloup expressed on one level the emotional response to the humiliation and horror of the war and Commune, while the government of Monsieur Thiers began to work on the more mundane problems of recovery and reconstruction. The balance sheet of 1871, indeed, did not contain many credits for the new provisional government. The Treaty of Frankfort, which required a huge war indemnity that in reality was tribute for "expenses" incurred by German occupation, demanded that France grant Germany the status of "most favored nation" economically and of course provided for the loss of two of France's wealthiest provinces, Alsace and Lorraine. After the country's greatest period of economic and industrial prosperity, her economic prospects looked less than impressive.

Politically the situation was no more promising. The defeat, capture, humiliation, and exile of Louis Napoleon Bonaparte seemed to offer little hope for political stability for some time to come. A remnant of the July monarchy, Adolphe Thiers, had been entrusted with the guardianship of a regime proclaimed the Republic on 4 September 1870, the legislature of which was dominated by the two royalist factions, Bourbon and Orléanist. Although the republican leader, Léon Gambetta, had valiantly tried to defend his country from the German onslaught, his party, if one may call it such, was more than divided over the events that came to be called the Commune of Paris. With socialism discredited, socialists exiled, republicans divided, and Bonapartists without a new Napoleon, the only question that seemed important was which pretender would no longer have to pretend.

Similarly, the legacy of the Commune presented a bleak future to a society that had been trying to reconcile, as some have noted, a revolutionary idea of sovereignty with government. To both Red and Black the Commune had been yet another episode in the unresolved class war to whose dates of 1793 and 1848 could now be added 1871. Given the important impact of the industrial spurt of the 1850s and 1860s, the divisions and tensions within French society—between worker and bourgeoisie, peasant and notable, town and country, Paris and provinces—augured poorly for France in the first years of the new Republic.

Yet appearances and reality are the juxtapositions of historians' revisionism. The interplays of continuity and change, so mysterious to contemporaries, often become strikingly clear in retrospect. Although the changes wrought by the years 1870-1871 were important, their importance was not that immediately apparent. To a certain extent, in fact, the impact of the economic, political, and social consequences of the war and Commune would not be felt until the early 1880s. Rather, the years from 1871 to 1878 can now be perceived, remarkably, as extensions or continuities of developments inherited from the Second Empire. To that extent, the recovery of France, her seeming stability in the first decade of the Third Republic, appears incongruous with regard not only to the conditions that prevailed at the regime's inception but also to the events which altered that stability in 1881 and 1882. Thus, the continuity of the 1860s into the 1870s served to check the full effect of the war and Commune for almost ten years.

Indeed it was with remarkable speed, energy, enterprise, and dedication that the provisional government of France set about paying off the German reparation. Set at five million francs, an amount designated by Bismarck to weaken but not cripple the defeated nation, the indemnity served as a focus for the financial and emotional recovery of France. Thiers and the government realized from the outset that an extension of credit was greatly needed. To obtain this would necessitate the cooperation of banking institutions and the public. In June 1871 the government offered bonds for sale to the public. To everyone's apparent astonishment the loan was not only picked up by the French population but in fact was oversubscribed by more than 100 percent.[1] France had not lost her banking credit. The growth of banking institutions, an integral aspect of the economic history of the Second Empire, bequeathed to the Third Republic a system of credit which was internationally acknowledged. In this respect the years 1870-1871 represented but a short interruption in this important development. In maintaining the capitalist prosperity of the 1860s, the early 1870s witnessed the opening of several additional financial institutions and the flourishing of older ones such as the Union Générale. This was especially true in the two short periods of marked economic prosperity—from 1871 to 1873 and 1878 to 1882.

Likewise the response to the offering of June 1871 indicated not simply a bourgeois approval of the incoherent regime of the era but more profoundly a patriotic ground swell of support for the nation. The humiliation occasioned by the losses of war and territory was, it seems, replaced by a public pledge to rebuild. The quick repayment of the loan, no doubt, only seemed to magnify this sentiment and contributed to the maintenance of a positive and stable patriotism throughout the decade. When Gambetta subsequently coined the phrase "Think of it always, speak of it never" as an appropriate response to the issue of *revanche*, he was articulating a sentiment shared by a great many of his compatriots. The prosperity of the 1870s appeared, then, as the necessary first step toward the international reclamation of French national pride.

In this context of international prestige the maintenance of French commercial relations with England, which continued the free-trade policy of the Empire and enabled the French debt to be converted on the London exchange, provided yet another framework for French recovery after 1871.[2] With a modern railway system essentially intact, a healthy (for the time being) balance-of-payments situation, a vigorous banking system, and a careful fiscal policy, the postwar economic "miracle" was built on the liberal policy established in the preceding twenty years. Even the loss of Alsace-Lorraine, which deprived France of a significant part of her natural and industrial resources, was compensated for by the simultaneous discovery of iron in French Lorraine and the application of the Thomas and Gilchrist method of smelting.[3] In the late 1870s then, following a two-year slowdown that had resulted from a recession in agriculture, these developments helped to restore the French economy.[4]

Although it is difficult to equate the Second Empire with mid-Victorian Britain, certain characteristics are nonetheless striking. "The Empire is peace" had been the official Napoleonic proclamation.[5] With peace and prosperity the Empire had indeed maintained a social cohesion. True, there were the forty-eighters whose voices would once again be heard in 1871, but the order of the Second Empire, whether it be attributed to centralization, authoritarianism, or prosperity, remained one of its dominant features.[6] Despite a significant industrial spurt, the France of the 1860s and 1870s retained in its social composition a curious mixture of the old and new: peasant agriculture and high finance, artisan hand crafts and new large-scale industrial organization.[7] Although the impact of the Napoleonic system was important, it did not transform the nature of French society overnight. Rather it provided for the gradual alteration of the traditional productive forces of handwork and workshop to modern ones of the factory and machine in the course of a generation. Thus, not only was the composition of the working classes at the origins of the Third Republic essentially similar to that of the Second Empire,[8] but "when the mason from Creuse gave up his biannual migrations and settled in Paris, or when the Breton peasant went to work at St. Denis, each brought with him the habits of the land. For to them the tools of labor represented the condition of liberty."[9]

Similarly, to the governments of the Second Empire and the Third Republic what was called the social question was ultimately seen as a political one. The new *couches sociales* of Gambetta were called forth to participate in a political and legislative process which would, by integrating the elements, solve their social isolation. Restraints, for example, on trade union activity and organization, although slightly altered in the mid 1860s, were not removed until the 1880s. The dominant economic and political liberalism with respect to the working classes remained in force throughout the period. As was true in England, however, when the prosperity of one era gave way to the decline of another, it came to be in the best interests of the middle and propertied classes and of the state to abandon to a significant degree a noninterventionist economic role. At precisely the time when the implications of the original industrial impact were most being felt, then, and before the economy was fully able to recover, the social question would indeed be a real one. But in the first decade of the Third Republic's existence it remained a ghost in the attic.

One of the important reasons traditionally given for the absence of socialist militancy and organization in the 1870s was the destruction of the Communards as a group and their subsequent death or exile. Although to a certain extent it is true that the French working classes were deprived of a leadership that had been prominent since 1848, there are several other factors that carry equal or greater weight in this matter.

Within what one might call the Left in France from 1848 to 1881 there were not only socialists—those who belonged to the Socialist International—but

Blanquists, Proudhonists, St. Simonians, and republicans. Opposed to the regime of the Empire, seeking a society of equal justice, these groups nevertheless represented a kind of intellectual and sentimental vision of socialism and were far from unified in their dealings with one another.[10] It is only with great difficulty then that one speaks of a French socialist movement prior to the 1880s. The experience of the Commune did not significantly alter this development except in a negative sense. Dispersing the Communards also eliminated their mid-century romanticism and small-producer mentality from the subsequent development of a more mature social and intellectual socialism.

Similarly, while one must not ignore the activity and protests of the working classes in the last years of the Second Empire, it seems clear that by and large the majority of the working classes saw their political aims as represented by the dominant anti-Bonapartist group, the radicals. The so-called Belleville program of 1869 announced by Gambetta for the radical or irreconcilable republicans represents the best example of working-class republicanism. Thus, in the 1870s when Gambetta spoke of both the existence of new *couches sociales* and of the nonexistence of the social question, he articulated the truth of his own political position. In addition he reflected the relationship that existed between the social and political components of the Second Empire's opponents.

Traditional accounts of the genesis of the Third Republic stress the failure and stupidity of the royalists, the role of Thiers, the unwritten "constitution of 1875," the Sixteenth-of-May crisis, and the perspicacity of Gambetta as the major factors in the establishment of that regime. Implicit is an argument that the Republic was a lucky accident and the result of the good works of some men in contrast to the stupidity of others. Equally important is the notion that the Republic was fundamentally different in its character from the regime that preceded it and from the remnants of its opposition. Liberal not authoritarian, republican not monarchial, parliamentary not Caesarist, anticlerical not Catholic, were the descriptive terms most enthusiastically identified.

A more careful look, however, reveals in political as well as in economic and social matters a strong continuity between the Second Empire and Third Republic. If one accepts the idea that the liberalization of the 1860s came about for reasons other than concessions of weakness in the face of political failure, one can begin to appreciate that the framework for the 1870s was indeed formed in the 1860s.

That Gambetta saw in Emile Olivier the making of a great liberal politician in the English tradition is an indication of the debt owed by the Third Republic to its predecessor.[11] In this sense the consolidation of the Republic was as much the victory by the loyal opposition of the liberal Empire as it was the vanquishing of the evil and insidious royalists. These latter merely provided a transition after which the republicans emerged with the political spoils. The great lawyers of the 1860s became the politicians of the 1870s, the radicals of Belleville the Opportunists of Paris.

Yet the republicanism that in fact emerged in the vital years between 1873 and 1878 was by no means a unified political force. True, republicans succeeded in the ad hoc establishment of a regime that following the crisis of the Sixteenth of May saw them dominate not just the Chamber of Deputies, but also the presidency and the Senate. This triumph was, however, the work of at least two men, Léon Gambetta and Jules Ferry, whose personalities and programs represented two very different versions of republicanism. In fact it would be not too strong to suggest that these men and their followers waged a significant battle over the nature of the Republic, which battle endured into the early 1890s.

In 1882 when Ferry (concerned with a recent measure barring Orléanists from accepting army commissions) uttered the phrase "Le péril est à gauche," he was not speaking of those recently returned and as yet ill-organized socialists who bore the legacy of the Commune, but of the Gambettist faction of the Republican party.[12] Having been allies in 1871, and sharing the view that republicanism had to be made respectable in the face of the Commune, the two men emerged as leaders of opposing factions by the mid 1870s. While Gambetta played the role of popular rhetorician, gathering crowds about him wherever he spoke, Ferry associated himself with more moderate political leaders, such as Jules Grévy. Gambetta earned a reputation for theatrical performance, Ferry for political astuteness. Thus, in the campaign of 1877 it was Gambetta who could proclaim that clericalism was the enemy while Ferry remained far more moderate in his attitude toward Orléanist clericalism. For him, the anticlerical aspect of republicanism would have to wait more than a decade when such a position was more respectable. Indeed, the contrast was more than political. Gambetta was southern and provincial, warm and outgoing, with a reputation for authoritarianism that contrasted with the proper, Parisian, bourgeois manner of Ferry.[13]

The Opportunists, as Ferry's group came to be known in the 1880s, had several goals whose rhetoric contained one fundamental principle: respectability. Central to their moderate position was a general acceptance of and support for the two founding acts of the Third Republic: the so-called constitution of 1875 and the Treaty of Frankfort. The maintenance of parliamentary supremacy and acceptance of Bismarck's Europe were to them the realistic *données* of the age. Domestic and foreign considerations hence were seen as ultimately interrelated not only by the Opportunists but by their revisionist opponents as well. The moderate political position of the late 1870s and early 1880s was quite simple: to retain those institutions that had been established at the regime's founding. France needed time to restore herself internally before she could begin to strengthen herself internationally. Moderate policy sought at all costs to avoid conflict with Germany, for "a Jacobin Republic would have fulfilled Bismarck's wish to keep France in diplomatic isolation."[14] Ferry's faction sought to avoid responding to the essential criticism of the Third Republic—that it was weak—in the belief that Caesarism at home or saber rattling abroad would only endanger, not enhance, the regime's possibility for survival. Thus, the Opportunists, to the chagrin of radicals, socialists, and nationalists, turned their efforts in the 1880s first to the clerical issue and then to imperial adventure.[15]

In contrast, the public support that Gambetta enjoyed served only to increase the fears and suspicions of his political colleagues. From the outset, indeed beginning with the Belleville manifesto, Left republicans called precisely for a Jacobin republic and a foreign policy which would entail reforms in both the constitution of 1875 and in the provisions of the Treaty of Frankfort. In the early and middle 1870s when France was engaged in the national enterprise of recovery, enjoying a consequent degree of economic prosperity and witnessing the republicanization of the regime, the differences between Opportunists and Left republicans were not noticeable. A common enterprise and enemy provided, along with economic stability, a unity of purpose and action. The patriot who sought above all the return of the Lost Provinces could support the republican attack on the Orléanist caretakers without having to consider the possibility that his dreams might be deferred for a lifetime. Even as late as 1881 those around Gambetta could and did assume that his impending "Great Ministry" would begin the process of revision. Thus, in the formative years of the political development of the Third Republic, there began to emerge two factions that centered on the personalities of the dominant men of the time: Léon Gambetta and Jules Ferry. Each stood for a different republicanism and each had an inner circle of friends and advisors who undertook to support publicly their leader's position.

While Gambetta, in his last years, tended to rely on the advice and counsel of his mistress, his collaborators included many who had met him either in his more radical days as an unflagging opponent of the Empire or as the "dictator" of France in the period of the Army of the Loire. "Red" republicans and patriots, these men and women behind the scenes, worked as publicists for the great man and for one another. Most often involved in Parisian literary or journalistic society, they saw their task to be that of keeping the public aware of the real Gambetta—the man of the people and the man of France—while the politician plied his trade. Through the vehicles of the *Nouvelle Revue* published by Juliette Adam, and the *Petite République Française* for which Arthur Ranc was an editor, there appeared article after article on the subject of revision. Alsace-Lorraine had to be kept in the public mind lest the new generation forget the true France, and Gambetta's pet political reform, the *scrutin de liste*, supported as the means by which France could strengthen her internal resolve. If only Gambetta could achieve power, maintained his supporters, then *revanche* and revision would surely follow.[16]

For these people there clearly was but one instrument for such a policy: the army. Representing a synthesis of revolutionary and Napoleonic traditions, the army of the Third Republic evoked both the ideal of the nation in arms and the concept of professionalism. No longer the elitist and hence royalist institution that it had once been, and yet not evoking the radical image of the National Guard, the modern French military concept was built upon universal training and an elitist officers' corps. Once again, as in so many other facets of French institutional development, the Second Empire had essentially created the army that the Republic was to inherit.[17] Domestic reform, recovery of the lost provinces, the strength of the army were all key provisions in the attacks mounted by Gambetta's associates against those who would weaken France and create an impotent version of a once proud and great nation. If for Ferry the peril was on the Left, Ferry himself was the real enemy for the Gambettists.[18] Within this circle, then, there was a community of opinion and an intense loyalty to the personal goals and qualities of the leader. People like Arthur Ranc, Joseph Reinach, Juliette and Paul Adam and even Paul Déroulède were all prominent in their own right. Others, and they are worth noting in this context, were less well known and had joined Gambetta for quite different reasons.

René Waldeck-Rousseau, a provincial lawyer whose career spanned the first three decades of the Third Republic, was recognized by Gambetta in the 1870s as a diligent, hard-working, sober young barrister of uncommon good sense. As was the case with many who surrounded the Great Man, the young lawyer had a specialty for which his advice was constantly sought: the social question. Having been previously interested in legal reform, Waldeck-Rousseau was expected to provide answers to the so-called question that his boss said did not exist. Though his ideas were never clearly formulated, Waldeck-Rousseau did, however, have an overriding social vision that would guide him throughout his imposing political career. The best society for him was one characterized by social peace, by harmony, cooperation, and equilibrium. Specifically the working classes had to be given more opportunity for *embourgeoisement,* with the state obliged to intervene in the social affairs of the nation in the name of social harmony. When Gambetta's "Great Ministry" was finally formed in 1881, his young expert was in fact the only later-to-be-prominent politician included. Increasingly as Waldeck-Rousseau's career unfolded, he began to sense that France's political weakness was the source of her undoing. In 1889, at the end of the Boulangist episode, he showed his disgust for parliamentary politics by retiring temporarily and urging his colleagues to adopt the English model in which practical men of affairs would replace professionals and intellectuals.[19] Only a true statesman at the head of a reformed parliamentary system could ensure the social harmony that Waldeck sought. It is not surprising, then, that in 1899 René Waldeck-Rousseau was called upon to form a united-republican defense government—a government that would include a socialist and an army general—to restore social peace to a France wracked by the tensions of the Dreyfus Affair and the machinations of the groups and individuals who sought to profit from those tensions. It is ironic, then, that one of the men with whom Waldeck-Rousseau would have to deal most severely in 1899 was in 1881 an equally young member of Gambetta's entourage.

Whereas Waldeck-Rousseau, like Ferry, was cool, impervious, and aloof, Paul Déroulède, veteran of 1870, poet, playwright, and lawyer, was by temperament and inclination like his idol and mentor, Gambetta. Tall and thin, dressed not unlike the Parisian dandy that he had been before the war, Paul Déroulède was in every facet of his life—his politics as well as his art—a man of the theater. Impressive in stature, given to rhetorical excess, he impressed his contemporaries above all with his presence. More than one youth who saw him perform in the years prior to 1914, when Déroulède was past his prime and no longer a significant personage, attests to his remarkable public display. Constantly in motion, calling forth the images of France's historical greatness from Joan of Arc to Napoleon, Paul Déroulède never failed to attract an audience. And as was so often the case in theatrical illusion, it was not so much what he said that counted but the way he said it.[20]

Yet in a nation, especially during the Third Republic, where the critic was so often the political man,[21] the performance was ultimately only as good as the first night's notice. Men like Paul Déroulède may indeed have had the audience on its feet during the show, but the critics invariably had the last word. Nevertheless, there were times, and the Dreyfus Affair was one, in which it became increasingly difficult for all concerned to distinguish between illusion and reality. For a moment Paul Déroulède contrived to suspend disbelief—for himself and those who followed him. To his chagrin it was to be Waldeck-Rousseau who turned up the house lights and pulled the curtain down.

Clearly, though, of all his contemporaries Paul Déroulède was eminently qualified to play this theatrical role. As early as 1868 the young man who was then twenty-three had mounted his first production at the Théâtre Français. Though he was by no means a young genius, this was, for the time, a considerable accomplishment. Although *Juan Strenner*, a one-act play in verse, was neither reviewed nor remembered, it was a beginning. Paul Déroulède, however, was not without his benefactors, even at the earliest stages of his career.

A year earlier he had approached his father, an *avoué* at the *cours d'appel* in Paris, and requested permission to embark on a career of letters. His parents' intent had been for the young man to follow his father into the law, a career for which he had been trained.[22] Disappointed, but hardly without further recourse, Déroulède was sent by his father to consult with one Emile Augier. Uncle Emile was a famous, prosperous, (and in retrospect, insignificant) playwright and librettist whose talents seem to have matched the artistic tastes of the latter half of the Second Empire. His advice, however, was reasonable. Told to absent himself from the distractions of Paris, young Paul set out for the family property in the southwest to contemplate his future in quiet solitude.

Whereas his mother's family was thoroughly Parisian, his father's was provincial, and during the course of the revolution a prosperous tailor and merchant called de Roullède had managed to acquire a small ecclesiastical farm in the canton of La Villette some thirty kilometers south of Angoulême.[23] Langely, as it is called, is a typical Charentais farm of some fifty hectares and an assortment of structures, residences, outbuildings, and a mill, all constructed of sandstone and topped with red tile roofs. The oldest and most important building dates in part from the thirteenth century and is complete with an (almost) Norman tower some seventy-five feet in height. It was to this place and this tower that Paul Déroulède made his retreat. In an apartment that gradually became part library, part billiard room, and part bedroom, Déroulède withdrew from the public for the first, but not the last, time. As a result of his efforts, and in no small sense his uncle's position, his first theatrical production appeared in Paris the following year. More importantly, the rhythm of Déroulède's life was established. Henceforth he would divide his time between the two worlds that his parents represented: Langely—warm, quiet, solitary, bucolic—and Paris—exciting and stimulating, a world of theater, women, intrigue, and acclaim.

Yet even with the credit of a theatrical production under his belt, Paul Déroulède could hardly have been considered *sérieux* by himself or his family. He had no political allegiance, aside from a rather vague preference for Republic rather than Empire, and seemed content with his life as a kind of playboy womanizer who had fathered a child as well as a *pièce du théâtre* while at Langely.[24] By all rights he ought to have vanished into the anonymity of the Parisian middle classes, raised and squandered a fortune or two, and died. By his own admission the promise of this unextraordinary life was significantly altered by the events of 1870–1871.[25]

Throughout his life Déroulède claimed that the experience of the Franco-Prussian War had been instrumental in converting him to radical republicanism and nationalism. While many of his comments on the war were made in the heat of political debate a generation later, it seems clear that for a young man of twenty-three, as for so many others of his and future generations, the experience of war left an indelible imprint. Though he did not say it in so many words, 1870 was the best year of his life. The Franco-Prussian War led Paul Déroulède on several simultaneous and indeed diversified pathways. The camaraderie, simple heroism, adventure, and collective enterprise were for him, as is so often true, the stuff of subsequent memories. As an officer who engaged in combat, he was decorated with the Légion d'honneur after a daring escape from a prisoner-of-war camp. As a man who celebrated the family as a social institution, he stayed behind enemy lines to save his brother's life. As a defender of his concept of the Republic, he risked a second capture and fought his way to join Gambetta's Army of the Loire. The virtues to which he would remain loyal for some forty years were forged in 1870: the army, the family, the Republic, the heroism of the simple man.

Yet besides these memories of honor and glory there stood for Déroulède the failure. France had been humiliated. Not only had she suffered the loss of a war, but her two eastern provinces had been taken as bounty. There was something more than a physical, geographical, and economic loss. To the French the nation is abstract and indivisible. It represents both the revolutionary concept of citizen and an idea whose mathematical symmetry is aesthetically pure. The German victory in 1870 was made all the more profound in contrast to the grandeur of war itself and the special concept that the French have of their nation.

For a man like Déroulède the war emphasized the values that he would hold dear. For if the nation was a unity whose violation was blasphemy, the cement of that unity—the individual, idealized as *paysan*-soldier in arms— could and must be the instrument for restoration. The true France, for Déroulède—the France of good honest men who believed in simple virtues of honor, family, the army, and the Republic (for it was the Empire that had strayed)—would surely win out.[26] What the Empire had surrendered, the Republic could restore.[27]

Yet Paul Déroulède neither supported nor participated in the radical experiment of the Commune. A soldier first, he proclaimed his loyalty to the government of Thiers and in fact took part in the storming of one barricade before receiving an insignificant wound. As he had done three years earlier, the young soldier-veteran returned to Langely to recuperate and once again ponder his future.

Within a year the playwright of 1868 and the soldier of 1870 became the poet laureate of his generation. Having decided to retain his army commission on inactive status, Déroulède dedicated himself to the fact and idea of *revanche*. Combining his earlier literary success with the indelible experience of the war, he published in 1872 a volume of poetry, *Chants du soldat*. *Chants* soon became one of the best-selling volumes in French literary history, earning Déroulède a reputation that rivaled that of Victor Hugo. Evoking an uncomplicated nationalist-patriotic sentiment, his poetry surged with the imagery of war and heroism to teach above all that Alsace-Lorraine must be returned, by whatever means necessary, to the nation. Though he would write several other volumes of patriotic poetry, none of them enjoyed the success of *Chants du soldat*.

By 1889 this slim volume had appeared in twenty-nine editions, become required reading in the primary schools, and made of Déroulède an independently wealthy and national figure.[28] Overnight he became the personification of *revanche*. For if Gambetta said, "Think of it always, speak of it never," Déroulède's efforts to keep the idea before the public were unceasing.

To so embody *revanche* was to provide Gambetta with a useful service. As republican victories in 1877 and 1878 began to ensure the ascendancy of the regime, it became necessary for Gambetta, especially in his struggle with Ferry and Grévy, to moderate his views. Generally it was assumed that revisions of the treaty and the constitution were necessary prerequisites for the reestablishment of French pride, but increasingly it became necessary for these reforms to be officially understated. In his association with the patriots of Gambetta's Republican Union, Déroulède could and did speak of those things that he imagined Gambetta could not.[29] He became identified not only with the notion of *revanche* but with the more radical anti-Ferryist faction of the Republican party. In addition Déroulède retained his political and social connections with the army. In retaining his commission, he became its unofficial spokesman and completed the circle that could still encompass the Republic, the army, and demands for reform.[30] Thus, while he did not actively participate in the political struggles of the day, he was the literary voice of a position that was both strong and current in the France of the late 1870s.

As Gambetta followed the course that would lead to his eventual though short-lived ministry, Déroulède and others became increasingly critical of the opportunism that they saw developing. Believing still that Gambetta was doing what he had to do, Déroulède became more outspoken in his reactions to Ferry's imperial policies in 1881. In that year French troops occupied Tunisia in a swift move designed to restore French prestige abroad and to bolster public support of Ferry's ministry.[31] Although there was potential conflict with Italy over the territory, clearly it was a maneuver that the government had decided would appear safe in Bismarck's eyes. When reproached by Ferry for opposing an active colonial policy, Déroulède was reported to have replied, "I have lost two children, but you, you offer me twenty servants."[32]

Despite the success of the Tunisian adventure, President Grévy in late 1881 felt compelled at last to call Gambetta to office. Having been the single most popular politician in France and having exercised an enormous degree of unofficial power as president of the Chamber, Gambetta, given a huge electoral victory in 1881, could no longer be denied. In November of 1881 the man who for countless others, including Déroulède, seemed to represent France's continued desire for *revanche* became prime minister. While the ministry of all talents was a distinct disappointment, Gambetta did persuade one of his friends, the strongly anticlerical but equally strong revisionist, Paul Bert, to assume the position of minister of public instruction.

Dedicated to the program that republican, patriotic, and positivist ideas had to be instilled in the French public at an early age, Bert created a Commission d'éducation militaire. Designed to promote military and patriotic values in the primary schools, the commission included three men of military-patriotic good standing—Félix Faure, a future president of the

Republic, Henri Martin, a distinguished historian, and Paul Déroulède. While Gambetta pursued his own political ends—curiously enough called opportunistic by those who opposed him—the Gambettist party set out to introduce those ideas one of which was to "speak never" to the French public.

The commission's existence, however, was as short-lived as the ministry that had proposed it, and as cries mounted in the Chamber accusing Gambetta of Caesarism, Déroulède, Martin, and Faure resigned their posts.[33] While their resignations preceded Gambetta's fall by several weeks, the latter was in no small part due to the constant criticism that the commission received from Jules Ferry.

By early 1882 the Gambettist experiment was over. Within the year Gambetta would no longer be living, and men like Paul Déroulède would find themselves loyal to an ideal that no longer had a leader.

NOTES—CHAPTER 1

[1] Shepard B. Clough, *France, a History of National Economics*, p. 204.

[2] Tom Kemp, *Economic Forces in French History*, pp. 219-221.

[3] Clough, p. 203.

[4] Kemp, pp. 228-229.

[5] René Rémond, *Right in France*.

[6] Theodore Zeldin, *France 1848-1945*.

[7] Georges Lefranc, *Le Mouvement syndical sous la Troisième République*, pp. 14-17.

[8] Duveau, Georges, *La Vie ouvrière sous le Second Empire*.

[9] Lefranc, p. 18.

[10] Georges Lefranc, *Le Mouvement socialiste sous la Troisième Republique* (Paris, 1963), p. 14.

[11] Zeldin, p. 550.

[12] Charles Seignobos, *L'Evolution de la Troisième République*, pp. 101-105.

[13] Ibid., p. 85.

[14] Frederich Seager, "The Alsace-Lorraine Nation in France 1871-1914," p. 116.

[15] See for example Thomas F. Foner, *Jules Ferry and the Renaissance of French Imperialism*.

[16] Tint, pp. 32-46, see also Déroulède archives (AD) 15,299, 1 March 1880, Paul Demeny, editor *La Petite République Française*, to Paul Déroulède; and AD 4,670, 19 February 1880, Colonel Henry to Déroulède.

[17] Zeldin, pp. 519-521; Raoul Girardet, *La Société militaire*.

[18] AD 11,318, undated but clearly October 1881, Juliette Adam to Paul Déroulède: "We must fight him [Ferry] for his acts, for himself, and that's enough!"

[19] Zeldin, p. 675; see also Pierre Sorlin, *Waldeck-Rousseau*.

[20] Interview, M. R. Gaget, March 1969.

[21] Before it became the "Republic of Pals," the Third was called the "Republic of the Professors."

[22] Déroulède had attended the *lycées* Louis le Grand, Bonaparte, and Versailles before receiving a diploma from the Law Faculty in Paris.

[23] L. Oliver, "Les Déroulèdes sons l'ancien régime," *Souvenirs et Mémoires*, pp. 1-28, 117, 141.

[24] Jean Langely, his only recognized child, died some twenty-five years later in military service but not in action. AD 43,317, the colonel of the Ninety-third Infantry Regiment to Déroulède, undated.

[25] Paul Déroulède, *1870-Feuilles de route*, pp. 31-40.

[26] Déroulède, *Feuilles*, p. 12.

[27] Ibid. In a characteristic touch Déroulède claimed that his knowledge of the real France had come as the result of a peasant's fiery look before his enlistment.

[28] For a general evaluation of Déroulède's literary talents, see the following: Françisque Sacrey, *Trente ans du théâtre*, pp. 169-71; Henri Bordeaux, *1913-1919* (Paris, 1920), p. 120; and the excellent study by Claude Digeon, *La Crise allemande de la pensée française.*

[29] Déroulède archives (AD) 939, 19 June 1878, M. Remeny to Déroulède.

[30] AD 23,711, 16 May 1882, Colonel Henry to Déroulède.

[31] Dennis Brogan, *The Development of Modern France*, 1:217-223.

[32] Jean and Jérôme Tharaud, *La Vie et la morte de Paul Déroulède*, p. 32.

[33] Ferry proposed and later succeeded in achieving the transformation of the commission's idea of patriotic education into mere physical education. See Déroulède's *De l'éducation militaire.* At the same time, ironically, it had been Ferry who had made *Chants* required reading for French primary schools.

CHAPTER

2

—

The Founding of the Ligue des Patriotes

DÉROULÈDE'S EXTRAORDINARY SUCCESS as a poet of popular patriotic verse had in the mid-1870s brought him to the attention of those closest to Gambetta. His literary and subsequently political and social association with the Adams, Arthur Ranc, and others became the vehicle by which he gained an appointment to Bert's commission. As guardians of the Gambettist political platform, Déroulède, Faure, and Martin were not only attacked by Ferry but forced to leave the official and protective umbrella of government sponsorship.

Déroulède's perception in maintaining a Gambettism without Gambetta was of course primarily political. A patriotic education, a Republican education to his mind, was to be the instrument for creating a citizenry capable of supporting the very reforms for which in his belief the Gambettist movement stood. France could become a strong and unified nation politically, and after 1882 economically, only as a result of parliamentary reform and strong leadership. From this conceit came a larger understanding of the social and economic relationships, changes, and problems whose solution lay fundamentally in the political realm.

The founding of the Ligue des Patriotes in 1882 was a continuation of Déroulède's loyalty to his understanding of the Gambettist program outside the framework of the political system. At the same time the Ligue's sudden appearance as a popular patriotic society was in response to the concurrence of several levels of change in French society.

The political crisis that resulted from Gambetta's failure and subsequent death was compounded by the economic failure of 1881-1882. The Europe-wide depression, which had begun in 1873 and was to last until 1896, did not affect France immediately. Certain aspects of France's relatively balanced economy, her traditional modes and classes, and a conservative fiscal policy all served to retard the effects of the slump. More importantly, however, the French response to the indemnity of 1871 and to the humiliation of the Treaty of Frankfort, as well as the lingering effect of the policies of the Second Empire, staved off economic disaster until the early 1880s. At the very moment of the triumph of the Parliamentarians—that is, of the liberal political regime that matched the liberal economic system inherited from the Empire—economic forces came into play which resulted in significant social and political adjustments within French society. Indeed, the years 1881-1882 appear to mark the beginning of the transition in French politics, economics, and society at large from those features that had dominated the mid-nineteenth century to those that would dominate in the twentieth.

For a man like Paul Déroulède, by now an established poet of national reputation, the relationship among Republic, revenge, reform, and regeneration would no longer be as easy to maintain in the 1880s as it had been in the 1870s. The full impact of the Franco-Prussian war and its domestic and international settlement would reveal itself in the 1880s and 1890s far more discordantly than the seeming harmony of the 1870s would have suggested. The end of economic prosperity, combined with a decade of Opportunist political dominance, made it increasingly difficult to accept Gambetta's dictum to "speak of it never." The Alsace-Lorraine question, although by no means the single most important issue of the day, nevertheless came to represent the combined frustrations of those who opposed the policies of a government that desired, more than ever, to play it safe.[1]

The economic troubles that ushered in the depression of 1882-1896 arose from two main sources: banking and agriculture. In both arenas, the ramifications were important socially and politically. The banking institutions of mid-nineteenth-century France bore the stamp of their Napoleonic sponsor. Engaged in large-scale credit extension, they financed railway construction, serviced a large *petit bourgeois* class of small investors, and pursued policies of expansion and growth.[2] Generally, these institutions were dominated by Jewish or Protestant financial wizards; witness the extraordinary success of

Freycinet, Rothschild, and the Péreire brothers. However, under the leadership of Eugène Bontaux a new bank, the Union Générale, emerged in the 1860s as the glamor institution of the industry. Representing Catholic, legitimist, and conservative middle-class financial interests, the Union Générale challenged traditional "foreign" dominance over banking.[3] In the years 1878-1882 it enjoyed an unparalleled prosperity in investments and returns, with its shares selling at a peak of some three thousand francs on a basic worth of only five hundred.[4] When its investments (directed to Eastern Europe) proved unstable, the bank suddenly collapsed, wiping out its investors and sending shudders throughout French financial circles. As subsequent investment declined, so did industrial production; a significant decline in prices for industrial goods ensued. The response of the banking community was the pursuit of the most cautious policies for the next twenty years, culminating in the politics and person of Jules Méline.

The episode of the *krash* ushered in a period not only of economic decline but also of social myth-making, which attributed the poisoning of the French economic reservoir to foreign interests. It is no small coincidence that Drumont's 1886 book, *La France juive*, treated the fall of the Union Générale in precisely this manner. Subsequent scandals such as the Wilson and Panama affairs, not to mention the Dreyfus Affair, all drew upon this most important event for inspiration.

In addition, under the direction of Charles Freycinet, an engineer and sometime minister of finance, in the late 1870s France had embarked on an extensive program of public works designed to add ten thousand kilometers to its rail system. The so-called Freycinet Plan was halted by the slump of 1882. Those who saw the German victory of 1871 as the first sign of France's decline were only reinforced in their perception that Germany was not simply challenging but actually surpassing France in every phase of industrial and economic development.[5]

Prior to the events of 1881-1882, French agriculture had experienced several crises, the most important of which was an outbreak of phylloxera which severely damaged viticulture.[6] There followed a general decline in agricultural prices, reinforcing the industrial slump. One result of this agricultural depression was a notable exodus from the countryside of rural residents, particularly to Paris—at precisely the time when conditions in the capital were least propitious for significant population growth.[7] Thus, in the 1880s not only did France embark on an economic pattern of declining prices and production, but also its already overcrowded cities had to absorb rural populations whose views of modern urban society necessarily were prejudiced by the general economic decline. Within a generation, the "new social groups" whose life was most disrupted by the financial and agricultural crisis of 1881-1882 would see themselves as victims of both the overall recovery of the 1890s and the militant working-class response to that recovery. The success of the department stores on the one hand and the socialists and syndicalists on the other, combined with the myths of parliamentary corruption and "foreign" influence, created a political environment permeated with tensions and uncertainties.

The response of the government in the early 1880s, however, was of a different, more prosaic order. Although the Empire had bequeathed to the Republic a policy of *laissez-faire* economics, many French political, industrial, and peasant interests continued to demand a return to protectionist policies. Thus, in 1880 the free-trade era came to an end. The tariffs of that year signified the beginning of a movement that culminated in the Méline tariff of 1892. That agriculture was "saved" by the return to protectionism probably was only coincidental. Prices continued to decline and the provincials continued to flock to Paris, but not at such an alarming rate.[8] As in fiscal matters, however, a pattern was established which would characterize French international economics into the twentieth century.

Small producers, new industry, and peasant proprietors all stood to gain from the new policies. With an economy still divided—between the old and the new, between workshop and factory, even between Paris and the burgeoning industrial centers—the tariff policies of 1880s and 1890s served both the traditional and the modern. To a certain extent, these policies preserved a social as well as economic equilibrium. Small landholders, merchants, and craftsmen who ordinarily would have been threatened by the onslaught of capitalist industry were indeed protected by conservative government policies. Yet when recovery returned in the mid-1890s, the very same constellation of Opportunists would be held responsible for not doing enough to stem the tide. The period in France from 1881 to 1896, then, was one in which the social and political consequences of the dominant economic patterns manifested the transition from traditional to modern. The political legacy of the 1870s—cautious opportunism—served only to make that transition more difficult.

It was the Opportunist faction of the Republican party which not only dominated but also profited from the economic pattern of the 1880s and 1890s. Led by Ferry, France embarked on a path of conservative financial policy, initiated a new Empire, and ignored the dicta of the 1870s—reform of the Frankfort Treaty and revision of the constitution of 1875. Neither the goal of a Jacobin republic nor of the nation in arms was deemed worth pursuing. Ironically, the Great Ministry of Gambetta, coinciding with the economic disasters of 1881–1882, marked the beginning of Opportunist dominance. Even more ironically, it was Gambetta himself who was seen as the first Opportunist.

In fact, Gambetta's popularity out of office had served to heighten the fears and suspicions of his political colleagues. Ensnared by his reputation as a fiery orator and as author of the Belleville manifesto, and by the political desire to obtain a majority, Gambetta had to tread cautiously the line that separated respectability from power. In so doing, he became vulnerable to the criticism of opportunism from within his own faction, the Republican Union. Fear, suspicion, animosity and envy all played roles in the Chamber's rejection of the Great Ministry of 1881 and in the political failure of France's most popular leader.[9] Obviously, Gambetta's fall represented a corresponding defeat for the reforms through which he hoped to strengthen a weak nation. When the French electorate failed to respond to Gambetta's ouster with indignation, his opponents and supporters alike were confirmed in their observation that in the French political system no man, no minister, was indispensable. Electoral reform, a strengthened executive, a popular regime, a vital continuity in foreign policy—in short, *une république pure et dure*—were to be avoided at all costs by those who had opposed the great man.

Thus, the France of 1882 was in many ways a less unified nation than it had been ten years earlier. The Republican party was split, not only between the Gambettists and Opportunists, but also among those who followed the radical policies but not the personal leadership of Gambetta. Radical Socialists, intransigent anticlericals—in general, anti-Opportunists and particularly anti-Ferryists—began to emerge as the opposition in the France of the 1880s. In addition, outside the Radical party fold a vociferous nucleus of men maintained a devotion to the personality and principles of their fallen leader. But as was true of the Radicals, the followers of Gambetta found their touchstone as critics of the man who, for them, symbolized France's waffling weakness: Jules Ferry.

Within the context of (*a*) the commencement of the depression of 1881–1896, (*b*) the abandonment of liberal domestic and international economic policies, and (*c*) the fall of Gambetta's government, the founding of the Ligue des Patriotes by Paul Déroulède assumes a significance that transcends that organization's meager beginnings. Prior to Ferry's assumption of governmental control, Gambetta's appointees to the Commission d'éducation militaire found themselves unable to develop the kinds of patriotic programs which they had hoped would revive French "national" education.[10] Paul Déroulède, Félix Faure, and Henri Martin resigned from the commission before it had been in existence long enough to submit any proposals to the government.

Within several days of their resignation, Faure (a future president of the Republic) met with Déroulède and recruited his help in forming a private association that would support the same programs that the committee had propounded.[11] Faure argued that the spirit of Gambettism should be kept alive, despite the Opportunists' unwillingness to do so. He proposed the development of a curriculum that would include physical and patriotic instruction of the French people by a national network of private clubs. This plan, Déroulède agreed, would circumvent the Opportunists' reticence, which was becoming increasingly apparent as Ferry undertook a policy whose only apparent goal was to avoid aggravating Bismarck.[12]

Déroulède was swayed further to approve Faure's proposal by the offer of Louis d'Hurcourt to place his weekly paper, *Le Drapeau,* at the disposal of the new organization. On the night of 18 May 1882, within weeks of Gambetta's resignation, Paul Déroulède thus joined a prominent list of speakers in proclaiming the organization of the Ligue des Patriotes. Presenting the Ligue's slogan, "Qui vive—France," the author of the *Chants du soldat* made his first public address:

Yes, gentlemen, it must be said and it must be known. For the past dozen years our vanquished country has lived in a state of dependence which is close to slavery. . . . Do you know what ought to be done? . . . There are three things which I recommend . . . to develop thoroughly in all Frenchmen the patriotic spirit which makes them passionately love their country; the military spirit which makes them serve patiently and willingly; the national spirit which is the exact knowledge of the interests and needs of the nation. . . . Consumed by the fever of fear the cowardly often die of their wounds, while the brave, they recover, withstand, return.[13]

While claiming loyalty to the person and ideals of Gambetta, Déroulède too had despaired of achieving a Gambettist program, even within a Gambetta government. Now that the government had been overthrown and the Opportunists brought to power—for what turned out to be an eighteen-year period—Déroulède's hopes for governmental action were rudely smashed. In Déroulède's eyes, "Tonkin-Ferry" was no more likely than Jules Méline to lead France successfully against Germany. To Déroulède, Gambetta was the first but not the last politician to embody the ideals of *revanche* and patriotism. Similarly, Gambetta's government was the first but not the last from which Déroulède would turn away, disillusioned and disappointed.

The Ligue, with Déroulède as its secretary-general, was an immediate success. Within a week, "good" republicans had rallied to its side and to Déroulède, who was recognized as its spiritual heir as well as its moving force. He devoted all of his energy to the newly founded organization, speaking to local groups on an average of every three days for a period of more than three years. Within that time, fifty-two regional committees were established and hundreds of thousands of pamphlets distributed.

From its very inception, then, and despite its apolitical self-proclamation—Déroulède often protested that the Ligue had but one political loyalty, France—the Ligue des Patriotes was indeed partisan. Founded by frustrated followers of Gambetta, it was a left-republican, nationalist-patriotic, indeed neo-Jacobin organization of the political opposition. It remained fundamentally tied to the ideals of the 1870s and opposed to the policies and personality of Jules Ferry and the Opportunists. Given the critical, even scandal-filled climate of opinion which would come to dominate French politics in the late 1880s, it is not surprising that the Ligue and its founder, Paul Déroulède, maintained their stance as members of the anti-Opportunist opposition.

Nevertheless, the rhetoric of the Ligue and of Déroulède attempted for a time to sustain a guise of indifference to domestic politics, insisting only on devotion to reeducation and patriotic renewal. Subsequent events would force Déroulède to abandon this artificial distinction.

For Déroulède and the Ligue, the years 1882 to 1885 represented a period of building and development of the principles on which the Ligue had been originally established. For example, article three of the Ligue's constitution, the only article not concerned with membership and dues requirements, stated that the Ligue would concern itself with neither internal French politics nor religious questions. "We are all," claimed Déroulède, "Frenchmen and brothers."[14] The Ligue existed to instill the spirit of patriotism in those who had either forgotten or never experienced the great humiliation of 1870. The logical fallacy in this argument, however, is clear: how could the Ligue propose to remain apolitical and still hope to encourage the restoration of Alsace-Lorraine? As early as 1884, Déroulède joined others inside the government in denouncing Ferry publicly as a pro-German. A year later, Déroulède labeled France's policy of friendship with the victors of 1870 as the beginning of her ruin. Had France already forgotten those who had died facing the enemy?[15]

By this time, because of his reputation as a poet and lecturer, Déroulède had become a public speaker of great appeal. He was a star attraction whose physical presence and delivery were guaranteed to bring out the crowds.[16] Often, the sound of his own voice, combined with the audience's response, no doubt convinced Déroulède that his ideas were more popular than he had a right to believe. Yet, as the generation of Gambetta republicans died out or changed political sides, Déroulède remained constant and provided the link between his generation and those too young to have shared his experiences.

Although he had resigned his commission in the army in 1877 to concentrate on his literary career, Déroulède continued his connections within the officers' corps and with veterans' groups. Many of these men saw him as the one figure in public life who supported their honor and prestige. In December 1885, as a result of both his sustained criticism of the Opportunists via the policy of *revanche* and his identification with the Ligue des Patriotes, Déroulède declared himself a candidate for the Chamber from Paris. Campaigning as a *candidat de la revanche*, with the slogan "You know who I am; you know what I want; those who think like me should vote for me," he received one hundred thousand votes, albeit in a losing effort.[17] Despite the respectable showing, it was clear that Déroulède was but one of many men still loyal to the Republic, dissatisfied with the parliamentary regime of the Opportunists. Neither socialist nor Opportunist, he and others like him needed a movement that would synthesize their dissatisfaction with the present state of affairs.

The original Ligue des Patriotes, however, did not emerge from thin air. In the 1870s, both Paris and the provinces had witnessed the organization of a loosely federated system of local gymnastic and rifle associations. The most important of these, the association of sixteen Sociétés de Gymnastique de la Seine was led by one Joseph Sansboeuf, an Alsatian whose moderation was as well known as his devotion to patriotic education. In addition, there existed the weekly newspaper, *Le Drapeau*, edited by Parisian nationalist Louis d'Hurcourt, which served as a kind of house organ for the association of these societies. The formation of the Ligue des Patriotes on 18 May 1882, thus represented the amalgamation of France's "patriotic" organizations and *Le Drapeau*, on whose editorial staff was—not coincidentally—Paul Déroulède.

Thus, the original membership of the Ligue des Patriotes comprised essentially the adherents of these older societies. Reports of a great groundswell of public response—one source claiming a hundred thousand members within a fortnight—must be evaluated with regard to the Ligue's origins. What *was* new, however, in the Ligue des Patriotes was the political intent of its leaders. The Ligue was to be, from its very beginning, not only an organization of national revindication but also a focal point of anti-Opportunist politics.[18]

Although the Ligue represented a federated association of local societies and membership in these local societies also entailed membership in the mother organization, within months of its founding, the central Parisian organization of the Ligue controlled and dominated the rest. With a central *comité directeur* of thirty and a *comité de permanence* (which met weekly) of five, the Ligue was centralized and controlled by a handful of dedicated men.[19] The president of the Ligue des Patriotes, the republican historian Henri Martin, was in fact a figurehead nominated to please public opinion. His academic reputation gave the Ligue its apolitical, *au-dessus de la mêlée* appearance. Martin retired from his position in 1885 to be replaced by another public patriot, Anatole de la Forge, who remained in office through 1887.

It was not until 1888, then, that Paul Déroulède became president of the organization that he had been instrumental in founding. This presidential succession has often been cited as evidence supporting an important shift in the Ligue's posture in its first eight years of operation.[20] In fact, although there was a change in leadership from Martin to Déroulède, it was the latter —along with two close associates—who undertook the day-to-day management of both the Ligue and its overall policies. Déroulède was aided by Henri Deloncle, a private citizen of bourgeois and Parisian background who performed almost all the busy-work of the Ligue in its first six years;[21] and Pierre Richard, a lawyer who later became the independent deputy from Paris. These two, along with Déroulède, actually constituted the Ligue des Patriotes in its early years.

The membership of the Ligue, which numbered about nineteen thousand in Paris prior to the Boulangist phase,[22] for the most part consisted of the lower and middle bourgeoisie, which is to say it seemingly had few peasant or working-class members. As one would anticipate, a great many were veterans, especially commissioned and noncommissioned officers.[23] Not surprisingly, the primary preoccupation of the Ligue was the foreign posture of France. Within months of the Ligue's formation, while arguing for revision of the Treaty of Frankfort and propagandizing concurrently for an alliance with Russia, Déroulède proposed formation of a citizens' police force to help internal security deal with German agents in France. The government neither acted on nor indicated any receptiveness to this suggestion; however, this did bring the Ligue to the attention of Bismarck and the German press.[24] To Déroulède and his closest collaborators, if not the Ligue as a whole, war with Germany was an eventuality whose historical and patriotic necessity was unquestioned. Each minor diplomatic crisis with Germany in the 1880s renewed hopes for a restoration of *la patrie*, while each Opportunist solution brought with it increasing dissatisfaction and despair.[25] Inexorably, dissatisfaction with French foreign policy led to increased dissatisfaction with French political leadership.

Although there were few if any working-class members of the Ligue, its activities in the years prior to 1888 reflect (*a*) the economic malaise of the depression and (*b*) the degree to which questions of politics and economics were intertwined in the minds of many of its members. Whereas it is difficult to arrive at a precise understanding of the effects of the slump of the 1880s, it is clear, for example, that there were declines in prices and in industrial and agricultural production. This decline meant a stagnation of net income between 1882 and 1892.[26] Not only was growth limited for France in general during this period but apparently Paris in particular was subject to a greater economic decline than France as a whole, especially in the years 1884 to 1889.[27] This was due to, among other things, the rapid urbanization of the Parisian area, whose population growth was triple that of any other French city during the same period.[28] One need not be an expert in political sociology to determine that economic deterioration combined with population growth made for increased political dissatisfaction. That the Ligue des Patriotes stood for a left-republican critique of Opportunism, for the continued vision of Gambetta, is particularly persuasive in this context. The "new social groups," the backbone of the Republic—in other words, middle class, provincials, and above all Parisians—surely felt increased dissatisfaction with an unreformed and corrupt Republic. The Ligue in those years articulated that distress.

By mid-1883, less than a year after its founding as a so-called apolitical organization to sponsor movements of patriotic education, the Ligue was indeed involved in full discussion of these issues. An "order of the day" from June of that year shows the Ligue forming a commission to study (*a*) the economic effect of the Treaty of Frankfort, (*b*) the degree to which French industrial products had been duplicated by "foreign" (especially German) competition, and (*c*) the ways in which French public opinion might be brought to bear on the government over these issues.[29] Of importance here is not only the political-economic concerns of the Ligue at this time, but also the emphasis that it placed on the relationship between educating the public and political change. Once again, the Ligue was committed to reform within the parliamentary-democratic system. This remained its goal throughout the decade.

Between 1883 and 1886, the Ligue established an economic section devoted to issues of unemployment, the increase in foreign workers, and the crisis (as they viewed it) of industrial labor-management relations. Calling for increased cooperation between *ouvriers et patrons*, the economic section pursued the goal of bringing together workers and industrial and commercial interests in order to propose solutions to French economic decline, especially vis-à-vis Germany.[30] The Ligue expressed special concern in those years with the interrelated problems of unemployment and foreign workers in France, urging perferential employment of French workers as opposed to foreign and "cheap" labor.[31]

It is tempting to deduce from these discussions a kind of native corporatism in the making, and surely these attitudes—when combined (as they would be in the 1890s) with virulent anti-Semitism and fear of socialism—had that potential. But in the 1880s, given the political intent of the Ligue and its solid bourgeois membership, such an interpretation would be premature. Rather, the Ligue's economic concerns reflected a critical attitude toward a conservative government that preferred to employ traditional fiscal measures as it sought to sidestep further trouble with Germany. What mattered to the Ligue specifically was France's growing inability in any sphere to compete with Germany. What Ligue members proposed was reform, made possible by the creation of an educated public that would elect representatives devoted to a strong and forceful France in both foreign and domestic policy. The key, then, for the Ligue was political change.

In sum, the origins of the Ligue des Patriotes are to be found in the interaction of economics, politics, and society in the first years of the Republic's second decade. With the passing of the republican conquests of the 1870s, the victors began to squabble over the spoils. Although the Opportunists gained the upper hand, they did so at the expense of a dedicated party of patriots whose frustration was manifested in the founding of the Ligue. Further, as the economic prosperity inherited from the 1850s foundered in the early 1880s, it became increasingly apparent that political and economic discontent were inseparable. The orientation of the Ligue des Patriotes in its early years reflected the confluence of these disruptions in the life of the Republic. For the Ligue and for its secretary-general, Paul Déroulède, political change awaited the emergence of a leader whose record as a republican and a patriot was as indisputable as the remembrance of a France *"pure et dure."*

NOTES—CHAPTER 2

[1] Tint and Seager, "The Alsace-Lorraine Question."

[2] Kemp, p. 261.

[3] Kemp, pp. 262-264.

[4] Brogan, pp. 170-176.

[5] Brogan, p. 168

[6] Charles Warner, *The Government and the Winegrowers of France* (New York, 1960).

[7] Louis Chevalier, *La Formation de la population Parisienne au XIX Siècle*, has the best information.

[8] Kemp, p. 239.

[9] S. A. Ashley, "The Failure of Gambetta's Grand Ministry."

[10] John C. McManners, *Church and State in France, 1870-1914*, pp. 47-48.

[11] See the very well-done and interesting piece of scholarship by Steven Englund: "The Grand Ideal, the Disillusioning Reality: The Ligue des Patriotes 1887-1888"; and also Déroulède's speech at Angoulême in *Le Drapeau*, 26 May 1883.

[12] Digeon, p. 328.

[13] Le Batonnier Chenu, ed., *La Ligue des Patriotes* (Paris, 1916), pp. 35-41.

[14] *Le Drapeau*, 21 July 1883.

[15] *Le Drapeau*, 31 January 1885.

[16] Interviews with M. Paul Heurtey, Mme. Phillipe Barbet-Massin, and M. Phillipe Gaget, Paris, 1968-1969.

[17] Camile Ducray, *Paul Déroulède*, p. 159; and APP B/A 1,032, 16 September 1885.

[18] AD 23,607, 11 June 1882, Louis d'Hurcourt to Déroulède.

[19] Englund, "The Grand Ideal," pp. 28-31.

[20] See Tint, chapter 2, for example.

[21] AD 15,322, 14 October 1886, Deloncle to Déroulède.

[22] AD 15,322, 14 October 1886, Deloncle to Déroulède.

[23] APP B/A 1,337, 13 June 1883.

[24] APP B/A 1,337, 29 and 31 August 1882.

[25] AD 14,680, 9 February 1887, Deloncle to Déroulède.

[26] C. P. Kindleberger, *Economic Growth in France and Britain, 1851-1950.* Cambridge: Harvard Univ. Press, 1964.

[27] Guy Chapman, *The Third Republic of France: The First Phase*, p. 358.

[28] Kindleberger, p. 253.

[29] APP B/A 1,337, 21 June 1883.

[30] APP B/A 1,337, 18 August 1883.

[31] APP B/A 1,337, 25 March 1885.

CHAPTER

3

—

The Boulangist Crisis

TRADITIONAL FRENCH ACCOUNTS of Boulangism often have stressed its frivolous aspects. The famous depiction of the general retreating to bed in the midst of his greatest potential victory in 1888 emphasized the *Mariage de Figaro* quality of the movement. Too, such histories have accounted for Boulanger's success by implicating royalist money as the fundamental power behind Boulangism. The resulting interpretations might suggest that the France of Ferry, Freycinet, and Clemenceau was saved in 1889 from a royalist opera.[1]

It was not very difficult for subsequent historians to eschew the opera and underline the royalist connection. In so doing, they stressed the Caesarist pretensions of Boulanger as well as the nationalist conversion of the Ligue des Patriotes and its similarly Caesarist leader, Paul Déroulède.[2] It was this line of thinking which prompted some historians to consider the Boulanger affair as a serious moment in the development of the political institutions of the Third Republic. Boulanger was viewed as the first in a succession of scandals which led to the eventual triumph of parliamentary democracy in France. Hence, the forces that most threatened that triumph in the 1890s were already stirring in the 1880s.[3] Again, the roles of the Ligue and of Paul

Déroulède were seen as critical in this context, marking the rightward turn of the movement.[4]

Most recently, this view of Boulangism as a precursor of the right-wing nationalists of the Dreyfus Affair has been revised. The oft-quoted (though, one suspects, rarely read) study by Jacques Néré has fostered consideration of the social and economic context in which Boulangism arose.[5] Subsequent work has identified not one but several Boulangisms; these efforts have resulted in a kind of classification in which Boulanger, by appearing to be all things to all men, took on the coloration of those who invested in him. Hence there was a Jacobin Boulanger, a nationalist Boulanger, a working-class Boulanger, as well as a royalist one.[6] The Ligue des Patriotes is seen as representing only the nationalist aspect of the larger movement.

Interestingly, irrespective of the interpretation, the Ligue des Patriotes has been viewed as a political organization of shooting clubs transformed into one that was militantly political. This metamorphosis was to have taken place either before or during its adherence to Boulanger, thus altering the nature of the Ligue in subsequent events. Additionally, the influence of Déroulède in this change has been linked with his conversion from a "liberal" to an "authoritarian" patriot.[7] Finally, in seeking to restore their reputation from the ignominy of failure and exile, Déroulède and his admirers a generation later attempted to magnify and indeed distort the role of the Ligue in Boulangism. Specifically, Déroulèdian mythology would have it that in 1886 the chief of the Ligue des Patriotes promised the new minister his support in a coup and in 1889 urged him to march on the Elysée.[8]

The reality, however, corresponds to neither extreme of the interpretative spectrum and must be examined in the broader context of the developments that led to the emergence of Boulangism in France from 1886 to 1889. In that three-year period, affected by the relative economic decline resulting from the financial-agricultural collapse of 1882, the republican alliance also seemed to be not merely stalled but on the brink of collapse. As Franco-German relations deteriorated in 1886 and 1887, the critique of the republican Left which called for *revanche, révision, constituante* found fertile ground. The call for a more democratic consultation, a constituent assembly, when added to the themes of *revanche* and *revision* here linked the political opposition in the eighties with the Gambettist and Déroulèdist themes of the late 1870s. The new slogan not only gained currency among those who still saw themselves as the real political heirs of Gambetta[9] but also among those who saw their economic position deteriorating while the Opportunists remained inert.[10]

Within the general economic arguments advanced for understanding the 1880s, recent statistical information makes it possible to delineate several cyclical fluctuations during the decade. The years 1880 to 1890 appear to constitute a ten-year period of stagnation. By applying indices of industrial production, cost of living, wholesale prices, and some information about wages, the decade appears to be one of no growth, with the figures in 1888-1889 showing but scant improvement over levels reached in 1880-1882. Within this ten-year period, however, several more significant observations may be made. Overall, the 1880s were a time not of simple stagnation but of modest initial growth, rather sharp depression, and then subsequent recovery, the effect of which was to leave the economy in a position only slightly better than at the onset of the decade.

For Gambetta's "new social groups"—industrial workers, Parisian tradesmen and craftsmen, and white-collar employees—the 1880s were a time of economic difficulty, indeed of relative hardship. The specific years of real depression, 1884, 1885, and 1887, saw the devastating combination of a rise in the overall cost-of-living index and the corresponding decline in both wages and industrial production.[11] Indeed, in some sectors of the French economy this situation characterized not only the depression years of the mid-1880s but the entire decade as well. There are indications that in Paris, with its enormous population growth throughout the last third of the nineteenth century, wages were lower in 1896 than they had been in 1880.[12] In addition, studies of viticulture and glass blowers establish that the downward trend continued throughout the entire time in question. Underproduction in agriculture, when matched with overproduction in bottles, produced not unemployment—for those statistics in nineteenth century France are misleading—but a depression, both material and psychological, along with political resentment.[13]

Recent research on salaries has established clearly that real wages in Paris measured in the years 1876, 1882, 1886, and 1892 showed either no gain or a serious decline. Bakers, tailors, cabinetmakers, masons, and carpenters all suffered a decline in real wages in 1886 as compared to those of 1882. In most cases, this pattern continued through the mid-1890s, with little relief during the so-called recovery of 1889-1892.[14]

Thus, while a decade-long picture of the French economy reveals a plateau of stagnation, two qualifications must be made in order to gain an understanding of this development. First, the era was marked by three stages— stagnation, depression, and recovery; second, the situation in Paris (as in agriculture) was considerably more difficult than in the nation as a whole.

Not surprisingly, the Opportunists' theme of "play it safe" was rejected by the voters in the election of 1885. Losing almost half their seats, they saw groups to their left and right obtain almost equal representation in the Chamber. The Opportunists' domination appeared to be over; instead, Parliament was divided among the party of Ferry, the radicals, and the conservatives with the latter two groups having doubled their representation. As a result, there was little upon which the legislature could agree. From a Chamber of some 543 deputies, fewer than two hundred votes were obtainable for any of the critical issues the Opportunists sought to pursue.[15]

Tactically, the Opportunists had few choices. To move to the Right meant abandoning the anticlericalism implicit in Ferry's reforms in education, while an alliance with Clemenceau's group implied the acceptance of social reforms that were in fact abhorrent. In addition, the impact of the economic depression, which coincided with these political developments, was such that the state began to suffer a decline in revenue, adding further difficulties to an already fragile situation. Moreover, the year 1887 saw the first of the scandals that were to shock and titillate France for the next dozen years. The Wilson fiasco not only revealed "Opportunist corruption" but also implicated the president of the Republic, Jules Grévy. That Grévy was the father-in-law of the infamous Wilson was no less important a fact that that Grévy also was a close associate of Ferry.

Contemporaries as well as later historians found it easy to conclude that by 1887 French politics were deadlocked, impotent, corrupt, and in need of considerable change. Clearly, the entire system of parliamentary supremacy and inactivity, ministerial dominance, economic conservatism, corruption, and diplomatic weakness were all subject to question. Revision of the constitution obviously was in order. What was needed was a man, a moment, and a movement. While these would shortly appear in the guise of a certain general, in retrospect it is clear that what the Opportunists needed to restore their dominance was a crisis that could be overcome successfully. As is often noted, the Boulanger episode provided a little something for everyone, but in the end the Opportunists "saved" not only the Republic but their skins as well.

In 1886, however, the Opportunists sought only to regain their parliamentary dominance. Faced with the dubious choice of Right or Left, they moved toward the Radical party. Thus, when Freycinet formed his government, he was obliged to include several Radicals to represent that alliance. While members of Clemenceau's party received portfolios for several "technical" ministries, such as posts and telegraphs, the most important appointment proved to be that of the forty-nine-year-old General Georges Ernest Boulanger to the war ministry. Known as a "clean" (that is, Republican) officer, Boulanger was also known to be a protege of another Georges— Clemenceau.[16]

Within a year, the brav general had become "General Revanche." Moving first to purge several royalists from their commands, Boulanger subsequently showed his republican sentiment even more strongly when the army was ordered to the Decazeville strike in 1886 and was urged not to take sides. Most importantly, however, in 1882 Boulanger was attacked by Bismarck for his military reforms that threatened the peace, and Boulanger's strong reaction to the Schnaebele affair earned him his nationalist reputation. Bismarck's label of General Revanche stuck![17] Thus, it is not surprising that Boulanger's inclusion in the government was greeted with approval by many outside the Opportunist-Radical alliance.

By his own account, Paul Déroulède met General Boulanger well before the latter's political star had risen. Greeting him in 1883, the never reticent and always enthusiastic Déroulède commented that he had known from the first that Boulanger was "his man."[18] If it was not love at first sight, it was at least a marriage of a very fortuitous convenience: a republican general who seemed to stand for reform, who was supported by the Jacobin press, and who appeared to be above mere politics, joined with the self-styled heir of Gambetta and his thousands of nationalist followers.

For if the key for the Ligue in its early years was an outspoken demand for political change, its antithesis was mere politicking. The Ligue and Déroulède never joined the Radical party precisely for this reason. A theme that pervades the entire episode is the increasing mutual enmity between Déroulède and Clemenceau. Of primary importance in understanding this hostility was the emergence of the Ligue not as a political party but as part of a larger political movement, which for a time attached itself to the person of Georges Boulanger. Loyal neither to a dynastic leader nor to the pursuit of political power, the Ligue des Patriotes from its inception and during the Boulangist phase displayed a consistent adherence to the principles of political, social, and foreign policy reform. As a nationalist movement within the Jacobin heritage, the Ligue stood above party while advocating a process that was at the same time democratic and Republican. To be sure, the tensions between these principles were considerable; but for the duration of the Ligue's involvement with Boulanger, those tensions remained harnessed. Given the controversy surrounding both the nature of Boulangism and that of the political influence of the Ligue des Patriotes on that movement, it becomes clear that an understanding of the Ligue illuminates and clarifies the larger political phenomenon.

As long as Boulanger was acceptable to Opportunist politicians as minister of war, he could be regarded as General Revanche. When his dismissal came, however, as it did within months of war tremors and the shock of the Wilson scandal, Boulanger became the focus of all anti-Opportunist sentiment in France. Further, the resignation of Grévy late in 1887 served to aggravate the crisis, and when Ferry—the embodiment of parliamentary opportunism—challenged for the presidency, Boulangism became a conceivable alternative.

But an alternative of what kind? As indicated, much of the literature that draws on political accounts of the time emphasizes the royalist-nationalist-Bonapartist aspects of Boulangism. In fact, the only threat that it posed was electoral. In several by-elections in 1887, the name of the then-inactive general was placed before the electors, with impressive results. But there is no evidence to support the conclusion that the advisors who made up Boulanger's electoral group—the Parti national—intended to act seriously on the popular cries of "To the Elysée" which echoed through Paris via the press in the days preceding or following what has been called the *coup manqué* of 27 January 1889.[19]

As a political movement that attached itself to a dim-witted general of equally dim political visions, Boulangism was an accident. In contrast, the protest of the anti-Opportunists and anti-Ferryists, calling for reform and revision, was not. Representing an alliance of forces that belonged to the nonsocialist Left, Boulangism without Boulanger spoke to the collective social, political, economic, and national grievances of many Frenchmen. It was, in short, an unsuccessful attempt to create a consensus and political equilibrium.

In the years 1888 and 1889 in Paris, the Ligue and Déroulède represented Boulanger's most militant adherents.[20] As in the case of Boulangism in general, however, historians have alleged that the Ligue's involvement with the general was the result of an important conversion engineered by Déroulède. The evidence most often cited is the supposed politicizing of the Ligue in 1887. Although it cannot be denied that the Ligue changed in this period, it now appears that this was as much the result of overall changes in the orientation of French politics as of the specific machinations of one man. In addition, the notion that the Ligue des Patriotes was founded as an "apolitical" association would seem to be of little value. More significant is the fact that as the anti-Opportunist coalition called Boulangism gained in popularity, particularly after the general's elimination from the cabinet, the Ligue mirrored the political tensions involved in this change.

The activities of Déroulède and the Ligue between 1885 and 1889 are an accurate indicator of the evolution and popularity of Boulangism itself. From early March of 1885 until April of 1887, the Ligue des Patriotes undertook a series of activities which paralleled the intensification of anti-German sentiment, the basis of Boulanger's initial popular appeal. From protesting German operas to writing articles attacking French weakness in the face of German aggression, Paul Déroulède led the Parisian Ligue's patriotic propaganda.

Déroulède's second in command and loyally obedient political servant was a former journalist, Henri Deloncle. It was he who attended to the daily affairs of the Ligue while Déroulède traveled, speechified, and generally made a name for himself.[21] Always referring to himself as a loyal and fortunate servant, Deloncle probably wrote many of the pieces attributed to Déroulède which appeared in the Ligue's journal, *Le Drapeau*.[22] Yet their correspondence reveals something less than a perfect relationship. Déroulède was arrogant, demanding, and insistent that his orders be followed; Deloncle, subservient, defensive, and constantly begging for praise and approval.[23] Their relationship remained on this level through the early months of 1887. Early in that year, however, and coinciding with Boulanger's dismissal from the government and the "scandal" of the Schnaebele fiasco, Déroulède resigned from the Ligue des Patriotes.

While many of his followers in Paris followed suit,[24] Déroulède's decision was meant to dramatize the gravity of the diplomatic situation. Not wanting the Germans to take Boulanger's dismissal as a sign of weakness, Déroulède in his own way hoped to continue the new *revanchisme* that the general had personified.[25] As a free-lance nationalist, Déroulède planned and then carried out a one-man diplomatic sideshow, trying to drum up support for France in her hour of need. By the summer he had arranged to visit many European capitals, with a special stop in Moscow. There, according to his own exaggerated accounts, Déroulède was granted "successful" audiences with not only Pobiedonostev and Mikhail Katkov (a Pan-Slavic journalist) but also the great novelist Tolstoy. Posing as a quixotic salesman for "la maison Boulanger et cie," the ex-president of the Ligue had cast his political lot with the ex-minister of war.[26] Indeed, just before his whirlwind and windbag tour, Déroulède had gained considerable notoriety by personally blocking the train that was to have taken Boulanger to his new post at Clermont-Ferrand.

As important as was his decision to rearrange the Franco-Russian alliance and stand tall against Bismarckian saber rattling, Déroulède's decision to resign from the Ligue was intended to prevent its division.[27] It is clear that those who left with him in the spring of 1887 did so in support of his nationalist rather than political ambitions. By the time of his travels to Moscow, resignations had begun to pour in, especially from the provinces.[28] By November of that year, given the impact of the Wilson scandal and the imminence of Grévy's departure from the presidency, the Ligue was as divided as the nation. With the provinces generally supporting the Opportunists, and Paris the Boulangists, the Ligue des Patriotes was split.[29]

As in the instance of the Gare de Lyon demonstration in July, Déroulède's personal activities did little to dispel the anxiety of those *ligueurs* who would have preferred a pro-Ferry organization. The evening before the presidential election, which was to see the Chamber follow Clemenceau's dictum to vote "pour le plus bête,"[30] Déroulède led hundreds of anti-Opportunist followers in a random series of demonstrations against Ferry.[31] Ferry had aroused the particular enmity of the Déroulèdian Ligue by preventing formation of a last-minute Great Ministry that was to have included Boulanger as minister of war. The police report of Déroulède's activity gives an excellent account of the extent of his involvement.

At this moment he was everywhere, at meetings which constantly multiplied, so that on 1 December he had himself arrested in front of the Hôtel de Ville for fighting and loitering. The next day he was again with the crowds, going to the Palais Bourbon, questioning the deputies and running down the rue de Rivoli at the head of groups of demonstrators.[32]

Within that week, many of Déroulède's closest followers submitted their resignations from the Ligue, which had now officially declared its political neutrality and was being guided by Deloncle.[33] In fact, the Ligue was to be divided for more than six months along at least three lines. There is good reason to believe that the schism between Opportunists and Boulangists, and that between Paris and the provinces, reflected the growing personal disagreements of Deloncle and Déroulède. After at least five years of being a very subservient second fiddle, Deloncle was finally in a position to free himself from Déroulède's domination.[34] Additionally, with his firm endorsement of Boulanger's Parti national, Déroulède had begun to emphasize the need for real political unity and authority within the Ligue. This insistence, which would increase with his control, became one of the hallmarks of the Ligue's participation in Parisian politics.[35]

By late spring of 1888, with the Elysée in the hands of the Opportunists, and with Boulanger's electoral victories in February rendering his bid for power all the more feasible, Déroulède announced the creation of a counter-*ligue*. Leaving the old offices and the newspaper, *Le Drapeau*, to Deloncle, the poet-patriot formed a "rump" version of the Ligue called the *groupe d'action dissidente*. Simultaneously, Déroulède declared that his aim was the presidency of the full Ligue, one currently committed to Boulanger.[36]

By early summer his task had been completed. The newly reconstituted Ligue had a new board of directors half of whom were the brain trust of Boulanger's Parti national[37] and the other half relatively new men who not only followed Déroulède through the hectic days of 1888 and 1889 but also continued with the Ligue for the next dozen years.[38] The rearranged organization was to be based on Déroulède's public statement of January 1888:

From now on we shall concern ourselves with internal and external policies, that is to say with the reorganization of the Republic. It is to this reform that we ought to consecrate all our efforts and all our forces. The leader we follow, General Boulanger, is the symbol of the Parti national. . . . We protest the usurpative constitution of 1875 and ministerial parliamentarianism.[39]

The transformation of the Ligue was complete. But what, in fact, had been transformed? Surely the Boulangist phase indicating support for a party and a leader or "symbol" was not new. But in 1888 Déroulède was being consistent with the *raison d'être*—both explicit and implicit—of the Ligue's founding. His pronouncement, consistent with the principles upon which the Ligue had been established six years earlier, also was a résumé of the program of the republican Left—in a word, of Gambetta's Jacobinism. "Dissolusion, Révision, Constituante," the battle cry of Boulangism, was neither new nor revolutionary.[40] The Republican party synthesis of 1878 had broken. The effects of depression, ministerialism, corruption, and diplomatic isolation had divided France again. The so-called split and transformation of the Ligue des Patriotes was nothing more than a reflection of this division. Déroulède had succeeded in maintaining the Ligue's anti-Opportunist stance and had prevented Deloncle's group from proclaiming an apolitical or Ferrist platform. By 1888, at least temporarily, the Opportunists had been expelled.

From this point on, the Ligue des Patriotes became the major movement of Boulangism, particularly in Paris.[41] In the nine-month period from late spring 1888 until the final days of January 1889, the Ligue's activities consisted primarily of supporting the electoral efforts of Boulanger, both in

Paris and in some provincial cities.[42] Significantly, there were few meetings or demonstrations of the kind that had characterized the years 1885-1887, few oratorical flights of fanciful rhetoric against Bismarck; rather, in the words of the police, all efforts were being made "to try to avoid scandal."[43] Not only were Déroulède's physical resources committed to this strategy but also large sums of money which he had inherited from his family or earned in royalties were spent either in Ligue activities or, in the fall of 1888, on his own unsuccessful candidacy for the Chamber from Angoulême.[44] In that attempt, as well as in his effort in the regular spring elections of the spring of 1889, Déroulède cooperated willingly with the leaders of Boulanger's party.

There is little reason to reject the thesis that the Ligue des Patriotes, which supported the aims (if not the person) of Boulanger, neither planned nor intended to achieve its aims by means other than democratic ones. The activities of Déroulède and the Ligue in 1888-1889 substantiate that argument. At a meeting of the twenty *comités* of the Ligue with Boulanger on 1 January 1889, the general addressed his followers with the following: "As for the election itself, you can rest assured, for I am absolutely sure of success. But what we need, and I emphasize, what we need above all else is a strong majority."[45]

What he needed, he got. In Paris on 27 January 1889, aided by an enthusiastic and well-organized political machine oiled by the Ligue des Patriotes and financed in part by money from the royalist "treasurer" the Comte de Dillon, General Georges Boulanger defeated his Opportunist opponent by almost a hundred thousand votes.[46] Legend has it that this was the opportunity missed. With Parisians swirling and chanting the slogans of victory, Boulanger exchanged the glory of a march for the warmth of his mistress.[47]

Three days later, Clemenceau called for the dissolution of the Ligue, and within a matter of weeks Minister of the Interior Ernest Constans—who would, curiously, emerge as something of a hero—initiated the government's counterattack. The first part of the Opportunists' strategy consisted of a two-month-long attempt to prosecute and hence dissolve the Ligue. It would appear that the government wanted to bring Boulanger himself to trial before the Haute Cour—the Senate sitting as the highest tribunal for crimes of treason and sedition—but held back, correctly surmising the general's popularity. Instead, the prosection of the Ligue was meant to break up the general's electoral machine and prevent it from operating in the legislative elections scheduled for later that year. In addition, it was a prelude to the alteration in the electoral laws which would prevent Boulanger from running in multiple districts and sweeping his followers to victory. Finally, the prosecution of the Ligue was intended to warn the general that the government, having figured out his electoral strategy, would one day nab him, though perhaps not immediately.

The ideal solution for the "defense of the Republic," as it fancifully was called, would have been for Boulanger to flee. He did. In April 1889, General Revanche quietly established his headquarters on the Channel island of Jersey. A month earlier, Constans had initiated proceedings against the Ligue des Patriotes, asking the prefect of police to dissolve the organization for having violated articles 291 and 292 of the Penal Code and the Laws of Association of 1834. Convicted of the first offense—that is, of never having received the necessary authorization—but not of the second (for being a secret society), the Ligue was officially dissolved and was fined the sum of one hundred francs.[48]

Although Boulanger's flight preceded the Ligue's dissolution by less than a month, both the organization and the movement still were two years away from extinction. In the elections that followed the Opportunists' recovery of March by six months, thirty-eight Boulangist deputies won seats in the Chamber, including eighteen from the Seine department. While far short of the Boulangists' goals, and influenced by the steady pressure of Constans, the results established that the movement nevertheless was alive and well.[49]

Again, the reality was something different. Some of Boulanger's support can be attributed to the economic uncertainties of the years 1885-1888; however, the fact that public opinion would fall away from the anti-Opportunists with the rapidity of the last leaves of autumn indicates that forces stronger than Ernest Constans were at work. By late 1888 and into 1889, the economy was recovering gradually from the previous years of depression. Industrial production rose by 5 percent and wages by 3 percent while the cost of living declined.[50] Real wages then experienced a sharp increase. Further, the success of the Universal Exposition of 1889, celebrating both the centennial of the revolution and the triumph of industrial technology, suggested that the "Republic of the Republicans" was stable and prosperous.[51] The crisis that had seemed so severe two years earlier was over.

Nevertheless, the thirty-eight Boulangist deputies hoped to use the Chamber as a base from which they could expand their appeal and power. Among them was Paul Déroulède, now deputy from Angoulême's second district. The parliamentary record of Déroulède and his colleagues for the two years after the general's retirement indicates considerable program cohesiveness. With many representing lower- and working-class districts in

Paris, and others standing for an older tradition of Jacobin nationalism, it appears that the Boulangists' program combined a desire for social reform with national revindications.[52] Meeting from time to time with the general at his island retreat, the group maintained the fiction of unity with its leader until he, Georges, ended his life in a maudlin homage to his recently deceased mistress without whom, he declared, he could no longer live.

Although the Ligue had been officially proscribed, Déroulède's enthusiasm stimulated him to try to become both a leading Boulangist deputy in the Chamber as well as a guiding force within the general's inner circle of Jerseyites.[53] Déroulède did become the spokesman for the faction within the group which most vigorously counseled the general to maintain the movement. Déroulède's proposals caused considerable disagreements with the more moderate Alfred Naquet and Georges Laguerre, who had urged the general to retire. The disagreement was so intense that it provoked a duel between Déroulède and Laguerre. Probably to the relief of the local cows, the duel was called off at the last minute.[54]

At the same time, the *rapprochement* between Déroulède and Henri Rochefort—ex-Communard editor of *L'Intransigeant*, and populist supporter of Boulangism—was coming to an end. Having once called Déroulède "butcher of the Commune" in reference to the latter's Légion d'honneur, by 1891 Rochefort was finding once again that he and the deputy from Angoulême had little in common. This was particularly true with reference to Rochefort's outspoken anticlericalism, which the practicing Catholic Déroulède did not share. In 1893, with Boulanger dead and the movement but a memory, Rochefort's pen created the epithet of "plebiscitory idiot" for his colleague.[55] Thus, although the Boulangist movement persisted until the general's death in 1891, the coalition of personalities which supported it began to split apart rapidly following the events of 1889. The economic and political crises that produced the movement's unity evaporated, leaving a disarrayed parliamentary group to squabble over the legacy.

The Ligue itself, although officially dissolved, continued to function well in 1891. Many adherents allowed their memberships to lapse, but the militants continued to operate in support of the Boulangist group of the Chamber. Prior to 1889, Déroulède had made provision for eventual governmental action against the organization by dividing the Ligue's *arrondissement comités* into four groups, each of which was divided further into four groups, each of which was divided further into four subsections. Each section, in turn, had one delegate who reported to the section directly above in the hierarchy, with no subsection having more than twenty members. Clearly, with this centralized organization, questions of authority and leadership which had been posed in 1887 were eliminated. *Le maître* was also the master. The *comités d'arrondissement* claimed ignorance of any central Ligue *comité*, and instead took titles such as Comité de révision du IXe arrondissement—thus posing as purely local electoral organizations.

Police estimates of the composition of the Ligue indicate that its members in 1890 were at least similar socially to those who had joined in the first years of its existence. Although the leadership under Déroulède had changed, the account also indicates the extent to which the Ligue was still an organization of the middle classes. "From a social point of view the militant *ligueurs* belong to the bourgeoisie," states one report, while another identifies a smattering of educated ex-officers along with functionaries, school teachers, and *voyageurs de commerce*.[56] On the one hand, this middle-class identification corresponds generally with the kind of support that the Ligue provided for Boulanger; on the other hand, it contrasts considerably with the composition of the Ligue less than ten years later, during the Dreyfus Affair.

While Déroulède obviously hoped to maintain the Ligue on a quasi-underground basis, at least until he was persuaded that Boulangism had finally failed, both the financial distress of the Ligue and the continued police surveillance threatened its continued existence. The disintegration of the Boulangist movement deprived Déroulède of funds that had swelled the Ligue's treasury in 1889-1890, and by 1891 the *caisse* had fewer than a thousand francs remaining.[57] At the same time, Constans—still minister of the interior—declared that the Ligue's defiance of the 1889 prohibition was intolerable, and in March 1891 he ordered that the Ligue's offices be searched and its officers fined for having failed to obtain government authorization. Constans's new directive, the death of Boulanger, and several seemingly anachronistic demonstrations at yet another performance of *Lohengrin* left the Ligue with few members and a diminished *raison d'être*. By early 1893, prefectorial reports indicated that the Ligue had all but ceased to exist.[58]

Déroulède's activities, too, had begun to change in the year following Boulanger's death. Déroulède increasingly directed his energy to the Chamber. There he sponsored child-labor legislation, a sign of his Boulangist attachment to reform; denounced cuts in the budget of the war ministry; and was censured mildly by his colleagues for preventing a fellow deputy from leaving the floor of the Chamber. It appeared in 1892 that the Ligue des Patriotes had seen its last days and that its leader, Paul Déroulède, was embarking on a new and calmer career more appropriate to the temper of the times.

NOTES—CHAPTER 3

[1] Dansette, *Le Boulangisme.*

[2] Tint, pp. 73-82.

[3] Rémond, *Right in France.*

[4] Brogan, pp. 211-213.

[5] Jacques Néré's unpublished thesis, "La crise industrielle de 1882 et le mouvement Boulangiste" (Paris, 1958), covers in extraordinary depth the kinds of economic information presented later in this chapter.

[6] Frederich Seager, the *Boulanger Affair* (Ithaca, New York, 1969.)

[7] Tint, p. 44.

[8] These "myths" are to be found in Henri Galli, *Paul Déroulède*, in the biographies by Ducray and the Tharauds, and in Dansette, pp. 63-64.

[9] AD 14,689, 9 February 1887, Deloncle to Déroulède: "We must continue to see that the Ligue fulfills its role to the end of [its] Gambettiste heritage."

[10] See the very fine work by C. S. Doty, *From Cultural Rebellion to Counterrevolution: The Politics of Maurice Barrès*, pp. 36-70, on the appeal of Boulangism.

[11] B. R. Mitchell, ed., *European Historical Statistics, 1750-1950*, pp. 185, 731, and 736.

[12] See Mitchell, p. 185, for statistics that contrast wages in Paris with those in the mining industry.

[13] Joan W. Scott, *The Glassworkers of Carmaux*, pp. 80-82.

[14] Jacques Rougerie, "Remarques sur l'histoire des salaires à Paris au XIXe siècle," *Le Mouvement sociale*, no. 63 (April-June 1968), pp. 71-108, esp. pp. 102-103.

[15] Zeldin, pp. 642-646.

[16] The fullest accounts of Boulanger's career are in Dansette, and Seager, *Boulanger Affair.*

[17] The Schnaebele affair, an episode in which a French customs official was enticed across the border and charged with espionage, Seager, *Boulanger Affair*, p. 64. See also Doty, pp. 25-26.

[18] See the accounts in both Ducray and the Tharauds.

[19] See the contrasts presented in Roger Williams, *Henri Rochefort: Prince of the Gutter Press*, p. 218, Seager, *Boulanger Affair*, pp. 203-210, and Dansette, pp. 239-259. The term *coup manqué* is Dansette's.

[20] APP B/A 201, Report: State of Political Parties in 1890. This long and thorough examination of all dissident political groups in France, which evaluates their strengths and programs, attests to the diligence of the police and is a source of extraordinary information.

[21] AD 14,704, 12 August 1886, Deloncle to Déroulède.

[22] AD 14,689, 19 February 1887, Deloncle to Déroulède.

[23] AD 14,734, undated, but 1887 by its number. Deloncle to Déroulède.

[24] APP B/A 1,337, 4 April 1887.

[25] Chastinet, 2:185.

[26] *Le Grelot*, 4 September 1887. The caricature of Déroulède as Quixote would forever remain in the minds of at least his detractors.

[27] APP B/A 43, March 1887.

[28] APP B/A 1337, 16 July 1887.

[29] APP B/A 1,337, 21 November 1887.

[30] Hence the arrival of the unfortunate Sadi-Carnot to the Elysée.

[31] APP B/A 1,337, 20 November 1887.

[32] APP B/A 1,033, report on Déroulède's activities during the whole period from 1887 to 1889, dated 1889 but citing surveillance on 1 and 2 December 1887.

[33] AD 16,928, 5 December 1887, Richard to Déroulède.

[34] APP B/A 1,337, 20 April 1888.

[35] Ibid.

[36] APP B/A 1,337, 24 April 1888.

[37] The names, especially Alfred Naquet and Georges Turquet, served to remind the public of the Boulangist connection.

[38] Marcel Habert, Henri Galli, Ferdinand Le Menuet, and Pierre Richard all compensated for Deloncle's defection.

[39] APP B/A 1,003, general report, 1889.

[40] Sternhell, "Barrès et la gauche," p. 78.

[41] APP B/A 1,337, 3 June 1888. This report established Ligue membership at one hundred thousand. Other estimates go as high as double that number, Chastinet, 2:185.

[42] Doty, *Cultural Rebellion*, pp. 187-188.

[43] APP B/A 1,337, 18 May 1888.

[44] AD K, checkbooks, 1885-1889.

[45] APP B/A 1,337, 2 January 1889.

[46] The royalists tried but never succeeded in converting Boulangism to their cause.

[47] Dansette, pp. 239-259.

[48] APP B/A 1,337, 12 March 1889.

[49] Doty, "Parliamentary Boulangism after 1889," pp. 250-269.

[50] Mitchell, p. 185.

[51] APP B/A 201, General Report: Situation, 1890.

[52] APP B/A 1,032, 11 November 1890. See also Doty, "Parliamentary Boulangism," and Sternhell, "Barrès et la gauche," for an analysis of the working-class support of Boulangism.

[53] Williams, pp. 244-245.

[54] APP B/A 201, General Report: Situation, 1890.

[55] APP B/A 1,032, 7 October 1898. This report like the one preceding is a summary of the Ligue's activities over a ten-year period.

[56] APP B/A 1,340, 13 December 1890.

[57] APP B/A 1,340, 1 March 1891 and 18 March 1891.

[58] Archives nationales (ANF⁷) 12,449, January 1893. See also APP B/A 1,340, May 1892.

PART
11
—
FRANCE DIVIDED: THE AFFAIR

CHAPTER

4

—

The Doldrums

THE TEMPER OF THE TIMES, however, was not one characterized by the golden haze of peace, progress, and prosperity attributed to it by subsequent generations looking back on the Belle Epoque. The victory of the Opportunists, rallying to defend their Republic against the onslaughts of a Caesarist general on horseback, proved to be short-lived. The recovery of the French economy, spectacular in 1888 and 1889, became fragile by 1893-1894. More important, although the first years of the new decade appeared to be tranquil ones, in truth they represent a time in which new forces were gathering in anticipation of events and conditions that would give them life. The failure of Boulangism, for example, while seeming to reinforce the recovery of the Opportunists, also created a political vacuum that the socialists would attempt to fill.[1] Although at least some of the working classes' requirements for social reform had been responded to by the Boulangist deputies, during the 1890s those classes were to look elsewhere for representation and support. Similarly, it has been claimed that the Boulangist crisis had been a school for the education of new men and new programs in the art of modern urban electoral politics.[2] This was true not only for the socialists but for the Ligue des Patriotes as well. Within five years a new Ligue and a newly vitalized French socialism would face each other—organized, disciplined, dedicated—in the energized political atmosphere of Paris. The experiences of 1889 might be forgotten, but their lessons were remembered. The Opportunists' victory, the Boulangist defeat, and the subsequent growth of modern French socialism were legacies of the late 1880s which were to unfurl in the late 1890s.

In 1893, however, the new parliamentary elections confirmed the Opportunist victory of 1889. The socialists had gained from twelve to forty-five seats; nevertheless, their growth was canceled out by the virtual extinction of parties "hostile" to the regime.[3] Despite several crises, the Opportunists controlled most of the ministries, and in 1896 Jules Méline became prime minister of the longest-lived government of the Third Republic. Political stability seemed assured, and the subsequent movement attempting to reconcile the "clerical" issues seemed to indicate that France shortly would solve a difficult and long-standing problem. The *ralliement* was an expression of this "new spirit" on the part of both the Church and the Republic.[4] Though this reconciliation would ultimately collapse at the time of the Dreyfus Affair, there is good reason to believe that consideration of these clerical issues represented an attempt by the republicans to avoid the commitment and reform necessitated by increasing industrial and economic pressures. In this respect the Opportunists had changed little.

In the years that divide Boulanger from Dreyfus the vicissitudes of industrialization and the growing force and organization of socialism produced a period of uncertainty, of change, and indeed of challenge for the victorious republicans. More than the origins of a Franco-Russian alliance, more than the establishment of neo-mercantilist economic policy of tariffs and empire, the social question and the anxieties it revealed characterized the "quiet" years.[5] The Belle Epoque was also the *fin de siècle*. The explosion of concurrent anarchist activity seemed to intensify not only the depth of the problem but also the indignation of a smug, though increasingly fearful, middle class.

Clearly, the evolution and development of French socialism, the increasing organization of the working classes, and the economic response of the government were all of a piece. Recalling the conservative fiscal response of Freycinet and Ferry to the crises of the early 1880s, the efforts of Méline in the 1890s exhibit a remarkable consistency. The expansion, contraction, and reexpansion of the French economy from 1889 to 1896 were all resolved with the institution of a tariff system that ended the fiction of free trade.[6] Rather than protect French industry in its effort to modernize, the intent of the Méline tariffs actually was to alleviate the tension of industrialization by what one historian has called a policy of "resistance to change."[7] Observing that working-class demands for higher wages, shorter hours, and increased state intervention in the social question would only step up the industrial pace that produced these demands, Méline and others sought to restore France's traditional economic balance of industry and agriculture. As conservatives, they believed that a stable political regime was best ensured by a tranquil social system. Ironically, within three years of the erection of the tariff wall, France would begin the most extensive period of economic growth in her history.

Eighteen ninety-six marked the beginning not only of that eighteen-year era of industrial expansion but also of a unified French socialism. Speaking at Saint-Mandé, Alexander Millerand announced the intention of French socialists to achieve their goals by the "conquest of public power through universal suffrage."[8] The agreement by the Guesdists (followers of Jules Guesde) and the independents to share one page of a single newspaper, *La Petite République*, added to the likelihood that the divisions of the 1880s soon would end.

Significantly, the announcement of a minimum socialist program was also a victory for Jean Jaurès, for whom a unified French socialist movement was both a life's work and an ideal.[9] Elected to the Chamber in 1889, Jaurès returned to the legislature in 1893, largely because of the role he played as an interviewer in the heated miners' strike in Carmaux in 1892.[10] By his support of the strikers, Jaurès had focused national attention on the social question, as well as upheld the workers' political aims. The strike at Carmaux, however, was more than a landmark in Jaurès's personal move toward socialism; it also marked the simultaneous emergence of the two political forces—one of the 1880s and the other of the 1890s—which addressed themselves to the interests of the working class. The strike of 1892 also marked the last instance of concerted interest on the part of the Boulangists in issues of social reform.[11] With no general, little money, their leadership quarreling, and their major political machine disbanded, the Boulangists had virtually completed the process by which the social question was passed to the socialists. It appeared that French politics had formed a new opposition to the regime of the Opportunists, just as the effects of industrialization had begun to underscore the widening social gaps in society. It is this double theme— the growth of socialist parties and unions and the recovery and expansion of the French industrial economy—which best characterizes the years between Boulanger and Dreyfus. That the Opportunists, and by now some of the Radicals who shared governing, reacted defensively is a measure of the conservative reflex of the social as well as political nature of the Third Republic.

Shortly before the elections of 1893 which established the social and political contours of the next five years, Paul Déroulède found himself without a political cause. For the first time in more than twenty years he was again a man of letters. In June of that year, the deputy from Angoulême, in response to an episode called the Norton affair, rose in the Chamber and stated, "All of you disgust me. Politics is the lowest of professions, politicians, the lowest of men. I've had enough. I resign."[12] The impotence of Déroulède without Boulanger had been clear enough several months earlier; then, in the midst of the debates set off by the revelation in *La Libre Parole* that a Jewish financier, Baron Jacques de Reinach, had corrupted several deputies who had supported the Panama Canal Company, Déroulède had set his sights on Georges Clemenceau. On 20 November 1892, during an exchange over what had become the Panama affair, Déroulède took the floor. He first launched into a long attack on Cornelius Herz, asking why this man, a "German" born in France, should be an officer of the Légion d'honneur. Receiving the applause of both the Left and Right, he speculated about who this man's patron could be: "But none of you will name him because he has three things which you fear: his sword, his pistol and tongue. Very well, I brave all three . . . he is M. Clemenceau."[13]

Clemenceau, himself on the fringe of politics, had little choice but to challenge his tormentor to a duel. Each exchanged three shots. There were six misses. Having been called not only a Panamist but an English spy, Clemenceau withdrew from active political participation for six months.[14] In an act of coincidental symmetry, Déroulède soon followed his rival into political exile. The day following his "resignation," the deputy from Angoulême received a visit from an old political ally and sometime friend, Lucien Millevoye. Trying to apologize for involving him in the Norton mess, Millevoye attempted to persuade Déroulède to return to the Chamber. His mediation was greeted, however, with the following: "You have made me look like a simpleton, you have discredited me."[15] Shortly thereafter, Paul Déroulède returned to Langely.

In the hagiographic biographies of the founder of the Ligue des Patriotes, Déroulède's principled pique is cited to illustrate the sympathetic and honorable qualities of *le maître*. In retrospect, it represents both more and less. Between 1889 and the illuminations of the Norton-Clemenceau affairs, in 1893 in fact, Déroulède had functioned as a member of the Chamber of Deputies. Dramatic moments aside, he did concern himself in those years far more with issues of revision than *revanche.* In continuing to label the constitution of 1875 royalist, Déroulède maintained his allegiance to the Gambettist-republican tradition. His ideas for reform centered on the creation of a strong executive, a belief in the purity of universal suffrage, and the liquidation of the colonial empire.[16] He was equally involved with social issues. Not only did he voice his district's concerns with the crisis in agriculture but he maintained and intensified this—the old Ligue's and the Boulangist group's attention to the plight of the working class. In both 1890 and 1891 Déroulède proposed significant social reforms that would have begun the process of state intervention in the creation of a primitive system of social security, financed by a progressive income tax.[17] In a word, as a parliamentarian between 1889 and 1893 Déroulède continued the reformist tendency of his past.

Thus, there is something almost pitiable and childlike in the cries of disillusionment and disappointment. "We are the party of the disgusted" was a phrase he often repeated. Déroulède's anguished pronouncements at the Chamber nevertheless contained certain elements that highlight the evolution of his political thinking. No longer a member of Boulanger's inner circle devoted to the strategy of electoral victory as a means to political reform, Déroulède was not yet a key figure in the nationalist and anti-Semitic leagues that formed the core of the anti-Dreyfus movement. In the mid-1890s he had discarded one set of allegiances without replacing it with others. Further, as a result of his reading of the Norton forgeries, he apparently recognized that if he truly was disillusioned with politics as well as disgusted with parliamentarianism, then he was too naïve to be successful at that game. The next several years, which were to bring complete withdrawal from public life, followed by an even greater political involvement and finally exile, severely tested his perception.

It was thus in 1893 that Paul Déroulède found himself almost entirely alone. The Boulangist combination, despite the opportunity that Panama had offered, had split away from him. His former allies, Millevoye, Rochefort, Thiébaud, Laguerre, Naquet, and in 1893 Pierre Richard, had now become enemies.[18] New stars were rising, such as the anti-Semites, Morès, and Drumont, and old ones correspondingly had dimmed. Only a handful of the Ligue's leaders remained faithful. Although in 1893 Déroulède seemed disillusioned and disappointed, his most loyal lieutenants were not. Often working without funds and under the most minimal conditions, these men—Paulin Méry, a deputy from the fourteenth *arrondissement*; Marcel Habert, Déroulède's lawyer in 1889 and also a deputy; Henri Galli, a newspaper man and ex-editor of *Le Drapeau*; and above all Ferdinand Le Menuet, a journalist and secretary-general of the Ligue—pleaded with their former leader that they and all of France needed him. They spent the next four years urging Déroulède to return to political life and re-create the Ligue. Then in mid-July 1893 Cuneo d'Ornano, the Bonapartist deputy from the first electoral district in Angoulême and an admirer of Déroulède, wrote him the following:

I think that, in returning to your native ground, you have, like the giant in the fables, regained your resolution. . . . Your return is what we need, if you do not wish to remain eternally identified with Millevoye in your retirement (you who never approved of his attitude and blind stubbornness) . . . you must take up the struggle again.[19]

Remaining at Langely, Déroulède, now forty-seven, strolled in the lush countryside of the Charente, read in his study, and resumed writing. He began work on a new play, *Messire du Guesclin*, and received word that a recent book of poetry, *Chants du paysan*, had been given an award by the Académie française. At the same time he remained involved in departmental politics, having been elected *conseiller général* in Angoulême in 1892, a position he retained until 1901. For the moment, his relationship with the Ligue or its remnants was nonexistent.

The mid-1890s promised little opportunity for Déroulède and the Ligue to aspire to return to their former political prominence. It would take an unusual and critical situation to rally and reform the old Boulangist forces into a new power.

The rebirth of the Ligue des Patriotes in 1897-1898 following the reopening of the Dreyfus case, at which time Déroulède reasserted his preeminent (though not universally accepted) leadership, represented a realignment of the French Right. This new formation on the Right, composed of men once associated with the Left—from Gambettists through Communards to Blanquists—combined with the alienated lower-middle-class youth of Paris and with the doctrines of nationalism and anti-Semitism, would be a force having considerable historical and contemporary importance. In 1893, however, realignment of right-wing forces was beyond the realm of possibility. Its leaders barely were on speaking terms, and from all appearances each was in the process of dying a slow death. The same was true of the "dynastic parties," each of which suffered from the lack of an effective leader or insufficient financial or political resources, or both.

Déroulède's complete isolation from Parisian politics was not long-lived.

In January 1894 the prefect of police in Paris received a petition from a group called the Ligue patriotique des intérêts français, whose charter was almost an exact replica of the Ligue des Patriotes' 1882 constitution. The new president of this organization was Ferdinand Le Menuet. By May of 1894 the prefect of police had given authorization to the Ligue, provided that it refrain from participation in politics.[20] Not to be deceived, by mid-July the police and the Sûreté had suggested that this new organization was but a cover for the rebirth of the old Ligue and that its leader, Déroulède, was preparing to resume his position as president.[21]

Apparently, the police were absolutely correct in their first assumption but quite premature in their second. Still at Langely, Déroulède was kept well informed of the process of reorganization by Le Menuet, who described in detail how Marcel Habert had been able to arrange an interview with Casimir-Périer, the prime minister, and had received the government's approval for the new Ligue. Le Menuet was also optimistic that when the time came for the Ligue to "march," the government would not be unsympathetic.[22]

In these as in future activities, Déroulède's ambivalence is quite clear. On the one hand, his literary success had allowed him to divide his time between the comfort of Langely and the stylish social world of Paris. On the other hand, he was still very much attached to his convictions. The idea of revenge, of the return of Alsace-Lorraine and political revision as the way to restore France both morally and politically, remained central to the image that Déroulède projected before his admirers and critics. During the 1893-1897 period he believed that his pen could best contribute to the public's awareness of the imperatives of revenge. At the same time, his vanity and naïveté told him that other options needed to be kept open and utilized when the situation permitted. It would be another four years before such a situation presented itself, yet the conflict between action and reflection was steadily becoming more pronounced.

The opening of his play, *Messire du Guesclin*, was greeted by many as the return of the true Déroulède, whose poetry could be far more effective than his politics in publicizing those ideas that were so important to him.[23] Du Guesclin was a symbolic leader of a France beset with anarchy. Disinterested, energetic, and enthusiastic, possessing the foresight to understand the need for strong government, the hero decides to commit himself to action to achieve his goals.[24] The popular response to the play was enthusiastic, and Déroulède ensured that free tickets would be dispensed to all the requisite politicians, army officers, and journalists.[25] Clearly, the play occupied all of

Déroulède's energy, and its reception prompted his hopes that the Académie française might soon open its doors to him.[26] His success was also financial; a receipt Calman-Lévy, his publishers, showed royalties on the *Chants du soldat* of almost six thousand francs.[27]

These successes apparently offset the series of attacks on the play which appeared in *L'Intransigeant* and even prompted Déroulède to speak with Millevoye for the first time in more than two years. When asked by Millevoye whether he had any plans to reenter political life, Déroulède replied that for the moment he awaited events that would call him back to duty.[28] Millevoye was not the only member of the old Boulangist coalition in touch with Déroulède in 1895. Several months earlier, Georges Thiébaud had written, exclaiming surprise that Déroulède's play was going to concern itself with "the end of democracy." Thiébaud noted that republican democracy had been their ideal, but the *haute bourgeoisie* were scared senseless of the idea. As for himself, he would work to represent the common and forgotten man.[29] The implication was that Déroulède should join him and possibly Drumont and Rochefort in these efforts. By 1895, those who considered themselves important revisionist leaders were seeking to resume their activities.

In addition to the urging of Déroulède's public and one-time political collaborators, his loyal friends within the Ligue also continually tried to convince Déroulède that the time was ripe to resume his activities.[30] The appropriate situation seemed to present itself in 1895. Early that year, the French government announced that it was sending a squadron of ships to attend the German celebration of the opening of the Kiel Canal, scheduled for the summer. To those (including the members of the Ligue) who were aware of France's diplomatic overtures toward Russia, this was yet another indication that French foreign policy was at best unstable and inconsistent. The Ligue quickly began to plan for protests against the French position, and Le Menuet wrote to Déroulède asking that he take part.[31] At the same time, Déroulède's closest colleague, Marcel Habert, wrote, "Only Paul Déroulède can usefully protest in the Chamber against Kiel, and since Déroulède is not there, no one will bring it up . . . your presence is urgent."[32] Despite these pleas, Déroulède remained behind the scenes, taking no active part in the Ligue's plans or demonstrations.[33] In fact, the Ligue had a great deal of difficulty in mobilizing the few members it could claim, even in the *arrondissements* where it was strongest.[34] This was due, no doubt, to the lack of a critical issue that might have served to stir up enthusiasm among potential supporters of the Ligue and also was the result of the bitter struggle for relative hegemony among the component parts of what would become the Parisian Right.

Drumont, whose *La Libre Parole* was beginning to decline with the end of the Panama scandal, was eager to amalgamate the disparate elements of Boulangism.[35] It appears that he was trying unsuccessfully to reconcile Rochefortist elements in Paris, represented by Jules Roche, with those of Déroulède, represented by Paulin Méry. At the same time, not yet aligned with either group, Millevoye had his own limited following and used his position as an editor of *La Patrie* to confuse the situation further. The complex sectarian problem began to resolve itself when Millevoye and Déroulède met in November of 1895, but the Drumont-Rochefort-Déroulède triangle of competition and jealousy was no more harmonious at the end of 1895 than it had been at the beginning of the year.[36]

To cloud further an already murky situation, early in 1896 Déroulède was approached by representatives of the Duc d'Orléans and the Bonapartists, who indicated a desire to reconstruct Boulangism under a dynastic leader.[37] Although Déroulède thought that some kind of alliance with the Bonapartists was possible, his reaction to the Orléanists was completely negative. His supporters in the Ligue, who were in the process of both revising the statute that forbade internal political participation as well as reviving the organization, were apprehensive of these overtures.[38] Their relief was apparent when Déroulède addressed their meeting with a telegram declaring, "Vive la République nationale."[39]

From 11 January to 30 April 1896 the government was in a state of constitutional crisis, stirring the Ligue and other opposition elements into a flurry of activity.[40] The Chamber wanted to continue its Radical coalitions, whereas the Senate desired a more moderate cabinet.[41] Le Menuet wrote excitedly to Déroulède, declaring that the system was rotten, ready to fall apart. "Your presence here is necessary," he concluded.[42] Aware of the situation and at this time receiving copies of all the Ligue's correspondence, Déroulède decided to visit Paris and, for the first time in almost five years, to take an active role in the Ligue's affairs.[43] Within several days he conferred with *arrondissement* leaders and told his close collaborators to keep themselves ready in case they were needed.[44] At the same time, he and Le Menuet decided that the Ligue would campaign for candidates in the coming municipal elections.[45] In addition, he pursued tentative arrangements for cooperation with *La Libre Parole* organization and entertained plans to edit a daily newspaper whose backers included Millevoye and the Bonapartists.[46] Déroulède was keeping all options open. Undoubtedly, what the revisionists were looking for was an indication that the crisis in the Chamber would present them with enough ammunition to rally public opinion and to attack the parliamentary system. Each group was willing, as it had been a year earlier, to cooperate with any other, but at the same time each hoped to become dominant. While occasionally giving the appearance of unity, these groups displayed conflicting purposes and expectations in the 1890s.

When the Méline government came to power on the last day of April, 1896, Déroulède and others saw their opportunity quickly fade. Déroulède returned to the countryside to resume the routine to which he had become accustomed and to finish writing his latest play, *La Mort de Hoche*. His supporters in Paris continued to implore him to reconstruct the old Ligue des Patriotes. Though informed of all events, Déroulède took no active role. He remained isolated and aloof, refusing even to answer the correspondence sent to him from Paris.[47] Nevertheless, by December 1896 Le Menuet, Habert, and Galli decided without public announcement that the Ligue Patriotique would become the Ligue des Patriotes—complete with its old slogans, organization, and constitution.[48] Though the Ligue lacked offices, its members met regularly at a café-restaurant as was, and still is, the custom of many Parisian political groups.[49]

The events of 1895-1896 illustrate very well the ambivalence Déroulède seemingly felt as he faced the future. Having decided to renounce active politics, he nevertheless remained attracted to its possibilities. With the ebb of the crisis that had led him to hope that action was possible, Déroulède retreated to his literary world, disappointed and wary. He must have realized that once his enthusiasm was released, it would have no bounds, and hence he was defensive and cautious. Similarly, those closest to him in the Ligue thought that the attraction of reestablishing the Ligue des Patriotes would ultimately outweigh their leader's caution. During the winter of 1896-1897 Déroulède's supporters decided to risk his disavowal and began work on reestablishing the Ligue des Patriotes.[50]

By late March 1897, Le Menuet and Gauthier de Clagny had arranged to rent a suite of offices on rue du Marche St. Honoré. Immediately thereafter, the prefect of police informed the government that for all practical purposes it should consider the Ligue des Patriotes to be reconstituted.[51]

On 13 July 1897 a small tabloid appeared for the first time since 1889 on the streets of Paris. *Le Drapeau* announced that the Ligue des Patriotes was re-forming in order to promote the ideals of patriotism and national reconciliation. "We have only one religion, the religion of *la patrie*; one goal, the reconstruction of her integrity; one hate, the hate of those who wish to dismember France; one love, the love of the flag." There followed an extract of the statutes of the Ligue, which declared that the organization had as a goal the revision of the Treaty of Frankfort and the restitution of Alsace-Lorraine. The inside pages of *Le Drapeau* contained several articles attesting to German military strength and population increase as well as a selection of poetry from the *président d'honneur* of the Ligue, Paul Déroulède:

> Au Drapeau! Que ce cri soit le cri de la France
> Le Prusse en tête acclame un futur conquérant
> Nous, les anciens Vaincus acclamons l'Espérance
> Ce que la guerre a perdu, la guerre reprend.[52]

Despite the call to the flag, the newspaper did not appear again, as announced, two weeks later. Parisians left the city for the month of August; the government too followed suit. Only those at the prefecture of police seemed to notice this latest journalistic endeavor. It was but the first of several false starts. By the fall of 1897 the Ligue was holding local meetings in the various *arrondissements* of Paris. Attendance was dismal, with between fourteen and forty persons present. Déroulède remained distant and came to Paris only to supervise the production of *La Mort de Hoche*, which opened in October with moderate success.[53]

Hoche was the last of the five plays Déroulède was to write between 1869 and 1897. Although none of them had the critical or popular, especially popular, success of his poetry, they reveal a political consistency that coincides with Déroulède's public career. In contrast with his poetry, entirely concerned with the vision of war, patriotism, sacrifice, and *revanche*, Déroulède's plays express his continued preoccupation with political reform and revision.

La Moabite, accepted for presentation at the Comédie-Française in 1880 and published in 1881 with a preface by its author, was nothing more or less than an open political attack on Ferry, who was treated as a dangerous atheist undermining the political vitality of the nation. Similarly *Messire du Guesclin*, written in the years following Déroulède's retreat from politics after the Norton-Clemenceau spectacle, reiterates Déroulède's plea for political reform. Where *La Moabite* was biblical in its historical setting, *du Guesclin* presents a Breton of the fourteenth century who restores his nation to order. In so doing he must choose between monarchy and anarchy, and he opts for the former as a means of preserving the political integrity of the nation in the face of foreign invasion and disorder.

Two years later Déroulède dealt with these same themes in *La Mort de Hoche*. Aware that *du Guesclin* might be understood as a monarchist plea, *Hoche* by its revolutionary analogy restored Déroulède's loyalty to the republican tradition. Yet beneath the plea for political restoration of republican virtues, *Hoche* reveals an increasing preoccupation with the theme of the necessity of revolution or counterrevolution as the only means of restoring what has been lost. Hoche proclaims his allegiance both to the revolution as it embodied the ideas of Rousseau and the Enlightenment and to the belief that Napoleon could restore that revolution. The corruption and decadence of the Directory was depicted as analogous to the parliamentary regime of the Opportunists and their successors.[54] As in *La Moabite* and *Messire du Guesclin, La Mort de Hoche* was a political drama that preceded Déroulède's reentry into the drama of politics.

As usual, Déroulède presented free tickets for his play to those who he deemed were important. The response was varied. Some praised his efforts and thought that the play indicated that the France of 1897 had a problem as serious as the France of Hoche.[55] Others, perhaps more discriminating, like the Duchess d'Uzès, sent their regrets, the duchess declining on three separate occasions.[56]

In December, *Le Drapeau* appeared once again, with a plea for those loyal to the Ligue to rally at la place de la Concorde on the thirty-first.[57] A week before the rally Marcel Habert, at a meeting of the *assemblée générale* of the Ligue, announced first that the treasurer reported a balance of 339 francs, and second that the *président d'honneur*, M. Paul Déroulède, was expected to attend the rally.[58] The demonstration materialized as a rather pitiful celebration of *la patrie*. It was dark and cold, a winter's day when all of Paris is a chilling grey—a day on which it would have been hard to believe that one was in perhaps the most beautiful city in the world. A delegation of seven members of the Ligue de Patriotes arrived in front of the statue of Strasbourg, la place de la Concorde, and replaced the seven flags that had flown there since July. The ceremony took fifteen minutes and apparently was observed by as many agents of the police and Sûreté as Ligue members. Speeches were left unspoken, and the *président d'honneur* did not appear. "The affair- . . . passed without incident."[59] As the *ligueurs* left, disappearing into the protective grey cloak provided by the weather, they distributed copies of *Le Drapeau* to a few onlookers.

All conditions being equal, the possibilities for the successful reorganization of the Ligue des Patriotes in 1898 appeared no better than they had during the previous six years. The possibility that Paul Déroulède would resume his political position within the Chamber or as president of the Ligue was similarly dim.

NOTES—CHAPTER 4

[1] Harvey Goldberg, *The Life of Jean Jaurès.*

[2] See the studies by Patrick Hutton, especially "Popular Boulangism and the Advent of Mass Politics in France."

[3] Chastinet, 3:52.

[4] See particularly, Alexander Sedgwick, *The Ralliement in French Politics,* and David Shapiro, "The Ralliement in the Politics of the 90's," *The Right in France.*

[5] Sorlin, *Waldeck-Rousseau,* pp. 354-364.

[6] See E. O. Golob, *The Méline Tariff.*

[7] Zeldin, pp. 647-652.

[8] Alexander Millerand, *Le Socialisme réformiste français* (Paris, 1903), p. 26.

[9] Daniel Ligou, *Histoire du socialisme en France 1810-1961,* pp. 122-139.

[10] Scott, pp. 133-136, and Goldberg, pp. 107-108.

[11] AD unnumbered, 20 September 1892, Pierre Richard to Déroulède.

[12] *Journal officiel (JO),* 21 June 1893, p. 1,794.

[13] *JO,* 20 December 1892, pp. 1,886-1,888.

[14] Déroulède's family says legend has it that Clemenceau backed down from a second round in fear of Déroulède's second, name forgotten, reputed to be a crack shot. Interview with M. Paul Heurtey, 5 June 1969, Paris.

[15] Tharaud and Tharaud, p. 96.

[16] *JO,* 8 November 1890, p. 373

[17] *JO,* 15 March 1891, p. 1,148

[18] Richard remained a personal friend of Déroulède, but as a moderately successful politician he was more and more becoming a member of the political fraternity. APP B/A 1,037, 1898.

[19] AD 8,156, Ornano to Déroulède, 16 July 1893.

[20] APP B/A 1,320, 28 January, 5 April, and 18 May 1894.

[21] AN F7 12,449, 4 July 1894.

[22] AD 17,889, 14 May 1894, Le Menuet to Déroulède. Almost immediately the Sûreté checked the identity of the prominent members of the "new" organization. To a man—there were only ten listed as militant in 1894—they were upper middle class, in their fifties, and destined to drop out of the Ligue by 1899. AN F7 12,449, 1894.

[23] AD unnumbered, unsigned to Déroulède, 12 November 1895: "If du Geschin [*sic*] knew how to lead an army, how well you know to electrify the heart."

[24] Tharaud and Tharaud, p. 98.

[25] AD 7,123, 26 October 1895, General Mercier to Déroulède.

[26] AD 17,952, 25 October 1895, Le Menuet to Déroulède; APP B/A 1,032, 25 December 1895.

[27] AD unnumbered, 31 December 1895.

[28] APP B/A 1,032, 25 October 1895.

[29] AD 9,914, 2 March 1895, Thiébaud to Déroulède.

[30] For the sake of convenience, the Ligue patriotique des intérêts français will be referred to as the Ligue.

[31] APP B/A 1,032, 9 March 1895; AD 6,857, 14 March 1895, Le Menuet to Déroulède.

[32] AD 4,046, 7 March 1895, Habert to Déroulède.

[33] Instead, he came to Paris on 20 June and then only to lay a wreath at the statue of Strasbourg, Place de la Concorde. APP B/A 1,032, 20 June 1895.

[34] APP B/A 1,340, 13 May 1895—the 5th, 11th, 14th, 18th, and 20th. AN F[7] 12,449, 13 April 1895.

[35] AN F[7] 12,449, 1, 2, 6 April 1895.

[36] AD 17,947, 5 November 1895, Le Menuet to Déroulède.

[37] AD 14,407, 14 March 1896, de Dion to Déroulède: "The Prince [who] has carried the flag of France . . . desires to talk with the one who personifies for all bravery, loyalty, talent, and patriotism." See also APP B/A 1,032, 25 March 1896. The delay of only a few days between a letter of invitation sent to Déroulède and the police's knowledge of a possible new relationship indicates the reliability of police information; AD 22,715, 27 January 1896, Baron de Breretz to Déroulède; APP B/A 1,032, 25 March 1896.

[38] APP B/A 1,340, 23 February 1896; AD 17,697, 16 April 1896, Le Menuet to Déroulède.

[39] AD 17,697, 16 April 1896, Le Menuet to Déroulède.

[40] Now the Ligue Patriotique, having again changed its name.

[41] Chastenet, 3:92-93.

[42] AD 17,796, 22 April 1896, Le Menuet to Déroulède.

[43] APP B/A 1,032, 20 April 1896.

[44] APP B/A 1,032, 28 April 1896.

[45] AD 17,572, 20 April 1896, Le Moine to Déroulède.

[46] APP B/A 1,032, 5 May 1896; APP B/A 1,032, 28 and 30 April 1896.

[47] AD 17,829, 25 January 1897, Le Menuet to Déroulède.

[48] AD 17,607, 7 December 1896, Le Menuet to Déroulède; AN F[7] 12,449, December 1896.

[49] The Ligue met at the Café de la Petite Bourse, 85, rue Richelieu, in the first *arrondissement*, not far from the Bibliothèque nationale.

[50] AD 1,819, 19 January 1897, Chevariat to Déroulède.

[51] AN F[7] 12,449, 20 March 1897. The police also noted that until such time as Déroulède resumed the presidency, which he would not do until he thought it necessary to take action, the Ligue posed little threat or danger. APP B/A 1,338, 21 April 1897.

[52] *Le Drapeau*, 13 July 1897.

[53] *La Patrie*, 7 October 1897.

[54] Those who have written admiring biographies of Déroulède, the Tharaud brothers and Ducray, see Hoche as Déroulède's justification for future action. Tharaud and Tharaud, p. 99. Although there may be a curious correlation between Déroulède's literature and action, the analogy, though simplistic, does indicate his tendency to act out his fantasies in his plays.

[55] AD 33,015, 7 December 1897, Foursin to Déroulède.

[56] AD 45,653; 45,654; 45,655; 8 October, 10 November, and 22 December 1897.

[57] *Le Drapeau*, December 1897.

[58] APP B/A 1,338, 23 December 1897.

[59] APP B/A 1,338, 31 December 1897.

CHAPTER

5

—

Anti-Semitism and the Affair

ALL THINGS, HOWEVER, were not equal. In 1897, three years after its initial disclosure in *La Libre Parole*, the Dreyfus case was reopened unexpectedly. On 31 October 1897 *Le Matin* leaked the story that the vice-president of the Senate, Auguste Scheurer-Kestner, an Alsatian and an "aristocrat of the Republic," had joined with a tiny minority in France who believed a certain Alfred Dreyfus to be innocent of the crime of which he had been convicted three years earlier.[1] Approached by Arthur Ranc and Joseph Reinach in the spring of 1897, Scheurer-Kestner had expressed his doubts regarding Dreyfus's guilt. After reviewing what he could about the case, he approached General Billot, Méline's minister of war, and was told simply not to meddle in the affair.[2]

At the time of *Le Matin*'s now-famous article, the Méline cabinet had been in power for more than a year and a half. The stability that it offered was the result of an alliance between Opportunists and moderate Radicals, whose political and economic conservatism was marched by at least a rhetorical willingness to move toward policies of social amelioration and religious moderation. Too, the discussions of social reform, from old-age pensions to the income tax, indicated that if the Republic was not interested in *egalité* it was willing to promote *fraternité*. But the fragility of Méline's government

71

was apparent, for it rested most profoundly on the false hope of a static (if not stagnant) economy. Yet beginning in 1896 increased industrial production, rural prosperity, and lowered unemployment were accompanied by the dynamics of a second, technological industrial revolution. The growth of business, bureaucracy, and working-class organization all affected, both materially and psychologically, not just French economy and society as a whole but particularly the class whose existence was most problematic in the context of industrial renewal—the urban *petite bourgeoisie*. And it was this social class above all which would play a significant political role in the events to come. The Opportunists, who saw France divided between moderates and socialists and who depended on the belief that if the socialists were to be out then the "Right" must be in, showed little understanding of the social and economic changes of the 1890s. Méline's position, so secure in 1896, would be shattered in less than three years; he seems to have been unaware of this, for his response to Scheurer-Kestner amounted to a request to leave well enough alone.[3]

Clearly, then, Méline's government was not disposed toward reviving the case of a Jewish army officer. Questions of justice aside, the army was a necessary ingredient in the recipe for political stability—and an overly hot oven would certainly burn the contents of the cooking pot. When Méline uttered his famous assertion that "there is no Dreyfus Affair" on 4 December 1897,[4] he anticipated—indeed encouraged—the 1899 proclamation of the anti-Dreyfusards that the army could not be guilty—and that statement followed the suicide of Dreyfus's major accuser!

Nonetheless, Scheurer-Kestner took up the issue with the president of the Republic, Félix Faure, who stated his neutrality. As a result, the vice-president of the Senate wrote an open letter that appeared in *Le Temps*:

New facts have been produced which demonstrate the innocence of the condemned. If I were convinced that a judicial error had not been committed, I would have remained silent. I can no longer remain calm with this thought.[5]

The following day, Mathieu Dreyfus, the brother of the convicted, wrote to the minister of war citing evidence of the *petit bleu* and accusing a Colonel Esterhazy of being the real traitor. In January the colonel was acquitted by a Council of War, while Emile Zola's *J'Accuse* was being printed in *L'Aurore* and Picquart, who had argued for Dreyfus's revision, was being arrested. All events were by no means equal.

The first public meeting concerned with the reopening of the Dreyfus case occurred in Paris within a month of Scheurer-Kestner's confrontations with Faure. On 22 November 1897 a group that called itself "Etudiants antisémites" gathered to protest the "campaign led by the Jews in support of ex-Captain Dreyfus." It appears that a man named Jules Guérin, totally unknown except to the police, was responsible for the rally. Guérin spoke harshly against the *syndicat judéo-financier*. Also in attendance was the editor of *La Patrie*, Lucien Millevoye.[6] The following day Déroulède received a telegram from *L'Agence Fournier*, a news service, asking for his "loyal opinion on this horrible Dreyfus Affair."[7] On the twenty-fourth, Déroulède was approached by the group that had organized the rally two days earlier and was asked to attend a planned meeting. Déroulède promised nothing, declaring not only that he had renounced politics but that he was also about to leave Paris.[8]

In 1898, the reopening of the Dreyfus Affair and the scheduling of legislative elections for May promised the opportunity for which the dissidents in France had hoped. Nevertheless, neither Déroulède nor the skeletal Ligue was the first to profit from the situation. That distinction fell to the various Paris-based anti-Semitic groups which directed their attention and energy toward the one area they knew best—the street.

Modern anti-Semitism, deriving from the nineteenth century, can be distinguished from earlier forms of anti-Jewish sentiment. The years between the Emancipation of 1791 and the formation of the Third Republic served as a critical watershed in this regard. Prior to the revolution, the Jew was responded to on religious grounds; anti-Semitism took the form of Christian theological attacks on the heretic. Accordingly, civil rights were denied to Jews on religious grounds, with conversion being the means by which the Jew could overcome his "disabilities."[9] The extension of civil equality in France along with the other effects of the revolution left the Jews equally free and poor.[10] In the course of the nineteenth century, however, the process of embourgeoisement and assimilation meant that for the older Jewish community, access to both wealth and society was possible. Yet concurrent with the Jew's increased social mobility and commercial, political, and artistic successes, there evolved a new definition of Jews as a race; thus, "at the very moment when they had begun to enjoy the fruits of emancipation and citizenship . . . the Jewish communities of France were confronted by a new test, an explosion of [modern and racial] anti-Semitism."[11]

In some sense, the "honor" of founding modern (and hence racial) French anti-Semitism must go to Comte Joseph Arthur de Gobineau. In 1859,

Gobineau published his infamous *L'Essai sur l'inegalité des races humaines*. Subsequently "substantiated" by the findings of positivist cultural anthropology, linguistics, and literary criticism, this essay stimulated the emergence of a theory and description of race and history. By identifying races whose intermixture would produce decay, Gobineau had anticipated the work of others, particularly Renan, who categorized two groups on the basis of "scientific" inquiry into the origins of language: the Arayan, or Indo-European, and the Semitic or Hebraic. The linguistic proof of racial types—with appropriate conclusions about the inferiority of the latter type—was sufficient to stir the imaginations of the fearful and the alienated.[12] When coupled with the then-fashionable classifications of biology, the anthropological/linguistic definitions of race became potent and virulent weapons for those who had grievances not only with the Jew but also with modern society, which had elevated the "racially inferior" to a position of civil equality.

Such a man, it seems, was Edward Drumont, whose book *La France juive* popularized the doctrines of modern racial anti-Semitism.[13] Drumont emphasized the role that the foreign and cosmopolitan Jew played in gnawing away at the material and spiritual wealth of France. Furthermore, in addition to being a creature of avarice and "foreign" allegiance, he claimed, the Jew was distinguishable by odor, facial characteristics, and fingers whose deformity were a physiological match for his greed. Displaying the subtitle, *France for the French*, Drumont's newspaper, *La Libre Parole*, carried forward the ideas presented in the book. Founded in 1892, the paper became the foremost artillery in the anti-Semites' arsenal.

Even though subsequent learned opinion and the investigations of Renan in the later part of his life sought to refute the bases of racial anti-Semitism, the Aryan myth was of sufficient power, resonance, and appeal to persuade many of its correctness.[14] Given the identification of the Jew with both the modern capitalist state and the foreign, subversive doctrines of socialism, one has little difficulty comprehending the appeal of anti-Semitism for those who saw their lives as threatened by the double-edged sword of contemporary economics and politics.

By January of 1898, with the flames of Zola's and Esterhazy's trials illuminating the issues that would make up the Dreyfus Affair, a new political group inspired by Drumont's decade-long efforts at propaganda appeared on the streets of Paris. The Ligue antisémitique de France, led by Jules Guérin, not only became the Ligue des Patriotes' main competition for the street vote but it also fashioned the link between nationalism and anti-Semitism during the Dreyfus Affair.

Jules-Napoléon Guérin was born in 1860. His father died before his birth, and he was raised by his mother and a family friend, a M. Mallet.[15] His mother resided in Paris, where Guérin attended school until he was sixteen. He then joined Mallet's firm and by the age of twenty-three had secured the post of managing assistant director, a position that paid six thousand francs annually. Two years later, in 1885, as chief of accounts Guérin suddenly left Paris for Germany, where he convinced two Germans to invest in his company. On his return it was disclosed that Guérin had fixed the company's books, pocketed a sizable amount of money, and defrauded the two Germans of two hundred thousand francs in order to cover up his embezzlement. In 1888 he lost a suit charging him with fraud and was fined five thousand francs, which somehow he avoided paying. During the same period, Guérin defrauded at least three other companies, set fire to one of his factories in order to collect the insurance, and with his brother bilked the post office of more than forty-four hundred francs, which he claimed to have lost in the mail. A police report on his business activity rather underestimated Guérin's reputation: "Most of the businessmen with whom he had contact considered Guerin to be a man of bad faith, lacking scruples and propriety."[16]

For most of his adult life, Jules Guérin lived in the nineteenth *arrondissement* of Paris, La Villette. There, in 1892, he tried to persuade the local Radical deputy to do him a special business favor. When he refused, the deputy was severely beaten, and as a consequence Guérin was sent to prison for a week. A man whose will and strength were feared, he dressed the part of a dandy: mustachioed, finely dressed, and always sporting a felt hat.[17] In his *quartier* he and his brother gained a reputation for their ability to organize street demonstrations, during which Guérin was always surrounded by an entourage of La Villette's wholesale butchers, who "escorted him, applauded him and when the need arose, supported him with their fists."[18]

Politically, Guérin was associated successively with Radicals, Boulangists, socialists, and finally anti-Semites. In 1893 Guérin became the friend and lieutenant of the Marquis de Morès, himself a swaggering and unsavory con man, who had been for a time a rancher in America. As Morès's subordinate, Guérin also became associated with Drumont and *La Libre Parole*, for which he wrote a series of articles denouncing the company of M. Mallet.[19] Upon Morès's death, Guérin found employment with Drumont, who encouraged him in 1897 to take over a small political organization called the

Ligue anti sémitique de France. Drumont allowed Guérin to use *La Libre Parole* to announce meetings and provided some money for the venture.

Thus, by November 1897 Jules Guérin was the *délégué général* of Drumont's political and electoral organization. The Ligue antisémitique became the first group on the Right to involve itself with public protest in the affair. Guérin's reputation as a street demonstrator and leader was borne out in February of 1898, when he led daily mobs of up to six thousand people in protests during Zola's trial.[20] Yet, as soon as the Ligue antisémitique began to enjoy some success, particularly as an instrument of propaganda for Drumont, Guérin began to draw away from his sponsor.[21] While Millevoye and Thiébaud appeared at Guérin's rallies, the other nationalist leaders—Déroulède, Rochefort, and even Edouard Dubuc of *La Jeunesse antisémite*—viewed him as wild, adventuresome, and self-seeking.[22] In mid-March, Drumont decided to seek election to the Chamber, representing Algiers. There the young mayoralty candidate, Max Régis, had been arrested for encouraging anti-Semitic riots, and Drumont was forced to go to Algeria himself to continue his campaign. Guérin was charged with Drumont's safety and organized a dozen of his La Villette butchers to assist him.[23] By Guérin's standards, his stay in Algeria was not without success. He led his supporters in a demonstration against the "anarchists." A violent riot ensued, and he was jailed for eight days.

Upon his return from Algeria, Guérin ordered the Ligue antisémitique to hold no more meetings. For the time being, he intended to reorganize. He planned to encourage the development of more local and autonomous sections, while the Ligue antisémitique itself would serve as a kind of financial and propagandistic clearing house. Guérin also wanted to start a newspaper called, bluntly, *L'Antijuif*.[24] To achieve these ends, Guérin desperately needed money. The obvious source was Drumont, now a deputy in the Chamber. Drumont, however, refused Guérin's requests not only for money but also for space in *La Libre Parole* for solicitations.[25] Drumont no doubt had achieved a measure of respectability which was now threatened by Guérin's thuggish nature. Furthermore, Drumont and the anti-Semites of the Right considered Guérin's appeal too radical. For Guérin, the opposite was true: Drumont was too old and too clerical.[26]

By mid-summer the split was complete and irreparable.[27] Guérin moved the headquarters of his Ligue antisémitique to new offices and began planning for the first scheduled appearance of his newspaper. It was noted that to undertake such a project Guérin needed close to two hundred fifty thousand francs. Since Drumont had refused him, and since the Ligue antisémitique had made no public appeals, there was considerable speculation concerning the source of Guérin's funds.[28]

Despite these problems, the first issue of *L'Antijuif* was a success. Guérin printed some fifty thousand copies and even planned to expand his enterprise to include a Sunday illustrated edition. The motto of the new paper could hardly be faulted: "To defend all workingmen. To combat all spectators." Guérin declared his goal to be the founding of a national organization that would defend the interest of "petit commerce, des employés et des ouvriers."[29] Soon he announced that *L'Antijuif*'s main campaign was to identify and unmask the Jews of Paris. Lists by professions were printed, exposing individuals who were Jewish. It was recommended that buildings with Jewish inhabitants be marked and the Jewish merchants be boycotted.[30] Despite the emotional intensity of his appeal, Guérin's anti-Semitism was suspect as being merely a vehicle for political advancement.

The editor of *L'Antijuif* and confidant of Guérin was Jules Girard. An undistinguished man, he had been rescued from the depths of financial failure in 1897 by the kindness of the Abbé Duvaus, the vicar of St. Germain de Charonne and editor of a small twentieth-*arrondissement* newspaper, *L'Echo de Charonne*. Girard became the *abbé*'s secretary and editor of the journal. In early 1898, Girard was active in the Catholic electoral organization, Justice Egalité, which was sponsoring a candidate in the twentieth against Vaillant, the Blanquist. Girard's position as treasurer of Justice Egalité proved too tempting, however, and he was soon helping himself to a share of campaign contributions. Girard was discovered by his protector, the good *abbé*, who refused to prosecute for fear of scandal. Subsequently, the *abbé* recommended Girard to Jules Guérin for employment. "Today Girard is Guérin's man, and Guérin can ask him to do whatever he wants."[31]

The other man close to Guérin was Spiard, a well-paid police informer. Spiard, however, had only begun to give the police valuable information in 1899. Prior to that date, Spiard (who used the code name Aspic) no doubt found it profitable to collect wages from both Guérin and the police.

In sum, the anti-Semitic movement in France in 1898 was split at least three ways. Drumont, the titular head, was in a position analogous to that of Rochefort among the ex-Boulangists. He concentrated on his newspaper and had little taste for direct action. Although an anti-Semite and nationalist, Drumont made few of the "socialist" demands that Guérin so much liked to include in his appeal.

Next, there was Guérin, essentially a con man out for himself, capable of the most violent action. In some ways the schism between Guérin and

Drumont was a conflict of generations; the Drumonts of the Right belonged to the nineteenth century, the Guérins to the twentieth. Perhaps their differences can be expressed symbolically in the clash between the printing press and the street. This conflict pervaded most of the organizations on the Right during the Dreyfus Affair—Bonapartist, royalist, anti-Semitic, Rochefortist—and yet it was absent in the Ligue des Patriotes, in which the leadership of Déroulède remained unchallenged. In the Ligue, the older generation's leadership—a combination of deputies, journalists, and lawyers—coalesced with the rank and file of young shop owners, clerks, and students, linking the two generations. It is not without significance that those who opposed Déroulède within the Right and those who feared him on the Left, notably Reinach and Jaurès, did so because they perceived that he was the strongest personality on the Right. Guérin wanted to avoid being incorporated into the Ligue des Patriotes for fear of losing his independence, while those on the Left saw in Déroulède the only chance for the Right to unify its purpose and action. Both perceptions proved to be remarkably mistaken.

Finally, there was Edouard Dubuc, the head of the Jeunesse antisémite, who split from Guérin in early 1898 and gravitated by the spring of 1899 to the Ligue des Patriotes.[32] If Déroulède was to assume unquestioned leadership of the dissident anti-Dreyfusard forces, he would have to face the challenge that Guérin posed. Both the intransigence and the popular demagogic appeal that characterized the Ligue antisémitique, would be a thorn in the Ligue des Patriotes' side for the following year and a half.

Nevertheless, as of the spring of 1898 Paul Déroulède had achieved a position that he would maintain for at least six months. The events of the spring and summer of 1898 moved him to a declaration of war on a society and a regime which appeared ready to reconsider the guilt of Captain Dreyfus. At that point, a judicial decision became the line of demarcation between those who wanted to revise the parliamentary system and those who, in demanding revision of the trial, also felt obliged to defend the Republic. The politics of "no enemies of the Right"—an essential feature of the Méline government—were ending. Revenge and revision, the slogan of the republican Left in the 1880s, became the cry of the anti-parliamentary, nationalist, and anti-Semitic Right of the late 1890s.

Passing through the stage of electoral maneuvering and entering the realm of direct action, Déroulède and the Ligue dominated the anti-Dreyfusard forces after September 1898. Their success was due in part to their ability to pursue their goals by means of street politics. This tactic had its precedent not only in the work of the Ligue but also in that of antirevisionist journalists who responded to the events of early 1898. By that time, with Esterhazy's acquittal and Zola's trial of January and February, the Dreyfus case had become the Dreyfus Affair. "I am, at the moment, completely absorbed by the Dreyfus Affair," declared Lucien Millevoye several days after Esterhazy's court-martial.[33] Anti-Dreyfusard newspapers began to cover the affair with banner headlines. A pattern emerged which was to continue for almost two years: sustained effort that coincided with a major episode in the affair, followed by periods of relative calm and regrouping. The contractions of excitement and relaxation on the part of the anti-Dreyfusards became more intense as the stimulus itself developed power and influence. Thus, when the affair first became public in January and February of 1898, politicians, polemicists, and journalists attacked the Dreyfusards as bourgeois, decadent, cosmopolitan, foreign, Jewish, elitist *sans-patries*.[34] Finally, in the midst of Zola's trial, Millevoye's paper, *La Patrie*, developed a theme that until that point had been used only by a small group of protesters, but which would become the core of the attack in the months to come.

The crowds, which in Paris, in the provinces, throughout the country, are burning, protesting, acting, are more useful in their instinct than those elites which bit by bit have constituted themselves into a caste of professionals, recruited by universal suffrage. . . . The street possesses a soul which the politicians do not have . . . *the street is incorruptible*.[35]

La Libre Parole was more direct in its analysis. "Rumors have it that in order to influence the jury in Zola's trial, Jewish money, stolen from Frenchmen during the past twenty years . . . is working to provoke, in the streets . . . demonstrations in favor of the traitor." The statement was signed by Drumont, Thiébaud, Jules Guérin, and Dubuc, as well as by those who identified themselves as "délégués des Organizations et Comités Républicains, Socialists, Antisémites, Patriotiques et Plébiscitaires."[36] Déroulède's name was not on the list, an omission for which *La Libre Parole*'s editors chided him severely.

For the past five years Déroulède has refused to leave his rustic manor of Langely where, hidden like a Druid in the depths of a forest, he expounds in poverty, beneath the humble roof, those mad ideas which his too liberal heart cannot help.[37]

In order for the anti-Dreyfusard leaders, nationalist and anti-Semitic, to reap the harvest of their campaign, they had to find a way of involving Déroulède. By late January all parties were in constant communication with the sometime-president of the Ligue des Patriotes, urging him to join them.[38] Rumors spread that he would soon announce his return to active politics, presenting himself for the legislative elections in either Paris or the Charente.[39] Members of the Ligue were particularly hopeful when Dérou-lède addressed their meeting of 11 February with a letter in which he expressed his indignation at the activity of the Dreyfus *syndicate*, and pro-mised to return as head of the Ligue to lead the protest against injustice.[40]

Déroulède's first tentative, cautious return to Parisian politics came toward the close of Zola's trial. Throughout the proceedings at the Palais de Justice, Jules Guérin had been leading his new organization, the Ligue antisémitique de France, in daily demonstrations. His success was consider-able; the newspapers covered the disturbances, and a new atmosphere, recal-ling the excitement of ten years earlier, prevailed. This was evidenced not only by the machinations on the part of the dissidents but also by the formation of the Ligue des droits de l'homme on the day following Zola's condemnation. In contrast, the government remained neutral—a posture that Déroulède and the Ligue viewed as benevolent.[41] Thus, with an indica-tion that the time had perhaps come, Déroulède returned to Paris on 22 February. On arriving, he immediately went to the Palais de Justice to witness one of the sessions in Zola's trial. Subsequently, he spoke with Georges Thiébaud about the possibility of a new nationalist newspaper and with Max Régis, the anti-Semitic mayor of Algiers and colleague of Dru-mont. Régis, proposed an alliance of the Ligue des Patriotes with the forces of Guérin, Ernest Roche (Blanquist), and Rochefort. A day later, Déroulède indicated that he was ready for a *rapproachement* with Rochefort. But when the latter declined, and Roche also announced that a combination with Drumont was impossible, the plans for a grand nationalist coalition disintegrated.[42]

Historically, the Left has been condemned as incapable of uniting its fac-tions. Certainly, during the period of "nationalist agitation" in France, the same must be said of the Right. There were almost as many factions as leaders. The close of the Zola trial simultaneously ended the first period of intense anti-Dreyfusard activity. The May 1898 election promised a new opportunity to act. In marked contrast with the Boulangist era, the dissi-dents of the 1890s never were tempted by the electoral strategy of the Comité national. There was no unity, in terms of a traditional political division, and little common activity in the electoral sphere. In 1898 the many fac-tions shared only a common disgust for those who would dare defend Dreyfus.

While the Ligues of Déroulède and Guérin emerged as the two major street movements of the day, two other political groupings also emerged from in part-Boulangist hibernation. The so-called Parti républicain socialiste, presided over by Henri Rochefort, and the Blanquist revisionists (a splinter group that did not follow the leadership of Vaillant), led by Jules Caron and Ernest Roche, had formed a wide range of electoral committees in Paris.[43] By 1899, however, both these factions and their leaders (except for Rochefort, who was well past his prime) abandoned their independence, merged with the Ligue des Patriotes, and delivered their memberships to Déroulède.

The government's official policy with regard to the Dreyfus Affair continued to be one of neutrality; the Chamber adjourned on 17 April with Méline's proclamation of "neither revolution nor reaction." Those members of the cabinet who may have favored revision remained silent, unwilling to risk their political careers.[44] Thus, to a certain extent the criticisms voiced by Déroulède and others cannot be dismissed as mere rhetoric. It was obvious that the government and the Opportunists in general did not want to make a campaign issue of the affair; after all, the Méline government had remained in power longer than any other cabinet in the history of the Third Republic.

Zola's condemnation was temporarily set aside in late April, and he was granted a new trial. Almost immediately, the minister of the interior, the young Louis Barthou, in defiance of the rest of Méline's cabinet, instructed the prefects to aid moderate republican candidates against the conservatives, even though the latter previously had supported the government.[45] In reaction to this, on 16 April 1898 *Le Drapeau* published an open letter by Déroulède addressed to the municipalities of France. Déroulède announced his decision to seek election to the Chamber, representing Angoulême.[46] Though his decision was late, he received considerable encouragement; his letter, which began with the statement that "the Dreyfus Affair has reopened," was designed to reacquaint the public with him quickly. He called for the elected officials of the municipalities to mobilize their forces against the campaign of the Dreyfusards, and urged these men to fight the "forces of Judas" in the name of the nation. The mayors and municipal counselors were reminded that in case of war they were the first to begin the mobilization against the nation's enemy, and that the time had come. The announcement of his candidacy also implied that Déroulède now conceded that the once-small band of Dreyfusards had grown significantly. Déroulède claimed to speak for the nation, represented by the patriots of France, in its hour of danger.

For Déroulède to have reasserted political interest, the enemy against whom the nation was supposed to rally had to be aggressive, numerous, clever, and well financed. In creating the myth of this adversary, the *sans-patrie*, Déroulède, the nationalist, inversely reduced the number of true patriots. Thus, the nationalism of Déroulède became increasingly exclusive and negative. It is quite possible, indeed probable, that the leader of the Ligue des Patriotes was unaware of such ideological implications. Rather, he understood that the elections, combined with the Dreyfus Affair, promised political opportunity from which he might profit. He also knew that his friends to the Right were spending a great deal of time and energy in rousing electoral support.[47]

During the elections, the Ligue itself suspended formal operations and played a purely electoral role. Perhaps Déroulède felt that he first needed to establish his position and investigate the possibilities for combination with others before reassuming his place at its head.[48] The *arrondissement* committees still operated under their 1893-1897 titles, and the members in Paris occupied themselves with campaign chores. At this time, the Ligue had committees in only eight of the twenty *arrondissements* (the first, third, seventh, eighth, eleventh, twelfth, seventeenth, and eighteenth), and it was far from being a national or even regional influence. In fact, individual *arrondissement* presidents often allied themselves with Blanquist or Rochefortist elements in endorsing and supporting candidates.[49] Nevertheless, Déroulède easily won his election on the first ballot, defeating two other candidates. His campaign was facilitated by virtue of his position as municipal counselor and by the activity of several close personal friends in Angoulême. Subsequently, *Le Drapeau* devoted its 16 May edition to the praise of its leader. As is often true, the qualities for which Déroulède was praised were those that made him so vulnerable.

In this time, the end of our century, when all is so demoralized and so demoralizing, it is good to hear a voice that speaks truthfully, to see a gesture that does not arouse apprehension. The gestures and words are the glory and honor of Déroulède. While others sow the seeds of skepticism and defiance and proclaim a state of decadence, Déroulède comes and follows the road of duty; he comes to preach the gospel of *la patrie*.[50]

A month earlier, however, the deputy from Angoulême had received a more prophetic tribute: "Without wishing it, Lamartine prepared the way for Napoleon III's success. I pray to God that you will be spared the playing of an analogous role."[51]

If Déroulède had hoped to make the Dreyfus Affair a national issue for the elections, he failed. Since parties were not organized nationally, the affair was significant only in several large cities and in Algeria, where Drumont had campaigned extensively. As a result, the nationalist success was only moderate. Déroulède, Millevoye, and Drumont joined de Clagny, Habert, Méry, Gabriel, and Roche, in the Chamber, but Thiébaud in Carpentras and Barrès in Nancy were unsuccessful. Some twenty nationalist and anti-Semitic deputies were elected; obviously, this was far from an electoral victory. It indicated that should the circumstances of the affair change, an alternative to electoral and parliamentary politics would be used by the Right to make its will known.

Within three weeks of the second ballot, the Méline government had resigned. When the Chamber (through the efforts of Jaurès and Picquart) persuaded Cavignac to have experts reexamine one particular piece of evidence, the result convinced the minister of war that the document was indeed false. On 30 August, in the minister's office, Colonel Henry admitted having forged the document. A General Roget was there to take notes on Henry's confession, and the same evening the government was informed. The period of relative calm which had existed during the summer and since the elections came to an abrupt end.

On 31 August, Colonel Henry ended his life. His suicide, saluted by the young literary critic Charles Maurras as an act of courage and proof of the army's innocence, was followed by a succession of resignations of war ministers as new accusations were made. By 23 September 1898 Mme. Dreyfus's formal petition for revision had been approved by Prime Minister Brisson, against the wishes of both Chanoine, the minister of war for September, and the minister of justice. Brisson clearly was confronted with a crisis. It is not unreasonable to suggest that the real politics of the Dreyfus Affair began with Henry's suicide.

Whereas the disclosures of 30 August troubled Déroulède and the nationalists, the events of September demonstrated that the key to bringing pressure on the government lay with public opinion. For a time, Déroulède considered that Cavignac was his man, but the events of September made him move cautiously.[52] Both Drumont and Guérin asserted in their respective newspapers that revision was simply a Jewish plot aimed at weakening France internally.[53] Déroulède's reasoning for the moment was uncharacteristically realistic: if the nationalists would be patient, there was a good chance that revision might be dropped, Brisson forced to resign, and Cavignac installed as either prime minister or minister of the interior. On the other hand, if revision were begun, more drastic action would be needed to force Brisson's precarious position.[54] In either case public opinion had to be aroused, and thus Déroulède made tentative plans for a series of mass meetings in which the intensity would mount as the date of the Chamber's reconvening drew near. Le Menuet reported that the Ligue was expanding rapidly, with seven thousand members in Paris, and the public was beginning to identify Déroulède as an important nationalist leader.[55]

Déroulède and the Ligue des Patriotes were now committed—the leader to his organization, the organization to internal political pressure. The affair was politicized; the nationalists' best chance lay with public opinion. For Déroulède, eight years of inactivity and caution were in the past. The struggle for him would be twofold: to achieve the significant position among the anti-Dreyfusards and to prevent the government from revising the Dreyfus decision. Dreyfusards also rallied to their cause. Neither side yet perceived the other's intent or devotion. With commitment came involvement, and with involvement came emotion, action, and then violence.

NOTES—CHAPTER 5

[1] See Joseph Reinach, *Historie de l'affaire Dreyfus*; Guy Chapman, *The Dreyfus Case*; Douglas Johnson, *France and the Dreyfus Affair*; and Marcel Thomas, *L'Affaire sans Dreyfus*.

[2] Chapman, p. 144

[3] Zeldin, p. 652.

[4] Chastinet, 3: 115.

[5] *Le Temps*, 15 November 1897.

[6] APP B/A 117, 22 November 1897. This series of reports contains daily summaries of police surveillance and activity in chronological order. Although little specific information is given, they provide a reliable index of public agitation over a given issue.

[7] AD 32,851, 23 November 1897.

[8] APP B/A 1,032, 24 November 1897.

[9] See Léon Poliakov, *L'Histoire de l'antisémitisme*, esp. 3: 458-472.

[10] Zosa Szajkowski, *Poverty and Social Welfare among French Jews 1800-1880*.

[11] Philippe Baurdrel, *Histoire des Juifs de France*, p. 205.

[12] See Michael Marrus, *The Politics of Assimilation*, pp. 8-20, and H. M. Sachar, *The Course of Modern Jewish History* (New York, 1965), pp. 221-240.

[13] See Robert F. Byrnes, *Anti-Semitism in Modern France*,

[14] See Peter F. Pulzer, *The Origins of Political Anti-Semitism in Germany and Austria*, for a comparative discussion.

[15] It is curious that Guérin's deprivation bears similarity with Drumont's origins as an orphan.

[16] APP B/A 1,103, report made 8 January 1899 which is the result of several hundred individual entries.

[17] APP B/A 1,103, 1 May 1899.

[18] APP B/A 1,103, 1 May 1899.

¹⁹ Byrnes, *Anti-Semitism*, pp. 176-177.

²⁰ APP B/A 106, for January and February 1898.

²¹ AN F⁷ 12,461, 5 February 1898.

²² AN F⁷ 12,882, 16 February 1898.

²³ They were described as having "the strength of Hercules" and as being "blindly devoted to Guérin." APP B/A 1,104, 30 March 1898.

²⁴ APP B/A 1,007, 3 June 1898.

²⁵ APP B/A 106, 29 June 1898.

²⁶ APP B/A 1,107, 28 May 1898.

²⁷ APP B/A 1,104, 20 July 1898.

²⁸ AN F⁷ 12,883, 2 and 19 August 1898.

²⁹ APP B/A 1,104, 21 August 1898. The last category was considerably less likely to accept such protection than the first two.

³⁰ *L'Antijuif*, 24 August 1898.

³¹ AN F⁷ 12,882, 10 February 1899.

³² Bibliothèque de l'Institut (BIMS) 4,577, 8 August 1899.

³³ Bibliothèque nationale (BN NAF) 25,101, 18 January 1898, Millevoye to René Dirant.

³⁴ See *La Libre Parole, La Patrie, L'Intransigeant*, for example, during January and February 1898.

³⁵ *La Patrie*, 21 January 1898, italics mine.

³⁶ *La Libre Parole*, 6 February 1898.

³⁷ *La Libre Parole*, 16 January 1898.

³⁸ APP B/A 1,032, 25 January 1898.

³⁹ APP B/A 1,032, 5 and 6 February 1898.

⁴⁰ APP B/A 1,338, 12 February 1898.

⁴¹ On 8 February 1898 Déroulède received the following telegram from Le Menuet: "Violent incidents at every instant . . . one does not know how the debates are going. Here is the declaration of Casimir Périer: 'I have confidence in the justice of my country . . . I shall say nothing.' " AD 37,952, 8 February 1898.

⁴² APP B/A 1.032, 22 and 23 February 1898.

⁴³ AN F⁷ 12,449, undated lists entitled "Old Boulangist committees which are currently Nationalist and to whom many Ligueurs currently belong."

⁴⁴ The *politique* of the Méline cabinet has been characterized as "creating policy day by day, occupied by administrative duties, devoted to the protection of material interests, and being only verbally attached to the Gambettist tradition." Chastenet, 3: 120.

⁴⁵ Chastenet, 3: 121.

⁴⁶ AD 8,131, 31 March 1898, Ornano to Déroulède.

⁴⁷ AD 8,437, 7 April 1898, Le Menuet to Déroulède, a letter noting Millevoye's petitioning of Rochefort and various patriotic groups for their endorsement in Paris.

⁴⁸ AN F⁷ 12,449, 23 March 1898.

⁴⁹ APP B/A 106, 17 April 1898.

⁵⁰ *La Patrie*, 5 April 1898.

⁵¹ AD 10,506, 7 April 1898, Dr. Visers to Déroulède.

⁵² AD 34,804, 2 September 1898, Habert wrote, "I approve of Cavignac and think that we ought to group ourselves behind him—he is an honest and courageous man."

⁵³ *La Libre Parole*, 5 September 1898; *L'Antijuif*, 11 September 1898.

⁵⁴ APP B/A 1,107, 14 September 1898.

⁵⁵ AD 40,957, 15 September 1898.

CHAPTER

6

—

The Republican Crisis

OF ALL HIS CONTEMPORARIES, Paul Déroulède in October of 1898 was best qualified to lead the movement of nationalist agitation which so alarmed the regime.[1] *Faute de mieux* perhaps, but nonetheless it was Déroulède—not Drumont or Rochefort, not Guérin or Barrès either—who had the energy, reputation, and organization to emerge in the forefront of the anti-Dreyfusard, antisocialist, and increasingly antiparliamentary groups which along with the anti-Semites composed what has come to be known as nationalist. He became, then, the head of a movement that in October of 1898, and again in December, made its politics known by way of an exhausting series of demonstrations, meetings, marches, riots, and secret midnight conferences. As the leader of the Ligue des Patriotes Paul Déroulède was a political personality whose career had been shaped not so much by the Chamber as by the stage—the theaters of Paris where so many had gone to hear and see his poetic praise of the nation. A man whose reputation owed so much to the soapbox and the stage, Paul Déroulède had grown accustomed to dramatizing his thoughts and actions. He had long since become used to the dynamic of performer and audience. His political activities were in many ways but an extension of his theatrical being. Acting out his moral and political positions became a means of expression which was acceptable to the crowds of Parisians who were treated to the *spectacle* at Salle Wagram or along the boulevards in the same way as if they had been attending the Théâtre française. After all, it was less expensive and no doubt equally entertaining.

The danger lay in the fact that the actors might take their roles too seriously. What had begun as a means of expression of political opinion when other outlets, such as the Chamber, proved unsatisfactory or unavailable, threatened to destroy itself when illusion gave way to reality. From September to December 1898 Déroulède produced his scenes on the streets, acted his revolution. As the crowds roared, he and his followers came increasingly to believe in themselves, to believe in their illusion. Subsequently, when it was clear that the pendulum for revision had begun to swing away from the anti-Dreyfusards, public opinion became their court of last resort. With legislative and legal action blocked, the street was the arena. Although the public enjoyed entertainment, it was not ready to accept the real political implications of the anti-Dreyfusard position. The bourgeoisie was fearful but not, as yet, foolish. By contrast those who followed and supported Déroulède to the end were not theater goers. Their impact would, however, be of enormous consequence. Nevertheless, in the weeks before and the months after 25 October, the performance continued. Few understood this better than one of Déroulède's most severe critics, Joseph Reinach.

Paul Déroulède was a pretender . . . he succeeded in combining, just as an actor would a set of astonishing contrasts in which one found the roughness of an ordinary soldier, the manners of elegance, a facile popularity, together with the allure of a Don Quixote who seemed mad only when he wanted to appear so, and the adventure of so many political intrigues. His rhetoric, drawn from the most common sources of patriotism, was unnecessary in its dominance of the crowds who saw before them a large man, arms waving in a huge unfashionable waistcoat. Yet he never lacked courage, nor feared appearing ridiculous. He was occupied completely with reputation. His stature was so strong that he was surrounded by admirers ready to follow him anywhere, ready to obey his slightest whim . . . he was a leader of men and would have been the most dangerous agitator if he had a cause. . . . Unfortunately Déroulède worked for himself . . . but never sold himself.[2]

Written within a few years of the events that it records, Reinach's sketch is a faithful depiction of the characteristics of the president of the Ligue des Patriotes. Others have chosen to interpret Déroulède as either absurd or simply self-seeking,[3] but Reinach's perspective is most revealing because it places Déroulède like a self-conscious actor upon the stage that he could and did so easily dominate. This element of conscious performance was not missing from his role in the turbulent events yet to come.

Indeed the last four months of 1898 saw a quickening of the rhythm of contractions which characterized the response of the Right to demands for revision of the affair. But it would be a mistake to see the acceleration of nationalist activity as the sole or even primary phenomenon operating in France, and patricularly in Paris. While the Dreyfus Affair would provide the framework in which great changes occurred, ushering in constellations that formed the basis of twentieth century politics and ideologies, the threads of change were already present, awaiting only the circumstance that would spin them anew. Since 1878 republican governments had devoted themselves to maintaining a social and political equilibrium. They had been opposed by a nonsocialist Jacobin opposition on the Left and a feeble royalist hope on the Right. The continuity of Opportunists, Ferryists, and Mélinists was matched by the criticism of Gambettists and Boulangists. Equally important, the plateau of economic stagnation, broken by two depressions and subsequent recoveries, provided the relatively stable base from which conservative fiscal and social policies could follow. The calculations that the Méline government followed—tariffs to protect France's "natural" economic balance, political alliance to the Right but not to the Left, gradual and moderate social reform, rapprochement with liberal Catholicism—represented an extension of the Opportunist political program.

In some ways, in fact, the vision of Méline and his Radical caretaker successors in 1898 was not incorrect. Speaking for what one might call the unarticulated fears of the bourgeois republic, the political device of no enemies on the Right was entirely appropriate.[4] From their perspective the enemy was *à gauche*. It is no less difficult to understand the attitude of the government in 1898 and 1899. The desire to deflect the pressure of the increasingly vocal Dreyfusards to reopen the case was itself a necessary corollary of the political balance that had been operating for two decades. Yet the events of 1898 which resulted not only from nationalist agitation, indeed not only from Dreyfusard insistence, began to exert enormous pressure on the position in which the government found itself. It became clear that those who dominated the Third Republic could not simultaneously maintain their political position and control the momentum of the affair. The convergence of social, economic, and political change in the context of the judicial process of the Dreyfus case produced a period of flux, uncertainty, and opportunity.

In the fall of 1898, then, the revelations and passions aroused by Henry's suicide, the *démission* of three war ministers, and the growing polarization of Dreyfusard and nationalist factions were made more acute by a significant diplomatic and military "humiliation" of French forces at Fashoda and the outbreak of two series of strikes whose intensity prefigured the wave of labor agitation which would engulf the last months of the affair a year later. The first of these *éclats*, the so-called Fashoda crisis, both fueled the fiery outrage of the nationalists and simultaneously forced them to reconsider the issue of empire. The second served to reawaken conservative anxiety, especially in Paris, about a revived and militant working-class unionism and socialist party. If Fashoda gave credence to the demands of the Right for revision and revenge as the antidote to a weakened national resolve, the strike of railway and construction workers in October 1898 challenged the social peace that the government needed desperately while it groped to maintain its balance.[5]

Furthermore these crises, foreign and domestic, when coupled with the agitation of street politics before the reconvening of the Chamber in late October 1898 as well as with the aftermath of that *journée*, impinged most of all on events in Paris. For it was in that city that the strikes, demonstrations, agitation, and political intrigue occurred. For all its good cheer, bright lights and boulevards, Paris was in 1898 and 1899 once again the center of a series of crises whose outcome was potentially and expectantly revolutionary.[6]

By the fall of 1898 the French economy was two years into the run of prosperity and growth which would last until 1914. In general, the effects of a second industrial revolution in electricity, chemicals, telephones, an infant automotive industry, and the discovery of coal deposits in French Lorraine had contributed to the first sustained period of economic growth since the 1850s.[7] Not only were indices of industrial production "encouraging" but real wages as well had begun to rise for the first time since the recovery of 1889-1892.[8] Yet in Paris, for the more traditional and skilled workers, particularly in the construction trades, the economic picture was not nearly so bright. Carpenters, masons, bricklayers, and house painters received wages in the late 1890s which were often at levels 10 percent lower than those of 1882.[9] In September 1898, nineteen thousand excavators, responding to calls for higher wages, had begun to strike against the International Exposition projects on which they were employed. Calling for a pay increase of ten centimes an hour and sustained by a vast array of socialist and trade union officials, the strikers had between thirty and fifty thousand men out of work by late October.[10] Workers' meetings at the local *bourses du travail* were often the subject as well of the increasing efforts of pro- and anti-Dreyfusard politicians. Although the socialists had not yet evolved an official position vis-à-vis the affair, the nationalists and anti-Semites were well aware that the convergence of labor agitation with Dreyfusard activity would exert great pressure on the government to reconvene the trial.[11]

The strikes of the construction workers not only affected the relative calculations of the government and the political dissidents of the Left and Right but also gave courage to the leaders of the C.G.T. Believing the notion that specialized strikes should serve as the impetus for the general strike, the C.G.T. in mid-October ordered the railway workers out in hopes of provoking a general strike. While their effort failed, in part because of the diligence of the ministry of the interior, the threat of the general strike, coupled with the agitation in Paris—political, economic and judicial—only heightened the tensions that surrounded the reconvening of the Chamber scheduled for 25 October.[12]

The Brisson government, besieged as it was by strikers, political manifestations, and a growing crisis in foreign affairs, responded with seeming force. Army contingents occupied, in early October, the vacant construction sites, while others were called to make rail connections to several Atlantic ports.[13] It was critical that such a railway strike not be allowed to cripple troop movements. On 14 October soldiers also occupied all major train stations in Paris. The presence of the army, comforting in some ways to the rhetoric of the nationalists, served on the whole to exacerbate the fear of working-class or socialist revolution in the minds of an already fearful bourgeoisie. Cries of a military plot, prefiguring the beliefs of more elaborate conspiracies which would emerge in the months to come, were echoed in the Parisian press.[14]

Although the decision to avoid armed conflict over Fashoda by recalling the military forces under Commander Marchand was not made until 7 November, a fortnight after the fall of the government and the demonstration of 25 October, the wavering of the government and the maneuvering of Foreign Minister Delcassé were well publicized in the midst of the events which composed the crisis of October. With the nationalists and anti-Semites championing Marchand and his expedition as a symbol of French national strength, the government, as in the instances of the affairs's revision and the construction strikes, was placed in the position of trying to maintain its equilibrium as it saw events polarize opinion. Fear and anger, from all sides and on all issues, had clearly replaced moderation and balance. The heirs of Méline surely could no longer claim that there were no enemies to the Right.

The first phase of this agitation took place between 25 September and 31

December 1898. It swirled around the manifestations of 25 October and, like a spark, it constantly threatened to explode the already volatile atmosphere. At approximately two in the afternoon on Sunday, 25 September 1898, Paul Déroulède arrived at the Salle Guyenet, 73, avenue de la Grande Armée. The first public meeting of the Ligue des Patriotes was to begin within the hour, and already the crowds were waiting.[15] The meeting hall eventually filled with between three and four thousand people; many more gathered outside on the streets. Periodically during the meeting cries of "Vive Déroulède!" could be heard outside the building, reverberating like the echoes of spectators' voices at a sporting event.[16] Inside, the loyal supporters of the Ligue were joined by a handful of royalists and a strong delegation from the Comités plébiscitaires, the activist element within the Bonapartist party. Earlier that day Baron Legoux, who, along with Cuneo d'Ornano, was the leader of this faction, had met with Habert and promised that he would support the Ligue and that "his men would be present not as *plébiscitaries* but as *patriotes.*"[17] It was even rumored that Rochefort had paid for the rental of Salle Guyenet.[18] Thus, within the meeting hall the imminent coalition of Rochefortists and Bonapartists was forming behind Déroulède. Outside, several buildings toward l'Etoile, Jules Guérin, accompanied by hundreds of his followers, including a bodyguard of La Villette butchers, told a separate meeting that if the Ligue des Patriotes wanted to march without his help, he would soon expose some of Déroulède's followers as Jews.[19]

During the meeting itself, Déroulède attacked Prime Minister Brisson for collusion with the Dreyfusard syndicate. He noted that France had come to be divided into two camps, with true Frenchmen on the one side and the Dreyfusards on the other. Finally, he proposed the adoption of the order of the day, which included the reconstitution of the Ligue des Patriotes and the commitment of those present to fight "as patriots against the campaign of demoralization and social disintegration which was being led by the Dreyfusards with the complicity of Brisson."[20] To the cries of "Vive Déroulède!" and the promise to repeat the procedure the next week, the meeting adjourned. About an hour later royalists and anti-Semites, separately, marched from l'Etoile to la place de la Concorde, demonstrated and dispersed.[21] If Déroulède was now cooperating with, or at least accepting the support of, Rochefort and the Comités plébiscitaires, he was having nothing to do with the other two groups. The anti-Semites and Guérin, despite their menacing statements, were content to wait and see what might happen, while the royalists appeared impatient, leaderless, and without plan.

As expected, the "great meeting of 25 September" resulted in a general cry of approval from the nationalist and Bonapartist press. Many editorial writers noted that while "we can no longer share all the opinions of Déroulède, not a man having at heart the love of his country can refuse to applaud the supreme address he gave yesterday."[22] Only two papers, the militantly Dreyfusard *L'Aurore* and the Bonapartist *Petit Caporal*, attacked Déroulède, the former for accepting the friendship of Rochefort in the light of their uneasy past relationship, the latter for being the senile dupe of the Dreyfusards. Those royalists who approved of the Ligue's new posture expressed their support privately, some with an ironic awareness of the awkward position in which their support put the deputy from Angoulême: "Let me thank you [for your speech] with all my heart (but only with my heart if more would be at all embarrassing to you or your numerous admirers)."[23]

In addition to the meeting that he announced for the next Sunday, Déroulède began to think in terms of a great nationalist demonstration to force the government to take a position opposed to revision. The Chamber was scheduled to reconvene on 25 October, and this date was the natural choice for a massive public protest. Immediately, Déroulède ordered a full rebuilding of the Ligue. With the goal of 25 October in sight, all other demonstrations and meetings would lead up to the main event.[24]

Despite this goal, the Ligue and its leadership were by no means sure of their preeminence on the anti-Dreyfusard Right, and many of their actions in the next month would be in reaction to movements on the part of their colleagues and adversaries. Within several days of the "great meeting," Déroulède learned that the socialists had rented Salle Wagram for 2 October and had appealed to the people of Paris to attend in support of Dreyfus and Picquart. Thus, the Ligue began to consider the possibility of annulling its own meeting and crashing the one at Wagram.[25] After several days of discussion, including secret rendezvous with the anti-Semitic leaders during which Guérin said that the Ligue antisémitique would "never march with the Ligue des Patriotes so long as it had Jewish members," Déroulède called an urgent meeting of his *quartier* representatives.[26] Gathered at the Hôtel St. James, the delegates were told that their meeting for the next day had indeed been called off and that they were to urge their followers to demonstrate outside the "anarchist" rally at Wagram. Toward the end of the discussion Déroulède announced that for the Ligue this demonstration was a matter of life or death. Furthermore, if fights erupted, well, *tant mieux*.[27] That same night the Ligue put up throughout Paris posters signed by Déroulède proclaiming:

The cosmopolitan anarchists who insult our soldiers have organized a public meeting . . . They have dared to convene the people of Paris to come and acclaim the TRAITOR DREYFUS AND HIS FRIEND PICQUART. I will oppose the cries of the "Sans Patries" with our triple cry of "Vive la France, Vive l'Armée, Vive la République." That is why our patriotic meeting which was to be held is now adjourned. I must go on Sunday to Salle Wagram. I WILL BE THERE.[28]

Rumors spread that upwards of twenty thousand people would appear, some to watch, most to participate. The police were well aware that the Ligue was now serious in its intent to reorganize.[29] In fact they had begun already to see Déroulède as a new kind of Boulanger, this time trying to create a "Déroulèdisme."[30] Thus, perhaps unwisely, the police ordered Salle Wagram closed to all parties. When both groups arrived to find the doors barred and guarded by the police, the demonstration quickly spread to the streets. That evening a series of clashes, fights, and arrests between *ligueurs*, Dreyfusards, and police took place at la place de la Concorde, l'Etoile, along boulevard Haussmann, and near Gare St. Lazare.[31] Déroulède had clearly made his point. With the reconvening of the Chamber only three weeks away, the activity of the Ligue on 2 October indicated the direction that other demonstrations would take.

Déroulède's impact was felt in three directions. His action forced the opposition—the militant Dreyfusards who indicated that had Wagram been left open, Déroulède would never have left it alive—to take the Ligue seriously.[32] Within a few days, in fact, *L'Aurore* began to publish articles implicating the Ligue in a plot to overthrow the government.[33] The police likewise now viewed the Ligue as something more than a minor and insignificant group.[34] Finally, the anti-Semitic leaders, Guérin in particular, saw that the Ligue des Patriotes and Déroulède were certainly strong enough to have an effect without merging with their forces. It was at this point that the policy of Guérin vis-à-vis the Ligue des Patriotes temporarily changed. For the next several months the Ligue antisémitique de France offered to cooperate with the Ligue des Patriotes, seemingly in good faith, without demanding that Déroulède declare himself an anti-Semite.[35]

Thus, on 7 October Jules Guérin was present at the Ligue's next meeting, at Salle Charras. Along with Georges Thiébaud and Marcel Habert, Guérin briefly addressed the five hundred *ligueurs* in attendance. Déroulède, however, was the featured attraction. He read an open letter to Brisson in which he deplored the violence in Paris due to the disorder caused by the Dreyfus Affair. Nevertheless, he continued, there was one man in France who remained faithful to the principles of law, order, and patriotism—the president of the Republic, Félix Faure. Déroulède proposed that the Ligue organize the people of Paris to demonstrate their support for the president, the army, and the Republic by greeting Faure when he returned to the capital on 9 October. For these purposes the Ligue was to be split into four groups, stationing itself at L'Etoile, the Bois de Boulogne, the Arc de Triomphe, and the Rond-Point des Champs-Elysées.[36] The day of the demonstration went smoothly, but the police, fearing more fights, were forced to call in more than two hundred men to guard the passage of the president.[37]

Brisson's government was clearly in trouble. "The unpopularity of the government is growing rapidly among the *petits commerçants* and among the workers. In the popular *quartiers* there is an open call for a general to take over."[38] The left-wing newspapers printed daily reports of supposed conversations between Déroulède and particularly generals Zurlinden, Cavignac, and Mercier, while the right promised to do all it could to force Brisson's resignation.[39]

Typically, *La Patrie* announced on 19 October: "The crisis is now a public peril. Dreyfusism is in power . . . we must dislodge it . . . the hour of decision is now. . . . On the twenty-fifth the Chamber will decide if France is to be freed or delivered." Several days later at a private meeting Déroulède spoke before one thousand *ligueurs*: "We have a government which seeks by any available means to dismember France and deliver her to the enemy."[40] These themes and phrases echoed throughout Paris as the twenty-fifth grew closer.[41] The Left replied in kind, charging that Déroulède was the true menace to the Republic. *L'Aurore* called on all republicans to demonstrate at la place de la Concorde on the twenty-fifth "to foil the plot of the reactionaries who have decided to seize power."[42] By 25 October no fewer than sixteen organizations had marshaled their members to demonstrate outside the Chamber. The police had more than a thousand officers on hand, and there was a feverish sense of preparation and excitement.[43]

By eleven o'clock on the morning of the twenty-fifth, the police had taken their positions along the streets leading to la place de la Concorde, around the Chamber, and on the Pont de la Concorde. When Déroulède, Millevoye, Drumont, and several dozen *ligueurs* arrived at 1:30 P.M., the crowds had already been waiting for more than an hour. Guérin's supporters were most vociferous, crying, "A bas les juifs," and causing countless fights. The jostling, shouting, fighting, and endless arrests extended throughout the afternoon. At one point Guérin himself was arrested for shouting, "Mort aux juifs," and subsequently kicking a police officer, M. Leproust, in the stomach.[44]

Inside the Chamber, as soon as the session was called to order, Déroulède requested the floor:

DÉROULÈDE: The cabinet on these benches was placed there three months ago by a republican majority of which I was a part . . . but it was formed around M. Cavignac. . . . After such a long recess . . . I should like for the Chamber, for all of us, to make known again our ideas and judgments.

VOICE: You were a Boulangist, don't forget.

DÉROULÈDE: Yes, I was and I remain Boulangist . . . I remain a Boulangist without Boulanger, because I serve my ideas, and not just a man. . . . What I want to ask now, in the light of the resignations of Cavignac and Zurlinden . . . is if the government has overstepped the confidence which we gave it.

To everyone's apparent surprise, General Chanoine asked to speak and, in a matter of seconds, offered his resignation.[45] Evidence suggests, however, that Déroulède, Guérin, and even Rochefort, as well as several members of the general staff, knew of Chanoine's intentions.[46] Nevertheless, Brisson's government was finished, and his cabinet resigned later that afternoon.

The crowds outside greeted the news of the ministry's defeat with new cheers and several serious brawls that required the intervention of mounted police. Yet the day was far from over. Many decided to wait for Déroulède to leave the Chamber before they considered dispersing. Finally, at close to nine in the evening, Déroulède appeared and, surrounded by hundreds of supporters, made his way to the Ligue's offices on rue des Petits-Champs.[47] This was the signal for those still in high spirits to spread the demonstrations to the boulevards.[48]

In Paris it was like a Sunday—everyone was on the streets. In front of the Bourse du Travail fifteen police walked two by two. The fifteenth was alone, perhaps because gatherings of more than three persons had been forbidden.[49]

The anti-Dreyfusards celebrated and hailed the new Boulangism, or, in this case, Déroulèdism. In contrast, the Dreyfusards, after weeks of rallying their forces for the "battle," responded by ridiculing the Right, saying, "One has never been able to take Déroulède seriously."[50] Déroulède, at least temporarily, thought that he perhaps held the political balance of power. With a ministerial crisis at hand, many assumed that the president, Félix Faure, would not be unsusceptible to Déroulède's anti-revisionist pressure.[51]

In retrospect, little had been resolved. Although the moderate Charles Dupuy replaced Brisson on 1 November, the movement toward revision was not checked. Dreyfusards and their opponents emerged from the 25 October conflict exhausted. The month of November was a period of rest and recuperation before agitation and activity were resumed. Direct action in the street had been added to the mood of the autumn of 1898. If meeting halls had dominated the Dreyfusard-anti-Dreyfusard conflict in September and October, the street became its major battleground in December. Of that time, Daniel Halévy would say, "Action dominated all."[52]

Halévy's statement is particularly relevant to Déroulède and the Ligue. For almost two months they had pursued an activist campaign in the street which aimed first at pressuring the regime and second at establishing their political position. Yet the stated goals of the Ligue had not significantly altered since 1897. Although the organization still claimed to represent France as an "apolitical" movement dedicated to *revanche*, its tactics had far exceeded the limitations of its program. Reacting spontaneously to the escalating process of revision, the Ligue had become an organization in which "action dominated all." For Déroulède, the pattern was much the same. A playwright whose fantasies had been played out on the stage, he now found himself in a situation in which the street replaced the theater. A romantic as well as a dramatist, he first responded spontaneously and then elaborated ideological justifications, a process he was to repeat several times within the next eight months.

Between 25 October and 4 December the Ligue des Patriotes held no public meetings. The month-long period of inactivity indicates the extent to which Déroulède and the Ligue were overtaken by events. After the victory of October, Déroulède did not have a plan with which to follow up the crisis caused by the demonstrations. Yet the success of 25 October brought new allies to the Ligue.

The Bonapartists, barely a political shadow, were deeply divided during the 1890s.[53] Prince Victor and his closest supporters, led by Paul de Cassagnac, were particularly addicted to inactivity, preferring to wait for their chance, which they estimated might come after the Universal Exposition of 1900.[54] The faction led by Baron Legoux and Cuneo d'Ornano was politically active and sponsored a group of Comités plébiscitaires in Paris. Since early 1898 Legoux had been urging his *comités* and Victor to take a position with respect to the affair.[55] Victor's unwillingness to offer either his approval or his purse to the anti-Dreyfusard side made matters difficult for Legoux, who was dependent on the pretender's treasury. By mid-July 1898, the Legoux faction was seriously considering full support of the Ligue. The decision was delayed, however, because of its unwillingness to support Guérin also, whom the Bonapartists viewed with great distaste.[56] The less support Legoux received from his leader in Brussels, the more the Comités plébiscitaires were drawn to the Ligue. Finally, Prince Bonaparte, in a message of considerable self-contradiction, told Legoux to announce that the *comités* "are not to hold any meetings for or against Dreyfus, not to cry, 'A bas les juifs,' but, nonetheless, may follow Déroulède and the Ligue."[57] Given Déroulède's appeal to authoritarian republican and plebiscitory practices, the politically activist Bonapartists did not find his leadership difficult to accept.[58] Thus, by December of 1898 the significant anti-Dreyfusard forces were those in Déroulède's coalition and Guérin's Ligue. The Orléanist royalists, led by André Buffet, did not appear important. Individuals such as the ubiquitous Millevoye and Thiébaud, lacking personal following, shifted in and out of each of the formations, depending on daily political fortunes.[59]

Despite the success enjoyed by the Ligue des Patriotes as a result of the October demonstrations, Déroulède found his organization beset with two related problems: organization and money. The Ligue had not yet been declared officially reconstituted, and, despite, a growing membership, several of the *arrondissement* committees still considered themselves autonomous.[60] One of the demands these *comités* made on the Ligue was that only Déroulède's permanent leadership would ensure their loyalty. In late November Déroulède called all the *arrondissement* leaders together and told them that the Ligue was in fact officially reconstituted and urged them to build up their organization at the local level.[61]

Having resumed the reorganization of the Ligue, Déroulède in late November 1898 called an end to the brief and somewhat artificial moratorium. As in October, rampant rumors stated that either Déroulède was acting in concert with Zurlinden and even Dupuy or that he had issued an ultimatum to the army that if it did not clear the streets of the Dreyfusards, the Ligue would do so.[62] The Left claimed that a nationalist coup was imminent and that it was ready to answer violence with violence.[63] The Ligue's leadership began to speak with much confidence. When questioned about the possibility of strong government action against the organization, Le Menuet said that "it would be necessary to convene the Haute Cour."[64] For the moment Déroulède felt that increased pressure, constant demonstration and disturbance were the best tactics to use in influencing the government to permit the prosecution of Picquart and prevent revision.[65] Rather than call another private meeting of the Ligue, he decided on a more theatrical gesture designed to dramatize his style of action politics.

On the evening of 10 December Salle Chaynes was the scene of a large and vocal Dreyfusard meeting to protest the arrest of Picquart. Sébastien Faure was speaking when Déroulède and Habert, having forced their way through the police barricades, entered the room.[66] Derisive cries from the fifteen hundred persons present greeted the two leaders of the Ligue, who dodged several attempts by the more excited spectators to strike them. Déroulède's attempt to speak was drowned out by the shouting. Faure addressed the crowd:

M. Déroulède tried to appear courageous in coming to this platform escorted only by M. Habert. To the contrary, however, it is his weakness which gives him immunity, for if he had come here with his hordes, the welcome would have been something else.[67]

As the crowd's vociferations grew louder, Déroulède left and was greeted by the tumultuous cheers of more than six hundred *ligueurs* gathered outside.[68] "What *ivresse!* Déroulède among two thousand *ligueurs* who waited to embrace him."[69] As in the past, the demonstrations spread to the streets. Déroulède led several hundred of his supporters in a torchlight parade down rue de Tanger, where he announced, "My mission for tonight is ended; do what you will, but above all, *conspuez les traîres.*"[70] Demonstrations, fights, and arrests continued well into the night.

Those who supported Déroulède cheered his "valiant" efforts.[71] Even *Le Figaro* reported, "Never has one seen a meeting as interesting, dramatic, and palpitating as the one held last night at Salle Chaynes in la Villette."[72] The preservers of public order could hardly fail to acknowledge the impact of Déroulède and the Ligue. "Those who are dominant are the majority of the members of the Ligue des Patriotes—a combination of veterans and students."[73] Déroulède decided that the Ligue itself would hold no more meetings for the time being. Rather, each time the Dreyfusards planned a rally, the Ligue was to attempt to break it up, responding to orders sent from the *comité directeur.*[74] Guérin, who had been speaking in the provinces during the past month, decided to follow the lead of Déroulède in an attempt to keep himself from being overshadowed. Although the Dreyfusards claimed a coordinated policy between the two Ligues, Déroulède was determined to maintain his distance from Guérin, content to let the anti-semites pursue parallel tactics.[75]

Given their success, the leaders of the Ligue began to make plans for a grand general assembly at which the Ligue was to be officially reconstituted and its presidency filled by Déroulède. The meeting was scheduled for 29 December at the Manège St. Paul. Concurrently, the Ligue's position with the Bonapartists was solidified,[76] and a campaign was begun to solicit funds for the widow of Colonel Henry. A new and insignificant organization, the Ligue des intérêts nationals, had been recently created. It was led by Colonel Monteil, whose support the Ligue des Patriotes was willing to accept.[77] Monteil preferred to remain independent, but for the moment his force was negligible. What is significant is the apparent effect that Déroulède had on public opinion. Within a month, Montiel's organization was joined by another new group on the nationalist front, the Ligue de la Patrie francaise. Its immediate popularity must be seen in relation to the atmosphere of excitement and polarization which Déroulède was instrumental in creating. If some of the intellectuals joined the Ligue de la Patrie française because they felt uneasy in the more militant Ligue des Patriotes, their increasingly active political response to the Dreyfus Affair owed a great deal to the lead prepard by Déroulède.

As the official voice of the Ligue des Patriotes, *Le Drapeau* proclaimed the renewed militancy of its program. If the nationalism of Déroulède had become more exclusive during the last months of 1898, the program of the Ligue until December remained, if not vague, then related still to the abstracts of *revanche*. By early December, however, Déroulède speeches, printed as editorials in *Le Drapeau*, indicated a "new" program more compatible with the militancy of the Ligue. It was clear to Déroulède that to preserve the honor of the army, the Republic had to be reorganized. The Dreyfus Affair was the responsibility of those evil men who wanted to deliver France into foreign domination. Such men—and their numbbers were growing—could no longer be called French. Obviously, there were many within the government who were likewise to be considered traitors. As long as the parliamentary system continued to protect these men from the people whose will might be expressed directly by plebiscite, the Republic was doomed. Thus, to restore Alsace-Lorraine, France had to honor her army and regain her initiative in foreign affairs. To do this, the Republic had to be reorganized, its authority strengthened.[78] The Gambettist strain had finally come to an end. *Revanche* and counterrevolution, not revision, were to be the new rallying cries.

More than four thousand people were packed into the Manège St. Paul on 29 December 1898. They came to hear Déroulède speak and to celebrate the definitive reorganization of the Ligue des Patriotes. Their enthusiasm was only slightly dampened when it was announced that the president of the Ligue, M. Paul Déroulède, was ill and that he had requested Marcel Habert to deliver his address:

> Whatever the future should bring, let us dare to continue up to the very end our double campaign of the defense of the army and the reorganization of the Republic.
> Believe me, the cosmopolitans will have good reason to curse, the anarchist good reason to strike out, the magistrates and politicians good reason to falsify justice and violate the law. The Party of France will vanquish the party of the foreigner.
> I know only too well that for a long time the state has ceased to exist, that there is no longer even a chief of state, but there is always the nation, always the army.[79]

The subsequent speakers only underlined the message that their president had sent. Although a specific program was not enumerated, it was clear that the Ligue des Patriotes intended to cleanse France of her decadent men and institutions. As one secondary speaker put it, a double revolution had to be created, the first to "tout renverser, l'autre pour tout rétablir."[80] It was also clear that these men considered the army to be the ally of the people in their struggle.

The police were anxious spectators at the meeting. Their anxiety was justified when at the sermon's end several hundred *ligueurs* demonstrated well into the night along the boulevards. Not all observers saw the meeting in the same light. "What a contrast to the Dreyfusard meetings. Here no aesthetes with long hair. . . only the faces of *brave gens*, of workers who, having finished their day, come to speak a bit about *la patrie* and their immortal aspirations."[81]

NOTES—CHAPTER 6

[1] APP B/A 1553, an entire carton of police reports charting the activities of the Parisian Ligues and socialists as well as the "military" plans of the police to avoid civil disturbances on 25 October 1898.

[2] Reinach, 3:300.

[3] APP B/A 1,032, 7 October 1898.

[4] See Robert E. Kaplan, "France 1893-1898: The Fear of Revolution among the Bourgeoisie." Ph.D. dissertation, Cornell University, 1971.

[5] Roger Glen Brown, *Fashoda Reconsidered*, provides an excellent analysis of the relationship between the Dreyfus Affair and Fashoda.

[6] Brown, pp. 8-9.

[7] See David Landes, *The Unbound Prometheus* (Cambridge, 1967), pp. 231-236.

[8] Mitchell, pp. 166, 174, 185, 737, and 743.

[9] Rougerie, pp. 102-103.

[10] APP B/A 1,396, 6 and 29 October 1898.

[11] Ibid., 8 October 1898.

[12] Edouard Dolléans, *Histoire du mouvement ouvrier, 1871-1920* (Paris, 1953), pp. 46-49.

[13] Joseph Reinach, 4:286-289.

[14] Brown, p. 105.

[15] APP B/A 1,338, 26 September 1898.

[16] APP B/A 1,338, 25 September 1898.

[17] APP B/A 1,338, 27 September 1898.

[18] APP B/A 1,338, 27 September 1898.

[19] Ibid.

[20] APP B/A 1,338, 25 September 1898.

[21] APP B/A 1,338, 26 September 1898.

[22] *Le Jour*, 27 September 1898. See also *Le Gaulois*, 26 September; *L'Intransigeant*, 26 September; *Le Petit Bleu*, 28 September; and *Le Figaro*, 26 September 1898.

[23] AD 15,664, 27 September 1898, Duchess d'Uzès, ENK, to Déroulède

[24] AN F7 12,446, 28 September 1898.

[25] APP B/A 1,338, 29 September 1898.

[26] APP B/A 1,032, 1 October 1898.

[27] APP B/A 1,338, 1 October 1898.

[28] APP B/A 1,032, 1 October 1898.

[29] AN F7 12,870, 1 October 1898.

[30] APP B/A 1,032, 2 October 1898.

[31] *Le Gaulois* and *Le Figaro*, 3 October 1898.

[32] APP B/A 1,032, 4 October 1898.

[33] *L'Aurore*, 6 October 1898.

[34] APP B/A 1,338, 8 and 30 October 1898.

[35] AN F7 12,451, 8 October 1898.

[36] AN F7 12,870, 8 October 1898.

[37] APP, B/A 1,338, 9 October 1898.

[38] APP B/A 1,032, 11 October 1898.

[39] AN F7 12,717. See various reports of the week of 6 October 1898, one of which is subtitled "On the hearsay of a usually reliable journalist," indicating that both the Left and Right were attempting to scare the government into some kind of action. See also APP B/A 904, 16 October 1898: "The so-called coup of the generals was one of the great 'stories' of the Dreyfusard press."

[40] APP B/A 1,338, 21, October 1898.

[41] APP B/A 107, 20 October 1898, and *La Libre Parole*, 24 October 1898.

[42] *L'Aurore*, 24 October 1898, and APP B/A 107, 24 October 1898.

[43] APP B/A 1,533, 25 October ; APP B/A 1,032, 22 October; and APP B/A 1,532, 18-26 October 1898.

[44] *Le Petit Bleu*, 26 October 1898.

[45] J O, 25 October 1898, p. 2,110.

[46] APP B/A 1,108, 1901; Johnson, p. 153, and Nicholas Halasz, *Captain Dreyfus: The Story of a Mass Hysteria*, p. 186.

[47] *Le Petit Bleu*, 26 October 1898.

[48] AN F7 12,461, 25 October 1898, 10:30 P.M.

[49] *Le Petit Bleu*, 26 October 1898.

[50] *L'Aurore*, 25 October 1898, and *Le Siècle*, 26 October 1898.

[51] AN F7 12,466, 27 October 1898.

[52] Chastenet, 3:131.

[53] See the thesis presented by John Rothney, *Bonapartism after Sedan*, which underlines Bonapartism's faliure as a political party.

[54] APP B/A 70, 4 December 1896. The Bonapartists had no special plans for that occasion; rather it had represented a distant point of departure, a rationalization for inaction.

[55] APP B/A 70, 26 January 1898.

[56] APP B/A 70, 21 September 1898.

[57] APP B/A 70, 9 October 1898.

[58] AN F⁷ 12,451, 7 December 1898.

[59] AN F⁷ 12,459, 3 November 1898, and AN F⁷ 12,451, 8 December 1898.

[60] AD 32,890, 26 November 1898, Comité du 17ᵉ arrondissement to Déroulède.

[61] APP B/A 1,338, 26 November 1898.

[62] AN F⁷ 12,717, 2 December 1898.

[63] AN F⁷ 12,451, 7 December 1898.

[64] APP B/A 1,338, 7 December 1898.

[65] AN F⁷ 12,461, 8 December 1898.

[66] APP B/A 1,032, 10 December 1898.

[67] APP B/A 107, 11 December 1898.

[68] APP B/A 1,032, 10 December 1898.

[69] Maurice Barrès, *Scènes et doctrines du nationalisme*, p. 229.

[70] APP B/A 107, 11 December 1898.

[71] AD 26,365, 11 December 1898, and 32,766, 30 December 1898.

[72] *Le Figaro*, 11 December 1898.

[73] AN F⁷ 12,461, 14 December 1898.

[74] APP B/A 1,032, 15 December 1898.

[75] APP B/A 1032, 14 December 1898; B/A 1,107, 15 and 18 December 1898.

[76] APP B/A 107, 19 December 1898.

[77] APP B/A 1,032, 21 December 1898.

[78] *Le Drapeau*, 4, 18, and 25 December 1898.

[79] *Le Drapeau*, 1 January 1899.

[80] *Le Drapeau*, 1 January 1899, "one to overthrow everything, the other to reestablish all."

[81] *Le Gaulois*, 30 December 1898, unsigned editorial.

PART
111
—

FROM THE RIGHT

CHAPTER

7

—

The Social Base

BY MIDWINTER OF 1899 the Ligue des Patriotes had become the foremost leader of the nationalist, and then anti-Dreyfusard, Right. Much of its success must be attributed to its organization and the loyalty of its members. Surely the cohesiveness of the Ligue was a factor in the emergence of Paul Déroulède as a dominant personality during the Dreyfus Affair. Yet, beyond its cries for counterrevolution the Ligue did not have a specific political program—Déroulède having abandoned his concern over the "social questions;" neither did it prepare to sponsor candidates for election. Rather, it posed as a movement articulating the concerns of its leaders on the one hand and the frustrations of its members on the other. While the nationalism of *revanche* appeared to be the touchstone for Déroulède and his closest followers, the social and economic anxieties of the rank and file focused attention on other issues. Collectively, these matters—ideological and socioeconomic—made the impact of the Ligue both important and, in the context of the late nineteenth century, unique.

The theatrical qualities of Paul Déroulède having been demonstrated, it must be recognized that the relationship between the Ligue's leadership and its members was one that spanned social class, generation, and the perspective that each category brought to bear on events. To appreciate, then, the

Ligue's and Déroulède's influence and mutual dependence better, it is necessary to examine the way in which the Ligue was organized and to determine
as explicitly as possible the social basis of its membership.

As of February 1899, the Ligue des Patriotes commanded a membership of
sixty thousand. The actual reemergence of the Ligue as an active element in
Parisian politics dates from only six months earlier. The suicide of Colonel
Henry, the resignation of four ministers of war, and governmental wavering
over the issue of revising Dreyfus's conviction all served to convince Paul
Déroulède that the Ligue could once again play a significant role.

By this time the Ligue was a well-financed, centrally organized, and
disciplined movement.[1] A *comité directeur* of fifteen, presided over by Déroulède, made all decisions, which were transmitted to the rank and file by
arrondissement and *quartier* delegates. Within the *comité directeur*, however, existed a small group of leaders who made secret and more significant
decisions. While operating on elective principles, the Ligue's Parisian
organization received its orders from the top—from *le maître*, Déroulède
alone, or in consultation with a handful of loyal followers known as the
cabinet noir.

Essentially the Ligue's membership can be divided into three parts: (*a*) its
top-level leadership, (*b*) its older and provincial members, and (*c*) its militants in Paris.[2] Within the first rank, two groups emerge: those who were
closely linked to Déroulède by friendship, profession, and class; and those
who had earned his confidence and represented the Parisian rank and file.

Second only to Déroulède in the Ligue was his constant and devoted
lieutenant, Marcel Habert. Almost twenty years younger than Déroulède,
Habert, like his friend and leader, was Parisian and bourgeois. His grand-
father had been the architect for the city of Paris; his father, a prominent
lawyer. Trained as a lawyer himself, Habert joined the Ligue in 1888 as a
supporter of Boulanger. A year later he served as Déroulède's counsel when
the Ligue was prosecuted by the state at the liquidation of the Boulanger
episode. Habert had become convinced that France's parliamentary decadence had contributed to the nation's international impotence, and as a
result he became one of several revisionists who worked to expose the Wilson
scandal. As a reward for his reformist zeal, he was elected to the Chamber in
1889, 1893, and 1898 and later served as the nationalist spokesman on the
Municipal Council of Paris. By the mid-1890s, his loyalty to Déroulède was
legendary, and he worked persistently to persuade his colleague to return to
active political life. The ultimate proof of Habert's devotion came in
December 1899 when, following the arrests and convictions for conspiracy of

many nationalists, royalists, and anti-Semites, he gave himself up to the police so that he might share his master's exile.[3]

Ferdinand Le Menuet, the secretary of the Ligue, was equally devoted to Déroulède and equally committed to urging him to take up the sword. The son of a republican mayor who had served briefly in 1848, Le Menuet was born in Saint-Lô and was a veteran of the 1870-1871 war. He joined the Ligue at the same time as Habert, in 1888. In fact, from its dissolution in 1891 to its refounding in late 1897, the Ligue des Patriotes was Le Menuet. Without his service as secretary-general, all continuity with the past would have been lost.[4]

If Le Menuet was responsible for the organization, continuity, and rebirth of the Ligue, it was Henri Galli who put *Le Drapeau*, the Ligue's newspaper, back on the streets of Paris. A provincial like Le Menuet, a lawyer like Déroulède and Habert, Galli was born Henri Gallichet in Chalons-sur-Marne in 1853. A brilliant student with interests in politics and journalism, Galli joined several radical republican groups in the late 1870s. Within a few years he became a reporter for, then editor of, *La Semaine républicaine*. An early member of the Ligue, Galli—like Habert and Le Menuet—was convinced of the veracity of Boulanger's republicanism, and he helped Déroulède swing the reluctant Ligue to the general's side in 1887-1888.[5] When the Ligue dissolved in 1891, Galli joined *L'Intransigeant* as an editor, a post he retained for the next decade. As the editor of *Le Drapeau* from 1897 to 1902, Galli was among the top three or four leaders of the Ligue des Patriotes. In 1900, Déroulède designated him as his spokesman in Paris. When the Ligue went into decline, Galli embarked on a successful political career, culminating in his election to the presidency of the Municipal Council of Paris in 1913. Like Habert, he lived well into the twentieth century and was known as Déroulède's most important protégé.[6]

Paulin-Méry was by origin a provincial, by residence a Parisian. Like others in the top leadership of the Ligue, Méry was a professional—a medical doctor by training and practice. At the age of twenty-six, in 1886, he became a member of the Blanquist organization in the thirteenth *arrondissement*. Originally associated with Edouard Vaillant, Méry then joined the party's faction that supported Boulanger in 1888-1889. At the same time, he organized a local committee of the Ligue des Patriotes and began to write for the local newspapers of the *arrondissement*. In addition, he opened a free medical clinic in his *quartier*, an act that earned him the reputation of an honorable and hard-working man of good conscience. Méry was elected to the Chamber in 1889, 1893, and 1898. Under his leadership, the Ligue des

Patriotes and the Blanquist revisionist groups in his *arrondissement* functioned as one organization in the 1890s; in fact, it was Méry who personally
brought the rest of this Blanquist faction into the Ligue in 1897.[7]

The similarities in background, profession, and class among the five top
leaders of the Ligue des Patriotes are striking. Between forty and sixty years
old, they were all professionals, all early adherents to Republican or socialist
organizations, all drawn to Boulanger and thus to the Ligue, and all served
(with the exception of Le Menuet) as deputies, municipal councilors, or
both. With their political origins on the left of center, later drifting to the
right, the leadership of the Ligue typifies the shift of the Ligue des Patriotes,
the major agent of French nationalism, in the late 1890s.

The more plebeian element of the leadership was represented by Edmond
Ballière, Edouard Barillier, and Pierre Foursin. When Déroulède began to
"militarize" the Ligue in the summer of 1899, he named these three men to
head the reorganized battalions.[8] The eldest of the three militant leaders,
Ballière, was born in 1840 in Calvados and was trained as an architect. Early
in 1870, he came to Paris and worked as a building contractor and as an
amateur actor. A supporter of the Commune, he was exiled in 1871 along
with his friend Henri Rochefort. Three years later, the two escaped and
Ballière lived the exile's life in London, Brussels, and Geneva until the
amnesty of 1883. Settling in Clermont-Ferrand, he resumed political activity
and gained election as the city's mayor, a position from which he was
removed in 1889 as the result of his support of Boulanger. Again, Boulanger
attracted another member who believed that the Ligue's cry of *revanche* and
revision echoed his personal political values. Remaining close to the Ligue
for a decade, Ballière was considered by Déroulède to be the organization's
most militant and devoted leader.[9]

Pierre Foursin, though ten years younger than Ballière, had also been a
Communard. A resident of the eighteenth *arrondissement*, Foursin worked
for France-Canada, a bureau that promoted cultural relations between the
two countries. Attracted to Boulanger's cause and thus to politics, he joined
the Ligue des Patriotes in 1888 while organizing a Blanquist committee to
his quarter. In his election to the Chamber from Paris in 1899, Foursin had
received electoral support not only from Déroulède but also from Henri
Rochefort and the Blanquist, Ernest Roche. Foursin's strength in the Ligue,
like Ballière's, derived from his ability to organize street demonstrations and
to mobilize his supporters quickly and effectively.[10]

The third of the battalion leaders, Edouard Barillier, was also the *porte-
drapeau*, a ceremonial position he filled proudly at all of the Ligue's public

functions. Barillier (the youngest of the three street leaders) was a wholesale butcher with reputation for solid honesty and reliability combined with a violent temperament. Prosperous enough to pay a rent of nine thousand francs a year, Barillier was one of those present at la place de la Nation in February 1899 when Déroulède and Habert were arrested for attempting a *coup d'état.* Typically, he too had been drawn into politics in support of Boulanger and joined the Ligue in 1888-1889. Remaining loyal to Déroulède in the days that followed, Barillier was reputed to have more than a thousand *ligueurs* ready to follow his call to action.[11] Barillier was arrested by the Waldeck-Rousseau government in August 1899 along with his idol, but he was acquitted by the same court that sentenced Déroulède to a decade's exile. Barillier's local popularity subsequently enabled him to seek successful election in the Parisian Municipal Council, a position he retained until his death in 1910.

Like those in the top leadership, the three street lieutenants of the Ligue also were drawn into political participation from the Left. Two were Communards; all three were attracted to the Ligue via Boulanger. Similarly, the parallel interests of the Ligue and the revisionist wing of the Blanquists seem to have attracted the same men. Although younger, with less formal or professional education, and addicted to the politics of the street, the three men of the second level in the Ligue's command provided a perfect communications link between those who made the decisions and those who would be called on to carry them out.

The rank and file of the Ligue des Patriotes can be divided into two elements: provincial and Parisian. Of the Ligue's total membership, the provincial adherents made up perhaps 25 percent.[12] Thus, at its height in February 1899, the provincial Ligue commanded a membership of ten to fifteen thousand. Of this number, however, between one-third and one-half belonged to the committees in Marseilles, where the membership is assumed to have been similar in its characteristics to that of the Parisian Ligue. In reality, then, there were fewer than ten thousand and probably only five thousand provincial and rural *ligueurs.*

Although the Ligue had been a national organization during the 1880s, its successive dissolutions in 1889 and 1891 destroyed its nonurban committees. Prefectural reports from 1893 show that only two departments, the Seine and the Gironde, reported the existence of organizations remotely resembling the Ligue des Patriotes.[13] With the exception of the organization in Marseilles, provincial committees did not begin to regroup with any success until the winter of 1898-1899. One of the great differences, then, between the Ligue of the 1880s and that of the late 1890s lies in its transformation from a national to an urban, and thus Parisian, political movement.

Of the provincial *ligueurs*, who constituted between 8 and 12 percent of the total organization, most were veterans of the war of 1870-1871, had joined the Ligue in the 1880s even before the Boulanger episode, and viewed Déroulède as the heroic incarnation of patriotism and *revanche*.[14] Many of these followers expressed their appreciation to Déroulède as the poet and politician of France yet in the same breath complained that the nation was threatened by the "masses of the Jews." Characteristic of the mentality of those who belonged to the provincial Ligue was the sentiment expressed by one who had been a *ligueur* for more than a decade: "I understand nothing of the words of nationalists or anti-Semites. I only know that *la patrie* is in shreds and that it is time for it to be saved."[15] Many of those who corresponded with the leader of the movement also included pleas for their own financial salvation, begging for assistance in obtaining licenses for *tabacs* or cafés, asking for job references and loans. These requests indicate the social and economic level of those seeking assistance as well as their belief that Déroulède, representative of the Ligue, would be responsive to their supplications. The correspondence of the provincial *ligueurs* reveals that a great many of them were veterans who viewed the Ligue des Patriotes as a kind of unofficial ministry of veterans' affairs. They thus belonged to the Ligue as individuals, rather than through local organizations, viewing their membership as a means of ameliorating their status as the nation's forgotten men.[16]

Although there were many *ligueurs* in Paris who were veterans and thus belonged to the generation of 1870, both the social profile and the organization of the Parisian Ligue differed markedly from the traits of its provincial membership. When the Ligue formed again in 1898, it was assumed to be simply the regeneration of the Boulangist Ligue—that is, resurrected on its old basis. In fact, the Ligue des Patriotes of the Dreyfus Affair was a combination of three organizations that had been allied in the 1880s but which did not merge until 1897-1898. Just as an examination of the leadership reveals lines of continuity extending to the republican and even socialist heritage of the Ligue, an analysis of the Ligue's component "committees" confirms its earlier left-of-center origins.

In reality, then, the Parisian Ligue des Patriotes was a melange of the remnants of the old Ligue, combined with two other political groups. Led by Henri Rochefort, the Parti républicain socialiste français was a loosely linked federation of electoral committees in Paris whose purpose was the support of candidates approved by *L'Intransigeant*'s editor. By the mid-

1890s, Rochefort's influence was well past its peak, and his group began to merge increasingly with the Ligue. As his biographer has suggested, by 1898 Rochefort was merely an old Communard neither willing nor able to participate in the street action that was forthcoming.[17] Rochefort's diminishing power and influence made it logical as well as likely that his following would be incorporated into the younger, more energetic Ligue.[18]

In addition to Rochefort's contributions, the Ligue des Patriotes benefited also from the absorption of a faction of the Blanquist organization. Claiming obligatory allegiance to the true revolutionary ideals of their founder-patron, the Blanquist revisionists had split from the party's central committee. When Blanqui's disciple, Edouard Vaillant, declined to support Boulanger, the revisionists—led by Jules Caron and Ernest Roche—joined forces with Déroulède and Rochefort.[19] Although retaining a separate identity and organization in the mid-1890s, the revisionists merged with the Ligue in 1897-1898. By the time of the Ligue's coup in February 1899, those who had once represented this faction of the Blanquist movement were among the most militant members of the Ligue.[20]

Thus, at its height, numbering upwards of thirty thousand members, the Ligue des Patriotes in Paris was a combination of Rochefortists, Blanquists, and Déroulèdists, whose political roots extended past Boulanger to the war of 1870-1871 and the Commune. Of crucial importance, then, in evaluating the significance of the Ligue—now the embodiment of nationalism and direct action on the Right—is the socioeconomic profile of its dominant, Parisian membership.

As noted, the characteristics of the Parisian Ligue differ strikingly not only from the provincial membership but from the leadership as well. However, a definitive assessment concerning this group is difficult to make because of the fact that the police were never able to obtain comprehensive lists of the Ligue's rank and file with names, addresses, occupations, and ages. The Ligue and Déroulède were more than cautious in ensuring that this information never left its various hiding places. Under duress, it appears, Déroulède ordered the membership lists either to be destroyed or to be removed from the country. Nevertheless, it has been possible, through announcements in the Ligue's paper, *Le Drapeau*, arrest records, or random membership lists obtained by the police, to obtain partial information on approximately five hundred persons identified as *ligueurs* during the years 1897-1899.[21] Even though the statistics on this sample of the Parisian Ligue are incomplete, they can give an approximate picture of the Ligue's composition.

The turmoil of the Dreyfus Affair spawned more than one militant street movement on the Right. The Ligue antisémitique de France, an offshoot of Drumont's *La Libre Parole* organization, formed and led by Jules Guérin, was Anti-Semitic first and subsequently anti-Dreyfusard. The Ligue antisémitique competed with the Ligue des Patriotes for control over the street and the nationalist movement. Jules Guérin, a man of little honor and character, was not nearly so careful as his counterparts in the Ligue des Patriotes. After his arrest in 1899, the police discovered his personal notebook containing several hundred names, addresses, and occupations of those who belonged to the Ligue antisémitique. Additionally, during the week preceding 23 February 1899, Paris was convulsed by a continuous series of demonstrations and riots by Dreyfusards and anti-Dreyfusards. Each side not only voiced its feelings concerning the election of Emile Loubet to the presidency of the Republic but also created an atmosphere best described as expectant. It was into this tense, emotionally charged, yet curiously theatrical setting that Déroulède and the Ligue would venture unsuccessfully. The week's activities, however, resulted in a considerable number of arrests of those who indulged in anti-Loubet statements or actions. Although it has been impossible to trace these individuals to either of the two revisionist Ligues, their names and relevant data were duly noted by the diligent police, making it reasonable to assume that those arrested had sympathies similar to those of the members of either Ligue.

By comparing the information available on the cadres of the Ligue des Patriotes with the data on the Ligue antisémitique and the arrests of February 1899, one can obtain a picture of the Ligue's membership. The Ligue des Patriotes was apparently composed of lower-middle-class Parisians. They provided the greatest percentage of the Ligue's membership in the Paris region and thus of the Ligue as a whole. Of the original sample of five hundred *ligueurs* who can be identified by address, occupation, age, or affiliation, approximately one-half can be located by *arrondissement*. If one compares the breakdown by *arrondissement* of the Ligue des Patriotes' members with the same distribution of the Ligue antisémitique and those arrested in the week of 18-23 February, an interesting profile emerges.[22]

A study made by a British historian serves as an additional reference point. D. R. Watson, in an essay dealing with the nationalists' electoral victory of 1900-1906 in Paris, utilized a statistical survey of the city made in the 1890s, which survey indicates the relative class composition of the twenty *arrondissements*.[23] Briefly, the study reveals that the wealth of each quarter decreased almost in proportion to its distance from the center, with the exception of the west end of the city, the sixteenth, and parts of the fifteenth and seventeenth *arrondissements.* Thus, one can perceive three U-shaped zones, each one blending unevenly into the other, containing essentially bourgeois, *petit bourgeois,* and working-class populations, respectively. By establishing the population patterns of the Ligue des Patriotes and comparing these patterns with the Ligue antisémitique, and then superimposing these onto the plan that Watson has proposed, it is possible to begin an analysis of the social profile of the Ligue.

The first two columns in Table 1 indicate the membership percentages, by *arrondissement,* of the Ligue des Patriotes and the Ligue antisémitique. The third column, used as a rough check, shows the arrests made for anti-Loubet actions in the crucial week of 18-23 February 1899.

TABLE 1

Comparison by *Arrondissement* of Memberships
of the Ligue des Patriotes and the Ligue antisémitique,
and Arrests Made Between 18 and 23 February 1899

Arrondissement	Ligue des Patriotes	Ligue antisémitique	Arrests
1	3.1	3.9	4.2
2	1.8	6.6	2.8
3	0.5	4.0	2.5
4	5.9	2.2	9.8*
5	0.5	3.7	2.8
6	5.6	5.1	2.8
7	1.5	3.1	7.1*
8	1.5	5.3	2.8
9	7.7*	12.4*	5.8*
10	6.4	5.6	4.2
11	11.8*	14.4*	21.4*
12	0.0	2.3	2.8
13	6.4	1.1	2.8
14	10.2*	2.2	2.8
15	0.5	2.0	2.8
16	3.1	5.0	0.0
17	11.8*	10.0*	5.6*
18	7.7*	9.9*	4.2
19	7.0*	3.5	0.0
20	4.1	1.5	4.2

* Indicates highest percentage.

In correlating the percentages, one finds that four *arrondisse-ments*—the ninth, eleventh, seventeenth, and eighteenth—contain the high-est percentages of memberships of the two Ligues and percentages of arrests. Further, the totals of these four *arrondissements* show their combined per-centage of Ligue inhabitants to be at least 100 percent higher than the average.

Percentages of Total Membership in
9ᵉ,11ᵉ, 17ᵉ, and 18ᵉ *Arrondissements*

Ligue des Patriotes 39%
Ligue antisémitique 47%
Arrests 37%

Thus, in the four *arrondissements* in question, the range is from just under 40 percent to almost 50 percent of the total for the whole city of Paris. Similarly, if the percentages for the ten least wealthy *arrondissements*—the ninth through the fourteenth, and the seventeenth through twentieth—are determined, the results are equally illuminating:

Percentage of Total Membership
for Ten Selected Arrondissements

Ligue des Patriotes 73.1%
Ligue antisémitique 62.9%
Arrests 53.8%

Indeed the statistical sample of fifty *ligueurs* who can be located by exact address, hence *quartier*, street, even side of the street, as well as *arrondissement*, only reinforces, in fact clarifies, the social profile that has emerged. In the ninth, eleventh, seventeenth, and eighteenth *arrondisse-ments* lived 56 percent of those *ligueurs* who can be identified by street address. Conversely only 14 percent lived in middle- and working-class districts in Paris. Of an even more startling and confirmatory nature is the pattern of residence of these fifty *ligueurs* all of whom were identified by the police in 1899 as militant and between the ages of seventeen and forty.

Three distinct clusters of Ligue des Patriotes can in fact be perceived. The first cluster lived exclusively in the Batignotelles *quartier* of the seventeenth, the southernmost "tier," just a few streets above the boulevards, in the eighteenth, and the three eastern *quartiers*, Rochechouart, Montmartre, and

St. Georges of the ninth. The second area of concentration was in the Roqueta *quartier* of the eleventh *arrondissement* contiguous to the artisan-trades area of the Archives and well removed from the working-class neighborhoods that linked the eleventh with the twentieth *arrondissement*. These two areas contained the four largest *arrondissement* totals of Ligue membership but included only one *quartier* in two of the districts, the eleventh and seventeenth *arrondissements*.

The third place where *ligueurs* were domiciled was an area that included parts of the second, third, and fourth *arrondissements* yet contained another 26 percent of the membership. Bounded by rue de Rivoli to the south, the boulevards that link the Bastille to la place de la République to the east, boulevards Poissonnière and St. Denis to the north and by rue Montmartre in the west, this third area contains the *quartiers* Mail and Bonne Nouvelle, Arts et Métiers, St. Avoie and Archives. Too, it contains within these boundaries both the "pletzl," or the area of eastern-European Jewish immigrant residence, and the shops and *ateliers* of the clothing trades which stretched along its streets from Bastille to la place de la République. It was in this latter section that the residents of the "pletzl" often worked.[24] The evidence of street, *quartier*, and area residence by members of the Ligue des Patriotes reinforces the information gathered from arrest records and *arrondissement* patterns.[25] The Ligue des Patriotes' rank and file was of neither the middle nor the working classes. Its membership, especially of its young, active militants, was predominantly lower middle class.

It appears, then, that the Ligue des Patriotes was not just a political phenomenon of the city of Paris, but indeed reflected the social, economic, and political developments within certain districts of the city. In some ways, this can be seen as obscuring one's perspective of the Ligue's significance in an understanding of the history of the Third Republic. However, this need not be the case; although the history of Paris does not necessarily reveal truths about the history of France, the forces in operation—particularly on the *arrondissements*, where the nationalists and anti-Semites found most of their members—were representative of those affecting French society as a whole. With the important exception of demographics, the Parisian *arrondissements* of the north and east can be viewed as a laboratory in which the major social, economic, and political tensions of the era were made manifest.

For if the population of France as a whole exhibited numerical signs of stability in the nineteenth century, a fact that the Ligue des Patriotes emphasized continually, the demographic distribution of the nation resulted, especially for Paris, in significant urban growth. In the course of a single generation, the population of Paris between 1872 and 1900 gained almost a million souls—from 1,850,000 in 1872 to 2,174,000 in 1900.[26] The shift in population mirrored the economic transformation of France from an agricultural to an urban-industrial society and also provided a source of growth, especially for the working-class and *petit bourgeois arrondissements* in the city of Paris. In the districts where the Ligues drew the major proportion of their members, there occurred both major population expansion and industrialization, and immigration, both internal and foreign.

Thus, into what traditionally had been lower-class, artisan, and tradesman *arrondissements* entered new populations: industrial workers, French provincials, and Jews from eastern France and (especially after 1881) from Russia, Poland, and Rumania.[27] This influx of social and religious newcomers coincided, then, not only with the industrialization of the Parisian *arrondissements* but also with the significant economic fluctuations of the era. Chevalier, for example, indicates that the years of greatest population change in the eleventh *arrondissement* were ones that also witnessed the largest shift from commercial to industrial occupations in that district.[28] It is not surprising to note that it was exactly during this time, from 1886 to 1891 to be precise, that there was a convergence between the economic and political crises of depression and Boulangism.

With the counterattack of the Opportunists and the upsurge of socialism, which in the early 1890s replaced the Boulangist claim to speak for the working classes, [29] the lower-middle-class population of these "laboratory" *arrondissements* surely began to fear for their position within bourgeois society. Their anxiety, manifested subsequently in their participation in the Ligue's activities in the late 1890s, no doubt was reinforced by the appearance of eastern-European Jews in the *quartiers* in which they lived.

Although it is estimated that only eight thousand Jews from Russia, Poland, and Rumania settled in Paris between 1881 and 1900,[30] two additional facts must be considered in order to appreciate the impact of the "great migration." Fully two-thirds of Parisian Jews lived in the ten *arrondissements* of the north and east, where in fact two-thirds of the members of the Ligue des Patriotes also lived. Further, these Jews settled in selected *quartiers* (in the ninth, eleventh, eighteenth, and twentieth *arrondissements*) in large numbers, again in areas in which the Ligue found itself especially strong. Equally significant is the fact that even though these five thousand "yiddish" Jews might appear to be numerically insignificant, the Jewish population of Paris had almost doubled, from twenty-four thousand in 1872 to forty-five thousand in 1897.[31] Thus, not only was there an influx of eastern-European Jews to Paris in the 1880s and 1890s but additionally their number was tripled by French Jews, for the most part Alsatians moving to the capital.

Also of interest is the social profile of the Parisian Jewish community in the generation between 1870 and 1900. During that time, despite the well-publicized success of a financial and industrialized upper middle class, there was a striking growth of a Jewish lower, though not precisely working, class. Comprising salesmen, tailors, shoemakers, lathmakers, occasional shop owners and rag pickers,[32] yet valuing upward mobility, skills, and educational achievement,[33] this new Jewish social stratum lived cheek by jowl and competed for jobs with those Parisians who by residence and occupation belonged to the Ligue des Patriotes and/or the Ligue antisémitique.

In the case of the Ligue des Patriotes, then, one finds that almost 40 percent of its membership lived in four *arrondissements*—the ninth, eleventh, seventeenth, and eighteenth—and almost 75 percent lived in ten *arrondissements* whose total population was considerably less than half of the total for Paris.[34] From these figures it can be concluded that the majority of the rank and file of the Ligue des Patriotes lived in lower-class neighborhoods but that the Ligue was somewhat less heterogeneous than, for example, the Ligue antisémitique. This conclusion is confirmed in a listing of the occupations of 113 *ligueurs*. Of this total, none can be identified as industrial laborers, but slightly more than 50 percent can be classified as *petit bourgeois*: tradesmen, florists, hairdressers, carpenters, butchers, and printers. In addition, fewer than a third of the sample were professionals: doctors, lawyers, teachers, architects, and accountants; 3 percent were army officers, 3 percent businessmen, and 2 percent students. The occupational profile makes clear the tensions indicated by the pattern of residence; that is, the Ligue des Patriotes was composed for the most part of lower-middle-class Parisians, with a smaller number of professionals, some of whom may also be considered as lower middle class, and a smattering of veterans and students.

In sum, the Ligue des Patriotes represented a basically lower-middle-class movement characterized by its internal discipline, its authoritarian organization, and loyalty to its leader, Paul Déroulède. In 1898-1899 its tactics and program merged, expressive of the Ligue's proclivity to seek redress of its grievances by direct, often violent action. While this tendency was related in part to the growing tensions of the Dreyfus Affair, the Ligue's tactics and program reflected not only the demands of the times but the social composition of its membership as well. Although not of the same social class as his followers, the leader of the Ligue nevertheless sought to dramatize his politics by action; it is worthwhile to recall that those who followed him belonged to a well-established tradition of urban violence and, at an earlier time, revolution. As the preeminent organization of the Parisian lower middle class, the Ligue des Patriotes facilitated the transfer of nationalism from Left to Right and at the same time represented an equally important and parallel political movement of a significant segment of that class. The participation of lower-middle-class elements in the anti-Dreyfusard movement foreshadowed their more complete adherence to the radical street leagues of the coming century.

NOTES—CHAPTER 7

[1] An F[7] 12,451, report of 9 February 1899 cites the figure sixty thousand, whereas F[7] 12,449, report of 26 August 1899 estimates thirty thousand. Given seasonal and political fluctuations, one has no reason to believe these figures to be inaccurate. The two largest contributors to the Ligue aside from Déroulède were Edouard Archdeacon, an ex-Ralle candidate, and Boni de Castellane, a social aristocrat of contemporary notoriety.

[2] Estimated by the police at 10 percent of the total membership. APP B/A 201, report on parties, 1870.

[3] APP E/A 49, report on Marcel Habert. Déroulède was sentenced to ten years in exile for his part in the disturbances in France in the summer of 1899. In fact he was apprehended to prevent what the government feared was a new *coup d'etat* designed to coincide with the opening of the trial of Dreyfus at Rennes.

[4] AD 17,952, 25 October 1895; 6,857, 14 March 1895; 17,687, 16 April 1896, all Le Menuet to Déroulède.

[5] See APP B/A 1,337, reports of December 1887, regarding the internal problems of the Ligue during the Boulanger affair.

[6] APP B/A 1,088, report on Henri Gallichet, 1914; *L'Almanach du Drapeau* (Ligue des Patriotes), 1900.

[7] APP B/A 1,182, reports: Paulin Méry, 1886-1899.

[8] See Chapter 9. The militarization was in response to Waldeck-Rousseau's announcement of a new trial for Dreyfus in July 1899.

[9] BIMS 4,577, 8 August 1899, papers of Waldeck-Rousseau.

[10] Ibid.

[11] APP B/A 947, 13 August 1899.

[12] AN F[7] 12,451, 9 February 1899, report on the reorganization of the Ligue des Patriotes.

[13] AN F[7] 12,449, March 1893, prefectural reports to the minister of the interior.

[14] AD 2,009, 24 November 1899, Paul Dacline, employee at PLM, to Déroulède: "You who have always given us such great examples of courage with your movement which I have always followed. . . . You are to me the incarnation of the French people."

[15] AD 32,670, 20 November 1898, letter of M. de Fauny to Déroulède.

[16] AD 32,766, 30 December 1898, M. F. Hautaire to Déroulède.

[17] Williams, pp. 249-250.

[18] AN F[7] 12,449, undated lists, late 1890s, entitled "Ex-Boulangist committees, currently nationalist, to which many Ligueurs now belong."

[19] APP B/A 201, 5 March 1890, Report: The state of various political parties in 1890.

[20] APP B/A 117, 19 November 1897; BIMS, 4,577, 8 August 1899, reports on Caron and Roche; APP B/A 106, A 107, A 108, 1897-1899, daily summaries of meetings which show the merging of the three organizations.

[21] Ibid. See also *Le Drapeau* and *L'Almanach du Drapeau* as well as diverse police reports APP B/A 107-109 and 1,072, of the 500 *ligueurs*, exact addresses on 50 "militants" in 1898-1899, lists by profession for 113, and *arrondissement* identifications for all 500 are available.

[22] APP B/A 1,072, entire carton devoted to events related to the death of President Felix Faure.

[23] Watson, pp. 69-85.

[24] See the excellent book by David Weinberg, *A Community on Trial: the Jews of Paris in the 1930s* (Chicago, 1977).

[25] I am indebted to Zeev Sternhell who kindly has pointed out some methodological problems in my earlier work "The Ligue des Patriotes" and who in his *Le Droit révolutionnaire* made use of that information. See especially Sternhell, Ibid., pp. 111-119.

[26] Chevalier, pp. 78-90, and Michel Roblin, *Les Juifs de Paris*, pp. 65-73.

[27] Mitchell, p. 78; See also E. A. Gutkind, *Urban Development in Western Europe*, pp. 257-262.

[28] Chevalier, p. 86.

[29] See Chapter 3.

[30] Roblin, p. 73.

[31] Roblin, pp. 60-61.

[32] Marrus, p. 31; See also Zosa Szajkowski, "The Growth of the Jewish Population in France."

[33] See for example Simon Kuznitz, "Jewish Emigration from Russia," and Thomas Kessner, *The Golden Door*.

[34] Préfecture de la Seine, Service de la Statistique municipale. *Résultats statistiques du dénombrement de 1896 pour la ville de Paris et le Département de la Seine* (Paris, 1896).

CHAPTER

8

—

The *Coup manqué*

BY THE END OF 1898, after four months of intense political activity, Déroulède had made clear once again the extent of his ideological evolution. The original goals of the Ligue, the return of Alsace and Lorraine and revision of the constitution, which represented the Gambettist vision of a Jacobin France, had been revised. Within the context of the Dreyfus Affair and the crisis of 1898 was added a new role, born partly of despair and partly of fear. What France needed, according to Déroulède's analysis, was a regime responsive to the will of the people. Instead all she had was a group of parliamentarians who represented not the nation but the cosmopolitan *sans-patries* who had but one aim: to see France weak and humiliated. The Republic was in danger and history demanded that it be wrenched from the hands of those who threatened it. "We must," Déroulède said, "restore the Republic of 4 September 1870."[1]

Indeed, although Déroulède was to justify his actions during the next eight months with the cry that the Republic was in danger, it is equally clear that his rhetoric concealed the new components that increasingly pushed aside the Gambettist and Jacobin origins of his nationalism. While awaiting, for the time being, involvement with the anti-Semitic Ligues of Guérin and Dubuc, Déroulède nevertheless had begun to employ the shorthand of racism: exclusivity, degeneration, conspiracy, the cosmopolitan *sans-patrie*. Despite calls for another 4 September, the Republic that Déroulède had in mind was increasingly of a different order than the one that his mentor, Gambetta, had hoped to create a generation earlier.

Similarly, the appeal of the Ligue des Patriotes reflected in part the magnetism and energy of its leader. Its growing popularity in 1898 was as well, however, a direct result of its enormous and widely publicized activity in the streets of Paris. It may be said that in all probability a significant number of those who belonged to the Ligue had only the vaguest sense of its ideological origins. At the same time it must be recognized that the popular element in the Ligue was itself exercising a more powerful influence than Déroulède either realized or was willing to admit. For it was the rank and file, the Parisian *ligueur*, who was most susceptible to the shorthand of racism and fear, and it was the Parisian *ligueur* who in the political marketplace had more than one group from which to choose.[2]

If during the fall of 1898 Déroulède's program had been vague, his tactics had been carefully considered and well planned. Designed to take advantage of the political opportunity that the Dreyfus Affair offered, the Ligue's strategy was primarily aimed at establishing its relative dominance over the wide range of anti-Dreyfusard forces. By December the success that the Ligue achieved in this area derived from both the activity of the Ligue—its meetings, demonstrations and street actions—and from its willingness both to court and to represent its "popular" constituency.

Clearly what Déroulède was calling for, and would increasingly contemplate in the weeks to come, was a revolution to restore order. France, he now declared, had become divided—and not just over the Dreyfus Affair—between those who spoke for the real nation and cosmopolitans who through the Parliament were destroying *la patrie* and hence were no longer worthy of the name François Politically it was thus evident that the Chamber had become the prisoner of foreign interests, slave to cosmopolitan thievery that was itself joined with international-finance capital.[3]

The Ligue's appeal, in the new year of 1899, began then to combine a kind of primitive anticapitalism and an unspoken anti-Semitism with an already explicit antiparliamentarianism. In January and February 1899, the theme of responding to the obvious vindications of the "common" man was echoed over and over in the meetings and literature of the Ligue.[4]

There is not a Frenchman today who does not condemn this regime . . . for it ruins us . . . it destroys our national organism and permits the enemy to place himself in our very midst . . . to wish to (conserve it) is to wish our *incurable decadence,* to wish the death of La Patrie française.[5]

The twin motifs of disease and decadence, the enemy within, the decline of the nation's powers to withstand the bacillus, implied but one thing: the need to act. By the second week in February the Ligue des Patriotes, with its regional affiliates in Marseilles, Limoges, Bordeaux, and Angoulême growing rapidly for the first time,[6] and with Paul Déroulède returned to Paris from a vacation in Nice,[7] began to contemplate some form of direct action.[8]

It is remarkable that at exactly the same time the Dreyfusard press, particularly *L'Aurore,* was convinced that the Right was planning a military takeover. The Left believed that arrests were imminent and that a combination of nationalists and clericals was about to act.[9] The government, as in October, was caught in the middle, and the prefect of police, Charles Blanc, as well as the premier, Dupuy, did little to restore order to the streets of Paris. In the first six weeks of the new year Dreyfusard and anti-Dreyfusard meetings doubled and redoubled, as did the accompanying invective and violence. "Given the current state of opinion a good *petit coup de main* adroitly placed will finish the Dreyfusards," wrote one of Déroulède's friends.[10]

Public opinion became even more polarized by the evolution of events closely associated with the affair itself. In late October the *cour de cassation* had recognized the petition of Mme. Dreyfus for a reopening of the case and indeed began to call witnesses. The court was presided over by Louis Loew whose connection with the bankruptcy of the Union Générale in 1882 made him an easy target for the anti-Dreyfusards who readily associated Rothschild's power, Fashoda, and Dreyfus with Loew's presidency.[11] As the attacks increased, other members of the judiciary joined in the criticism of the case. In early January Quesnay de Beaurepaire resigned his position as president of the civil appeals court in protest.[12]

Almost simultaneously, on 31 December 1898, under the initiative of three professors—Jules Lemaître, Albert Sorel, and François Coppée—came the announcement of the creation of a new league, the Ligue de la Patrie française.[13] By its declaration in *Le Soleil,* the new league attempted to rally the intellectuals of the Right in much the same way that the Ligue des droits de l'homme had rallied those on the Left. Within three days twenty-five Academicians signed its appeal.[14]

The undersigned, troubled at the prolongation and aggravation of the most disastrous agitation, persuaded that such prolongation can only compromise the vital interests of the *patrie française*, particularly those which are under the glorious protection of the national army . . . are resolved: to work within the limits of their professional power to reconcile the progress, ideals, morals and traditions of the *patrie française*; to unite and group, devoid of partisan politics, in order to act usefully against the situation by word and by example.[15]

Thus, at first appearance the Ligue de la Patrie française promised to represent attitudes similar to those expressed by the Ligue des Patriotes. In placing itself above the Dreyfus Affair, it claimed to recruit its members from all political parties. Within several days the new league collected the signatures of forty thousand persons. With most of its founders opposed to revision, however, the Ligue de la Patrie française announced on 4 January that it could no longer accept "any . . . of those who had supported Dreyfus or Picquart."[16] A new league thus joined the mounting public protest of anti-Dreyfusards.

The Ligue de la Patrie française also temporarily absorbed l'Action française, a small committee created in May of 1898 as an electoral pressure group. As a result, Lemaître and Coppée were joined as founders by Maurice Pujo and Henri Vaugeois.[17] On 19 January the Ligue held its first public rally under the presidency of Coppée, attracting more than fifteen hundred persons. Lemaître delivered the main address, which was but a restatement of nationalist and antirevisionist arguments which had been advanced for more than eight months. Although Lemaître and Coppée praised Déroulède as the nationalists' greatest leader, it was clear that the new organization posed a potential threat to the position enjoyed by the Ligue des Patriotes. Such a rivalry, however, did not develop for more than a year. In one sense the Ligue de la Patrie française complemented the Ligue des Patriotes. Déroulède's group was popularly based and action oriented, while the new Ligue had a greater intellectual appeal and was significantly less militant.[18] In addition, as the Ligue de la Patrie française emerged, it began to develop fully a precise anti-Dreyfusard program, which gave a direction to the nationalist movement. Finally, little conflict existed between the two groups not only because Coppée and Déroulède were on extremely good terms but also because the Ligue des Patriotes did not see the other group as heavyweight competition.

The Ligue de la Patrie française . . . *ne me dit rien.* . . . It is like rose water which will not enter into the fight and which repudiates anarchists and anti-Semites alike, as if there were a parallel established between the two parties.[19]

The presence of a new formation on the Right, however, especially one that appeared powerful, did not help to decrease the tensions that were so intense in Paris.

If the creation of a new *Ligue* served only to add to the expectant atmosphere in Paris during the first six weeks of 1899, the actions of Jules Guérin's Ligue antisémitique de France made no less a contribution. Early in January Guérin's men began to circulate in cafés and restaurants in the ninth, tenth, eighteenth, and nineteenth *arrondissements* and threaten their owners with violence unless they agreed to exclude foreigners and Jews from their clientele.[20] At the same time Guérin attempted to play on working-class anti-Semitism, trying unsuccessfully to draw support away from Jaurès and Gérault-Richard. Guérin said: "They [the socialists] denounce the evils of the *patronat*, but only the French. When it is a question of a patron juif-. . . that's something else again."[21]

Déroulède's temporary absence from Paris led Guérin to hope that he and his Ligue could dominate anti-Dreyfusard forces. He began to talk openly of finding "his" general and promised the worst kind of violence should Dreyfus ever set foot again on French soil. It was announced that the circulation of *L'Antijuif* had recently reached one hundred fifty thousand, an indication that more than five hundred francs a day were being provided from a source as yet unknown.[22] In response to this influx of money and intensification of activity, Guérin grew increasingly authoritarian and arbitrary. By late January he appeared less conciliatory than ever, imagining himself the force behind all nationalist and anti-Semitic efforts. As a result, several deputies who had previously considered themselves to be Guérin's legislative spokesmen quietly withdrew their support and gravitated to Déroulède's faction.[23] Despite his financial independence, Guérin could not ignore the Ligue des Patriotes. Thus, in late January *L'Antijuif* began a campaign attacking Déroulède and his Ligue.[24] Simultaneously, Guérin had posters affixed throughout Paris, announcing the imminence of civil war and the defeat of the Dreyfusard enemy.[25] Although the Ligue antisémitique de France at its height had only eight thousand members in Paris, its militancy and capacity for action made it a formidable political force.[26]

Tensions had been building since early September of 1898 and reached a climax in February of 1899. The activities of the Ligue des Patriotes, the Ligue antisémitique and the Ligue de la Patrie francaise had become more frequent and violent. The Left had responded in kind and the equilibrium that the government had hoped for was destroyed. The anticipation of both sides was that surely someone would act. The only question was who and when. This anticipation was heightened when on 16 February 1899 Félix Faure, president of the Republic and founding father of the Ligue des Patriotes, died from what was called an attack of appoplexy.[27] The occasion seemed ready-made for a decisive move to seize control of the slack reins of command.

Following the death of President Faure, the agitation, excitement, and violence which had characterized Parisian politics reached their climax in the events of 23 February. The disputed election of a new president of the Republic touched off mass protests by the Right and dire warnings from the Left. The three major groups on the Right, the Ligue des Patriotes, the Ligue antisémitique, and a wealthy though ineffective royalist organization, all attempted to take advantage of the situation with which they had been presented. The Orléanists, having been quiescent at best since their flirtation with Boulangism a decade earlier, had by the summer of 1898 reached an agreement with Guérin, who agreed to act in the interests of the Duc d'Orléans in return for between two and three hundred thousand francs.[28] Using the Comte de Sabran-Pontevès, who controlled a group of wholesale butchers in the nineteenth *arrondissement,* as a go-between, the royalists hoped that Guérin would be able to infiltrate the Ligue des Patriotes and convert it to their use.[29] With the Duc's money Guérin moved to new quarters on rue Chabrol and increased the circulation of his newspaper, *L'Antijuif,* to fifty thousand copies.[30] The royalists were initially encouraged in their strategy by the fact that whereas Déroulède himself was not publicly anti-Semitic, many rank-and-file members of the Ligue were. This insight was essentially a valid one, but those opposed to Déroulède failed to account for both the personal loyalty engendered by Déroulède and the evolution of the Ligue's rhetoric, which in late 1898 began to sound more and more like that of Guérin. Most importantly the decision to bank on Guérin was finally an indication that the Orléanists had money and little else.[31] Nevertheless, their relationship with Guérin cast a mysterious shadow over the events that followed Faure's death.

Yet the death of the president caught the nationalists and Déroulède by surprise. Although there had been discussions concerning the possibility of a *coup d'état,* there were no definite plans to put into immediate operation. The Ligue had openly proclaimed the need for a preemptive coup, but it was not ready to mobilize. The reaction of the Ligue's leadership was to wait for Déroulède and his orders for future action.[32] The same mood of enthusiasm and turmoil affected the other groups on the Right. Immediately they resolved to demonstrate in protest against the probable election to the presidency of Emile Loubet, whom they considered to be a Dreyfusard and a Panamist. The Ligue des Patriotes began to plan for a series of demonstrations to be held on Saturday, 18 February. Déroulède was expected to return from Nice that morning, and the voting for Faure's successor was scheduled for the afternoon at Versailles. Le Menuet even proposed that if Loubet were elected, the Ligue try to stop his carriage at la place de la Concorde and take him back to Versailles.[33]

The atmosphere in Paris was tense. The two pretenders, Orléanist and Bonapartist, were reported to be on France's borders awaiting a signal from their followers in Paris.[34] The Left proclaimed the Republic in danger.[35]

Félix Faure has just died. He has gone at the moment when crushing revelations were about to discredit him. Already the monarchists and clerical bands are mobilizing. . . . Democrats awake! Revolutionaries alert![36]

Despite the great tension, both the Left and the Right awaited Déroulède's arrival. If any specific action were to be taken, it was expected that the deputy from Angouléme would be its inspiration. This attitude was particularly true of the Guérin-Orléanist cabal which was committed to taking action only if the disorders were initiated by the Ligue des Patriotes.[37]

On Saturday, 18 February 1899 at 9:30 A.M. greeted by more than one hundred of his followers, Déroulède arrived at the Gare de Lyon, where twelve years earlier he had organized the famous Boulanger demonstration.[38] Quickly entering a carriage with Habert and Thiébaud, he made his way to the Gare St. Lazare and immediately proceeded to Versailles. Declaring that he had no intention of voting in the election whose result was already assured, he approved of plans to pay homage to Faure by placing a wreath at his grave following the funeral on the twenty-third. For the moment, although he threatened that "force can take the law by the hand and lead it to justice," Déroulède had no other concrete plans for the Ligue.[39]

Despite Déroulède's abstention, Loubet was easily elected to the presidency of the Republic, receiving 483 votes on the first ballot. The approval of "Clemenceau's candidate," however, gave credence to the nationalist attack on parliamentarianism. Upon his return to Paris after the vote, Déroulède stated,

In effect, I find it absurd to support a man whose ideas and sentiments on major issues are unknown. One asks even the least significant candidate to propose a program, yet one asks nothing of a man now mandated to direct the destiny of France. That is profoundly ridiculous, and even more, it is the vice, the evil, in our dying Constitution from which the Republic will expire if nothing is done. That is why, once again. . . I am giving my abstention the character of protest against an electoral system which I consider dangerous for my country.[40]

The speech was enthusiastically received by a crowd of *ligueurs* who awaited Déroulède at the Gare St. Lazare. Their response encouraged the Ligue's president, who saw the crowds grow larger and more vociferous as he and his entourage made their way to the Ligue's offices. There, demonstrations accompanied by cries of "Vive Déroulède" and "Conspuez Loubet," flared up all through the night.[41] In the space of several hours the police were forced to make almost three hundred arrests, usually of young men in their early twenties who had defamed the name of the president of the Republic. As a weary *agent* reported at 2:30 A.M. on 19 February: "A great animation reigns on the streets of Paris at this moment."[42] Urging his followers to wait for the right moment, Déroulède promised something would be done by Friday morning. "In the face of the imposing demonstrations that will occur, the government will be forced to call out the troops, Paris will be under a state of siege, and that will be the moment to try a *coup d'état.*"[43]

As a practitioner of theatrical politics Déroulède knew how to arouse public opinion, but his performance left no room for decisive action. At this point the danger of his believing too fully in himself became apparent. The logic of his stand and the direction of his rhetoric dictated that he act. In truth he had no specific plans. Those that he had fell far short of the meticulous calculation of a trained revolutionary, yet they encompassed one significant point: the necessity of obtaining the army's support. On the other hand, if Déroulède was conspiring with the army directly, why did he not announce his intentions to those closest to him? Several answers are possible. Most probably Déroulède planned to act, but as of 18 February he knew neither how nor when. An upsurge of popular protest accompanied his return to Paris and supported his anti-Dreyfusard and anti-Loubet positions. Once again it is not difficult to see his intentions being influenced by the reaction of the crowd. With all sides expecting someone to do something, the audacity of a dramatic act appealed more strongly to him. Drawn into political discussion and activity, he became intoxicated by the atmosphere of excitement that permeated Paris. That he had contemplated such an action for more than two months made it all the more appealing.

Meanwhile, the police and Sûreté were aware of Déroulède's intentions. Perhaps the reports sent by individual agents were lost or delayed in a bureaucratic process, but the preparations for the funeral on 23 February are strong indication that the forces of public order were prepared for the threat posed by the anti-Dreyfusard Right. Certainly, the Left proclaimed daily that such a threat was in the offing.[44]

The activity and excitement of 18 February were matched by the events of the next day. All dissident groups held secret meetings and inspired evening demonstrations that resulted in numerous arrests just as had occurred the day before. Everyone's attention was focused on the events anticipated for Thursday the twenty-third. Once again, expectations contributed more to the events that unrolled than premeditated plans did.[45] Leaving the anti-Semites to put up inflammatory posters and provide the *camelots* for the nightly demonstrations, the Ligue des Patriotes sent out more than four thousand *petits bleus* calling its militant members to a meeting at the Salle Charras on Tuesday 22 February.[46] Concurrently, Le Menuet began distribution of the Ligue's membership lists, and Habert telegraphed Dupuy in Marseilles, telling him to be prepared for Thursday.[47] Despite all this motion and activity, it appears that as late as 22 February nothing specific had yet been decided.[48]

Three days earlier the Ligue had petitioned the government for permission to participate in the funeral of the president, but its request was denied. There was even speculation that before the twenty-third the Ligue des Patriotes would be dissolved.[49] Nonetheless, the tone struck by Déroulède at the Salle Charras meeting on the evening of 22 February was calm and dignified. Some *ligueurs* wanted to organize themselves into cadres of brigades and sub-brigades, with the aim of combatting the *gauchistes* rather than the police, but Déroulède ordered them simply to appear at 8:30 A.M. and respectfully acknowledge the passing of one of their former founding fathers.[50] Looking tired and worn after three days of furious activity, Déroulède told his followers that if there was to be a demonstration it would occur after Faure was put to rest. Any directions for the Ligue would be given during the course of the procession and not before.[51]

By early evening on 22 February 1899 the basic pattern from which all parties would act the next day had been established. Everyone expected that some element or combination on the Right would attempt to turn Faure's funeral into at least a massive antirevisionist, anti-Loubet demonstration and at best into a coup designed to overthrow the government. One of the questions that remained open was, for whose ultimate profit might this coup operate? Of all the groups on the Right, it was assumed correctly that the Ligue des Patriotes was the most likely to act. The organization had been discussing the possibility for months, and recent events established Déroulède as the prime candidate to initiate such a venture. If other elements on the Right hoped to reap the fruits of the Ligue's initiative, they planned to let Déroulède begin the process over which they might subsequently gain control. In effect, however, the royalists and Guérin were the only ones with the capital and organization to capture movement. The Ligue de la Patrie française was neither oriented nor organized toward direct action. The Bonapartists were penalized by their leader's *immobilisme,* and the Roche-fortists and Blanquest revisionists had long since allied themselves with Déroulède.

The Left was no less certain than the Right that 23 February would bring an attempt by the nationalists to wrench power from the government. Dreyfus was still their symbol, yet his cause was largely forgotten between 18 and 23 February. The Republic was in danger, the Dreyfusards proclaimed, and they would defend it with all their energies. The police, too, were aware of the dangers presented by Faure's funeral. They ordered preventive arrests of anyone shouting seditious slogans, bearing equivalent emblems, or using the streets for political purposes.

The Prefect of Police counts on the energy of his subordinates to assume, against any attempt, whatever its origin, the respect and loyalty due to the government of the republic. (signed) Charles Blanc, Prefect of Police[52]

In fact, since 19 February, the date of Loubet's election, the prefecture of police had been assailed by letters predicting that on the day of Faure's funeral an attempt to restore the monarchy would be made.[53] The police believed that the Ligue des Patriotes had asked to join the funeral with plans to turn the procession into an attempt to march on the Elysée. They were also aware that the Duc d'Orléans was planning to come to Paris during the night of 22-23 February. Their information was quickly turned over to the Sûreté, whose men took positions to counteract an Orléanist presence in the city. Nevertheless, the police reasoned, "Nothing sure, formal, or precise has yet appeared."[54] This conclusion seemed to be substantiated when the Ligue did not insist on its part in the funeral.

Following the rally at the Salle Chaynes on the twenty-second, Déroulède and Habert began to draft a telegram that would be sent out to more than four thousand Ligue des Patriotes militants.[55] The *petits bleus* called the *ligeurs* to come in four groups to the Bastille, la place de l'Opéra, la place du Roule, and la place de la Concorde.[56] Because the telegrams contained no other information, the police interpreted them as confirmation of a prearranged plan.[57] Quite the opposite was true. Déroulède and Habert were still in the process of formulating their ideas and intended solely to have the Ligue des Patriotes out in force ready to respond to the orders that the two men decided to keep to themselves until the next day.[58] Habert busied himself with a map of Paris, pinpointing areas to be occupied, while Déroulède directed Caron to inform his militants of the convocation order.[59] Similarly, some fifty *ligueurs* were sent out to inform their colleagues of the order in case the *petits bleus* failed to reach their destination.[60] This in fact proved to be an excellent measure, as many of the telegrams were misaddressed and found their ways into the hands of the police.[61]

After midnight Déroulède and Habert retired to a small room. Working over the map of Paris prepared by Habert, the two men talked and planned until well past two o'clock in the morning. At that time their friends in the outer offices walked in and asked, "Well, is it for tomorrow?" Déroulède replied that it was. He did not elaborate.[62]

Thus, the machinery was set in motion for the events of the next day. Déroulède was committed to some kind of action, though he would not divulge the where, when, and how of his plan. Guérin and the royalists were now sure that Déroulède would attempt to overthrow the government. They were also sure that he was unwilling to accept any royalist role in his operation and in fact suspected that he was working for Prince Victor. This being the situation, the royalists and anti-Semites would try either to take over Déroulède's movement without his knowing it or to cause it to fail.[63] Finally, during the early morning of the twenty-third, the military governor, Zurlinden, changed the relative troop displacements for the funeral procession: Generals Pellieux, Florentin, and Roget had their routes slightly altered.[64]

Although it is difficult to imagine that Déroulède was unaware of the possibilities of cooperation with the two other important groups on the Right, the anti-Semites and the royalists, that he did not anticipate the role of the royalists is a perfect example of his political simplicity, and naïveté, a naïveté that was in fact his undoing and which was perhaps responsible for the only attempted *coup d'état* in French history between 2 December 1851 and 13 May 1958. Ironically enough, the plebiscitory authoritarian inspiration of the first bears some relationship to Déroulède's attempt, although at the same time there have been more than a few observers who have seen something of Déroulède in DeGaulle. It was within this spirit that he said to his closest followers on the night of 22 February, "If you have confidence in me, and if you love me, do not ask what I have done and what I am going to do. Just come tomorrow at 3:00 P.M. to la place de la Bastille."[65]

The members of the Ligue des Patriotes were to witness there the passage of Faure's funeral on its way to the Père Lachaise Cemetery. They arrived in small groups, and by the appointed hour some five hundred *ligueurs* were present.[66] Other members of the Ligue were in a café at la place de la Nation and the remainder on the corner of the avenue Philippe-Auguste and boulevard Voltaire.[67] Déroulède joined this last group at 3:45 P.M., appearing nervous, pale, overexcited, and annoyed at the Ligue's disorganization.[68] With him were Marcel Habert, Barillier, and Maurice Barrès, as well as several hundred additional *ligueurs* who had been told by the police to vacate la place de la Bastille.[69] Still more *ligueurs* were in front of the Hôtel de Ville and at the Bastille despite the fact that by midafternoon Déroulède had called them all to la place de la Nation.

Similarly, Guérin and about sixty members of the Ligue antisémitique were waiting along the boulevard Charonne, but without any orders from their leaders.[70] The royalists, organized by the Jeunesse royaliste, were assigned la place de la République and la place de la Bastille, while the Bonapartists of the Comités plebiscitaires gathered at Nation with the elements of the Ligue des Patriotes.[71] Guérin himself sent messengers scurrying down boulevard Charonne, kept a constant eye on Déroulède's movements, and held a carriage containing several dozen rifles and revolvers in a neighboring street.

By the time Déroulède arrived at la place de la Nation, the ceremony at Père Lachaise had ended, and the troops accompanying Faure's casket were returning to their barracks. One company, commanded by General Florentin and made up in part by the Eighty-second Regiment, of which General Roget was the chief officer, proceeded down boulevard de Ménilmontant into avenue Philippe-Auguste and to place de la Nation. There it was to follow boulevard Diderot to the Casserne de Reuilly where it was barracked.

As Roget's regiment approached la place de la Nation, Déroulède reportedly told Habert and Barrès to have the *ligueurs* begin singing "Vive l'Armée" but to await his signal before doing anything else.[72] Seeing Roget emerge in front of his troops, Déroulède, as well as Habert and more than two hundred *ligueurs*, jumped into the street. The *ligueurs* merged with the regiment as Déroulède placed himself between Roget and his column.[73] With the members of the Ligue des Patriotes continuing to shout "Vive l'Armée," Déroulède reached for the bridle of Roget's horse and cried, "To the Elysée!" Roget, who had been reaching for his sword, either in salute or to ward off Déroulède,[74] raised his arm, forced Déroulède to release his grip, and signaled his troops to continue on their way.[75] The regiment then proceeded to la place de la Nation, while the *ligueurs* continued to shout "To the Elysée" and "Vive l'Armée."

At the intersection of rue du Faubourg St. Antoine and boulevard Diderot with la place de la Nation, Habert suddenly shouted, "Block the street," referring to Diderot, which led to Reuilly. At this point, not understanding, the *ligueurs* closed off rue du Faubourg St. Antoine, which led back to central Paris, and the combined swarm of Déroulède, Roget, the Ligue des Patriotes, and the army troops of the Eighty-second Regiment was swept quickly along boulevard Diderot and into rue de Reuilly.[76] There, before the entrance to the barracks, Déroulède and Habert once again appealed to the general, saying, "It is not there that you must go, but to the Elysée."[77] With the crowd and the troops pushing Déroulède, Roget, and Habert into the courtyard, Roget ordered his men to enter the barracks, close the gates, and force the crowd to remain outside.

Suddenly Déroulède and Habert were alone within the barracks walls, the Ligue outside still chanting and Roget ordering his men to remain calm. Déroulède and Habert started to plead with the troops and urge them individually to revolt and join in proclaiming a new regime. Then, by the command of the regimental colonel, the two men were moved to the library where they were confronted by Roget himself. Refusing to leave, Déroulède declared that he wished to be arrested by the army for having tried to "incite the troops in an insurrectional movement and to reverse the parliamentary Republic, substituting for it the République plébiscitaire."[78] With Habert concurring, the two leaders of the Ligue des Patriotes were duly arrested and sent to the salle d'honneur of the regiment. There they calmly conversed with officers, dined comfortably, and, upon being left alone, burned many of the papers that Déroulède had carried with him.[79]

One set of papers contained the names and addresses of all known Dreyfusards, with the notation, "To serve the flag freely for one month." Included among the seventy-five persons enumerated were Ranc, Waldeck-Rousseau, Scheurer-Kestner, Clemenceau, Zola, and Jaurès.[80] On another paper was a proclamation that Déroulède planned to make after the revolt:

TO THE NATION

The usurpative Constitution of 1875 is abrogated;
Restricted suffrage is abolished;
Universal suffrage is re-established;

The Republic is again French and Republican.
A government of privilieged and corrupt men has
    exploited the nation and degraded La patrie;
With the aid of the people of Paris and the Army
    of France we have thrown them out.
The Parliament is dissolved;
The President of the Republic is overthrown.
There will no longer be an assembly without mandate
    which governs the state;
There will be Frenchmen who will be the representatives
    of the people, invited by them in constituent power;
No longer will a parliamentary coalition elect the
    Chief of State; instead, it will be all France.
In a few days the people will be called;
They will make their will known to us and we will
    respect it.
From now on we will see the maintenance of order
    and the defense of our reconquered liberties.
We are not usurpers; we are the guardians of peace,
    the sentinels of the country.
The parliamentary Republic is dead. Long live the
    plebiscitory Republic.[81]

Word of Déroulède's detention but not his arrest was spread to the boulevards by those who had witnessed the action at Reuilly. Among the militants of the Ligue and other dissident groups there was commotion and demonstration. By evening's end more than 250 persons had been arrested.[82] Having observed the day's events, Guérin and his royalist friends concluded that their opportunity had passed and dutifully telegraphed their contact, urging the Duc d'Orléans to remain in Brussels.[83] With Guérin left controlling the financial resources of the Orléanists, 23 February 1899 had rightfully earned the epithet "la journée des dupes."[84]

At approximately the same time that the demonstrations began near the offices of *La Libre Parole*, the Sûreté was informed of Déroulède's arrest. The prefect of police, however, did nothing save inform the prime minister of the matter. Dupuy took no further action until 11:00 P.M. when the chief of the Sûreté was finally sent to arrest Déroulède and Habert, who were enjoying the last of their after-dinner cigars. They were charged with "trespassing and refusing to leave military property."

Two years after the coup, both Paul Déroulède, then in exile, and René Waldeck-Rousseau, who had been prime minister since June of 1899, came to similar though independent conclusions about the bizarre events at la place de la Nation. The latter, learning of the Orléanist-Guérin connection, correctly observed that indeed there had been not one but two plots of overthrow the government[85] and that the reactions of Dupuy, Blanc, and the magistrature in the aftermath of the *événements* exhibited a "softness which cannot be too severely judged."[86] Waldeck-Rousseau's implication is clear: the government acted both laxly and without vigor, as if it had known all along what was going to happen.

Also in 1901 Paul Déroulède, in a speech delivered at St. Sébastien, claimed that he had failed because he had been betrayed, the government informed, and the general with whom he was to have collaborated taken off the parade route at the last minute.[87] Although it is impossible to determine which general might have been involved, or indeed if Roget simply lost his nerve,[88] what seems clear is that, for reasons upon which one can only speculate, the government of Dupuy knew of Déroulède's coup but did little either to stop it or to prosecute its leaders severely after its failure.

In response to Déroulède's accusations Waldeck-Rousseau in 1901 reopened an investigation of the Reuilly events. After questioning General Zurlinden, Waldeck concluded that the parade routes had been changed at 10:30 A.M. on the twenty-third of February and that General Pellieux had been relieved of leading the troops at his own request![89] Roget, therefore, must not have been aware of any specific plans whereas Pellieux and Zurlinden could well have been. Déroulède in 1910, however, disclosed that General Florentin, Roget's direct superior, was the one "who had us arrested."[90] Charles Blanc, prefect of police with his own tracks to cover, blamed Roget. In both cases one suspects a false scent. Given the entrapment practiced by Dupuy and Blanc, and given Zurlinden's political position in the face of massive political failure of the military during the past year, one can finally find it reasonable to presume the following: Zurlinden, who controlled Pellieux, had him contact Déroulède and encourage him to act, then in concert with Dupuy and Blanc, Pellieux was pulled out only when they learned not only what Déroulède but what the anti-Semites and royalists intended to do.

The government, under constant pressure from the movement for revision, still harbored the illusion that it could tread a middle ground between Dreyfusards and the militant nationalist Right. The *immobilisme* of the government, in part due to the heritage of Opportunism, in part due to the circumstances of the day, determined the way in which the specific events of 23 February 1899 were handled. The contrast with the counterattack of

Constans only ten years earlier underlines the actions of Dupuy and Blanc. In 1889 Boulanger's challenge had been both legal and electoral; in 1899 Déroulède had attempted to overthrow the government and the constitution by violent means. In 1889 Boulanger was forced into exile; in 1899 Déroulède was held for trespassing.

Yet Déroulède and his fellow *ligueurs* were not professional revolutionaries with the mental discipline, organization, and ruthlessness necessary to achieve their goals. In this respect, as well as in his political naïveté, Déroulède was a failure, and his coup had the flavor of *opéra-comique*. His failure represents a response by an individual and a movement, both radicalized by the highly charged climate of opinion, the general political confusion, and the unstable social situation. In one sense Déroulède's coup can be seen as an act of self-delusion. Could he have hoped to unite the army and the people against parliamentarianism? On a higher plane his coup was also an act of national delusion. The atmosphere surrounding the events of 23 February 1899 had led everyone to expect something. It may have induced Déroulède to believe he could succeed, but surely it convinced everyone that he would try. As a political act, the coup was a failure; as a psychological one, it represents a scene in a drama whose consequences were profound and far-reaching. In this sense, Déroulède's adventure was an episode in the whole array of events which made up the Dreyfus Affair. His movement was created, mobilized to action, and finally liquidated by the affair. The interrelationship was an intimate one, though most did not comprehend this at the time. Thus, given the tensions that had been building since September of 1898 and which were extreme during the week of 18-23 February 1899, the reactions to this attempt to overturn the government are at the same time incredible and understandable.

The immediate aftermath of the "Affaire de la place de la Nation" prompted the Left to exclaim "we told you so" to the government and to ridicule the actual coup.[91] The threat had been defeated, and Déroulède was once again the Don Quixote of France. Curiously, many on the Right reacted in the same way. Characteristically, articles in the nationalist press expressed regret and attacked the government but also implied that Déroulède was either a bad planner or stupid.[92] The reputation of 23 February 1899 as comic or farcical was thus begun with the reactions of both the Left and the Right which followed the event itself: "Déroulède est un grand coeur, mais c'est un naïf."[93] Once the immediate danger passed, the Left found it useful to discredit the man whom it had most feared as a mass leader. The Right, riddled with false alliances, jealousies, and less-than-honorable leaders, was likewise pleased to see one less horse in the field, at least for the moment.

Déroulède's failure, then, seemed to split the Right further and rally the Left. Finally, Déroulède's historical reputation dates from this period. The contemporary journalistic reaction can be seen as the origin of this reputation. The Left has since continued to ridicule, while the Right and its historians have chosen to deny the existence of a French fascism and thus have had to ignore its antecedents.

NOTES—CHAPTER 8

[1] *Le Drapeau*, 25 December 1898.

[2] See Chapter 7 for a detailed social profile of the Ligue des Patriotes.

[3] AN F7 12,466, 14 January 1899, private meeting of the Ligue.

[4] See for example AN F7 12,870, 25 January 1899, and *Le Drapeau*, 19 February 1899.

[5] *Le Drapeau*, 19 February 1899.

[6] AN F7 12,449, July 1899, report of prefects.

[7] APP B/A 1,032, 28 December 1899, which reported a duel in which Déroulède was wounded, for which report there is no corroboration. AD 41,089, 28 January 1899, Le Menuet to Déroulède, refers only to fatigue.

[8] AN F7 12,451, 11 February 1899.

[9] AN F7 12,717, 10 February 1899.

[10] AD 42,943, 7 January 1899, Rolland to Déroulède; AD 32,028, 22 January 1899, Devilliers to Déroulède: "Do you think there is a chance to make a coup?"

[11] Johnson, pp. 152-155.

[12] Beaurepaire had ten years earlier signed the arrest warrants for Boulanger and Rochefort.

[13] APP B/A 1,336, 7 January 1899.

[14] Eugen Weber, *L'Action française*, p. 17.

[15] APP B/A 1,336 17 February 1899.

[16] APP B/A 1,336, 27 February 1899.

[17] Weber, *L'Action* française, pp. 19-20. Charles Maurras was to meet Vaugeois in January 1899, and they in turn, agreeing that the Ligue de la Patrie française was too vague, began to plan for the independence and reemergence of l'Action française.

[18] Barrès, *Scènes et doctrines*, p. 80; Robert Cornilleau, *De Waldeck-Rousseau à Poincaré*, p. 61.

[19] AD 32,030, 31 January 1899, Devilliers to Déroulède.

[20] APP B/A 1,104, 6 January 1899.

[21] APP B/A 1,104, 15 January 1899.

[22] APP B/A 1,104, 19 and 30 January 1899.

[23] APP B/A 1,104, 23 January 1899.

[24] *L'Antijuif*, 29 January 1899.

[25] APP B/A 1,104, 6 February 1899.

[26] APP B/A 1,104, 8 February 1898.

[27] The real cause of Faure's death is uncertain. *La Libre Parole* claimed that he was poisoned while others in a more Gallic spirit indicated the presence of a young woman in the president's chambers. APP B/A 904, "Death of President Faure," 1899-1908.

[28] BIMS 4,577, undated report on royalist activities from July 1898 to August 1899.

[29] AN F7 12,451, 12,874, 12,459, all 15 October 1898.

[30] AN F7 12,883, 2 August 1898, and APP B/A 1,104, 21 August 1898.

[31] BIMS 4,578, detailed report on royalists, March 1899, included in the papers of Waldeck-Rousseau.

[32] AD 41,174, 17 February 1899, telegram, Le Menuet to Déroulède.

[33] AN F⁷ 12,870, 17 February 1899.

[34] APP B/A 1,034, 18 February 1899; *La Réforme*, 17 February 1899.

[35] *Droits de l'Homme*, 17 February 1899.

[36] *Journal du Peuple*, 17 February 1899.

[37] APP B/A 1,034, 18 March 1899, and B/A 1,104, 18 February 1899.

[38] AN F⁷ 12,870, 18 February 1899.

[39] AN F⁷ 12,870, 27 February 1899.

[40] *Le Drapeau*, 26 January 1899.

[41] APP B/A 1,338, 18 February 1899.

[42] APP B/A 905, 18 and 19 February 1899, and *Le Matin*, 19 February 1899.

[43] AN F⁷ 12,451, 20 February 1899.

[44] See *L'Aurore, Journal du Peuple*, and *Droits de l'Homme*, 18 and 23 February 1899.

[45] APP B/A 1,072, 20 February 1899.

[46] AN F⁷ 12,451, 20 February 1899.

[47] AN F⁷ 12,870, 20 February 1899; BIMS 4,577, 21 February 1899, Commission spéciale, and AN F⁷ 12,462, 21 February 1899.

[48] APP B/A 1,338, 22 February 1899.

[49] APP B/A 1,338, 22 February 1899, telegram of foreign correspondent.

[50] APP B/A 1,338, 22 February 1899.

[51] APP B/A 1,338, 22 February 1899.

[52] APP B/A 905, 22 February 1899.

[53] APP B/A 1,072, report of March 1901, p. 1.

[54] Ibid., p. 2.

[55] AN F⁷ 12,451, 23 February 1899.

[56] APP B/A 1,072, report of March 1901, p. 5.

[57] APP B/A 1,072, report of March 1901, p. 4.

[58] AN F⁷ 12,451, 23 February 1899.

[59] AN F⁷ 12,870, 23 February 1899.

[60] AN F⁷ 12,451, 23 February 1899.

[61] APP B/A 1,072, report of March 1901, p. 4.

[62] Paul Déroulède in a speech delivered at St. Sébastien. Manuscript AD, 23 February 1901. This also appeared in most newspapers during the week of 23 February 1901, and its disclosure prompted a governmental review of all materials regarding Déroulède's role in 1898-1899, including a full reevaluation by Waldeck-Rousseau.

[63] AN F⁷ 12,882, 2 March 1901, "Note blanche . . . Extraits du livre de M. Spiard sur les agissements de Jules Guérin." Unpublished.

[64] BIMS 4,577, March 1901, statement of Zurlinden: and APP B/A 1,072, report of March 1901, p. 8.

[65] *Le Drapeau*, 9 April 1899, "Les événements du 23 février," by Maurice Barrès.

[66] APP B/A 905, 23 February 1899.

[67] AN F⁷ 12,449, 23 February 1899.

[68] APP B/A 1,338, 24 February 1899.

[69] APP B/A 905, 23 February 1899.

[70] AN F⁷ 12,882, 2 March 1901, Spiard.

[71] APP B/A 1,034, 23 February 1899.

[72] APP B/A 1,072, 24 February 1899.

[73] AN F⁷ 12,717, 2 March 1899.

[74] APP B/A 1,072, 24 February 1899.

[75] BIMS 4,577, report of 7 March 1899, testimony of Roget.

[76] *Le Drapeau*, 9 April 1899, Barrès.

[77] APP B/A 1,072, 24 February 1899.

[78] BIMS 4,577, 7 March 1899, report of the Procureur de la République to the Procureur Général.

[79] BIMS 4,577, report of 7 March 1899; *Le Drapeau*, 9 April 1899, Barrès.

[80] AD, unnumbered, undated, unsigned.

[81] AD, unnumbered.

[82] AN F⁷ 12,449, 23 February 1899.

[83] APP B/A 1,072, 25 February 1899.

[84] APP B/A 1,103, report of June 1900, p. 13.

[85] BIMS 4,600, March 1901, notes. Also BIMS 4,577, "So it appears that there were two plots, parallel but not connected."

[86] APP B/A 1,072, report of March 1901, p. 12; Abel Combarieu, *Sept Ans à L'Elysée*, p. 116; and BIMS 4,600, March 1901.

[87] Barrès, *Scènes*, p. 256.

[88] *La Patrie*, 24 February 1899.

[89] BIMS 4,660, Waldeck's notes.

[90] *La Liberté*, 4 October 1910.

[91] *Le Petit République*, 24 February 1899; *L'Aurore*, 24 February 1899.

[92] *La Patrie*, 24 February 1899.

[93] APP B/A 1,034, 24 February 1899, Joseph Lassies.

CHAPTER

9

―

"France for the French"

By THE END OF February 1899, the activities of the Ligue seemed over and the credibility of the government restored. The nationalist Right was shown to be, if not foolish, then harmless. It is reasonable to assume that the Opportunists' hopes of heading off revision, preserving the regime, and maintaining the social equilibrium rested to some extent on the way in which they dealt with the event of la place de la Nation.

Yet these calculations, if they indeed were conscious, came to naught. The staging of a *pièce*, either for distraction or profit, resulted in the characters' reevaluation of their performance and only heightened their desire to be more effective the next time. The six months that followed 23 February 1899, then, witnessed both a continuation and a revision of the actors' positions and motivations.

The industrial recovery, now in full swing, was to make 1899 a year of labor militancy and strikes, thus both continuing and amplifying the events of October 1898—events that can be regarded retrospectively as a stimulus to the agitation at the end of the century.[1] The social and political pressures exerted on the two antagonists of mid-1899, Déroulède and Waldeck-Rousseau (who was to become premier in June), cannot be underestimated.[2] Similarly, the economic and social tensions of the lower middle class of

Paris, which as a group provided the backbone of the Ligue des Patriotes, contributed significantly to the vocal and visceral anti-Semitism in that social stratum. The response of the Ligue and Déroulède to the increasingly strident activism of its members would present a sharp counterpoint to Waldeck's desire to preserve social peace.

The months of February to June 1899 witnessed the swan song of Opportunism. Having "eliminated" a threat from the Right, the Dupuy cabinet nevertheless found itself unable to complete the circle of heading off the process of Dreyfus's revision and simultaneously preserving the Republic of Ferry and Méline. The presence of enemies on both the Left and the Right, compounded by the problem of an unresolved question of justice of international importance, paralyzed the government even more, if possible, after 23 February than it had before that date. Once again, then, the stubborn presence of an issue that transcended politics prevented the conducting of political business in the Third Republic. The Dreyfus Affair, looming over the usual problems of economics and society, simply would not go away. It had to be resolved.

A generation earlier, René Waldeck-Rousseau and Paul Déroulède had been young and talented colleagues of their mentor, Léon Gambetta. By June of 1899, with Déroulède acquitted of any wrongdoings at Reuilly and the government discredited—not only because of its less-than-vigorous prosecution but also because it had been unable to slow down the process of revision—both the Ligue des Patriotes and the government of the Republic were determined to terminate the affair. For Waldeck, the Republic would indeed be in danger, and the thought of a two-front war against militant, counterrevolutionary nationalists on the Right and the well-organized working class on the Left was horrifying. Conclusion of the Dreyfus Affair, and thus accommodation of the Left and the "social question," meant that the Ligues would have to be eliminated.

For Déroulède, the failure of February 1899 was one of both organization and ideology. Not only would the Ligue have to be recast, but also its appeal broadened; only then could the abominable process of revision—a process that would only hasten France's decay and humiliation—be stopped. The result of the clash would be a revolution in the politics of the Republic, a change in the perspective of what that Republic meant; the significance of this alteration would be felt for a generation.

On 24 March 1899, with Déroulède and Habert awaiting their trial before the *cour d'assises* and the Ligue having been officially proscribed,[3] *Le Drapeau* sponsored a conference to which concerned citizens had been invited to express their support for the two deputies.[4] After a series of speakers had railed against the betrayers of the Republic, a clamor arose from the rear of the hall, demanding that Jules Guérin be permitted to speak. Henri Galli, editor of *Le Drapeau* and chairman of the meeting, closed the session rather than permit the leader of the Ligue antisémitique to have the floor.[5] The incident was neither isolated nor without significance.

Several days earlier, twenty members of the Ligue had asked Déroulède's permission to join Guérin's organization.[6] With the "nationalist" trial scheduled for late May and the government indicating clearly its reluctance to press the case, it was apparent to all that a full-blown revival of the Ligue's activities was a real possibility by early June. Yet demands for Guérin and solicitations to join the anti-Semitic organization posed a threat to Déroulède's leadership of the nationalist Right. It was not so much that Guérin was a real alternative to Déroulède but more that anti-Semitism had a potent appeal for the rank and file of the Ligue des Patriotes. As of May, it was evident that without the leader of the Ligue des Patriotes, the nationalists lacked the power and prestige necessary to have a significant effect. As in early February, Déroulède's allies realized that they needed him perhaps more than he needed them.

Jules Guérin, but more importantly the urban anti-Semitism that he represented, remained the one exception. In fact, Guérin's organization was exceptional for several reasons. In mid-April the illegal Ligue vacated its offices and moved to new quarters at 51, rue Chabrol.[7] At a time, then, when antirevisionist forces appeared to be at their weakest, Guérin's group— renamed the Grand Occident de France[8]—suddenly was transplanted into luxurious quarters. Surely the five centimes that each of its fifteen hundred regular members paid each month in dues could not have paid for the gold-inscribed marble plaque that marked the entrance,[9] not to mention the rent of fifteen thousand francs.[10]

In addition to the exorbitant rent, the building at rue Chabrol had other exceptional features. Apart from extensive office space, Guérin installed several game and billiard rooms and a handsome apartment for himself. More curious, however, were the ironworks protecting all the windows and doors on the ground floor, and the front door two meters thick, itself protected front and back by iron-grilled gates. Three other iron gates guarded Guérin's private offices against unwelcome guests. Upon completion of his monument, appropriately named "Fort Chabrol," Guérin told his associates that he had finally taken ample precautions against those, particularly the police, who were out to get him. A bountiful supply of food stored in the basement supported Guérin's claim that he could withstand a siege of more than three months.[11]

The funds that enabled Guérin to embark on this extraordinary undertaking continued to come from the Duc d'Orléans. The royalists eventually realized that it was they who had been the real dupes in February, but they remained ignorant of that sad state of affairs until Agusut 1899. The royalist-Guérin strategy had been to take over and complete any successful action that Déroulède began. Déroulède's failure, then, was Guérin's excuse for having done nothing on 23 February; in fact, it became the main reason for the continuation of the partnership. Yet the duke was a reluctant pretender.[12] Why did he not seek to disengage himself from the agreements with Guérin? The answer must lie with the cooler, more calculating heads that surrounded His Majesty and prevailed upon him: "It is known that Mme. la Duchesse d'Orléans is very ambitious. If it were up to her, she would like nothing better than to engage in political intrigue."[13] The combination of the duchess, the still-militant Comte de Sabran-Pontevès, de Plas, and the Duc de Luynes held sway over the gentleman who probably preferred the role of pretender to actual ruler. Within two weeks of Déroulède's arrest, Guérin was again receiving large sums of money from the royalist treasury.[14] One could conclude then that Fort Chabrol was apparently as much symbolic of Guérin's independence from the Right as it was representative of the success of his efforts to pick the pockets of the Orléanists.

The militant counts and their organizations increasingly began to couch their rhetoric in anti-Semitic terms.[15] As a result, the parliamentary royalists became indignant with Buffet, whom they considered responsible for the anti-Semitic emphasis in their party.[16] Certainly this new tendency did not represent the historical traditions of Orléanism. By late May, the moderates within the party had persuaded the duke to terminate Buffet's *carte blanche* on royalist funds.

Yet as luck or politics would have it, Boni de Castellane (who had been the Ligue's major contributor), not at all pleased with the results of his February investments, was searching for yet another way to spend his money. Guérin readily responded to Castellane's generosity by receiving his new friend at Fort Chabrol several times a week, proudly pointing out the features of his most recent acquisitions.[17] Despite his support of Déroulède, Castellane had not maximized his political fortunes. When it became known that Guérin planned to make *L'Antijuif* a daily newspaper, Boni perceived that by backing the anti-Semite he could gain a political base from which a seat in the Chamber would surely be the outcome. The royalists suddenly saw

Guérin in a new light and gave him an additional fifteen thousand francs within days of Boni's hundred-thousand-franc contribution;[18] the royalists feared Guérin's being co-opted by another competitor, and so they raised the stakes themselves.

Guérin's isolation from the nationalists, a situation that had been evolving slowly and predictably since early in 1898, was complete by the time of Déroulède's trial. Yet Guérin's enclosure at Fort Chabrol symbolized both his strength and his weakness. That he had an impregnable refuge, a frightening reputation, and good financial resources was balanced by the rejection he evidenced toward, and received from, other nationalist leaders. Still, the Grand Occident was not called on to demonstrate during the court proceedings against Déroulède and Habert. Guérin's potential and appeal were ever-present. If Déroulède was going to try again to unite the anti-Dreyfusard forces of the Right, he would have to come to terms with both of those attributes of Guérin.

Déroulède's trial itself consisted of a parade of witnesses who attested to the honesty, loyalty, and devotion of the two deputies in question. On the last day, both men were given the opportunity to address the court. Marcel Habert spoke first, emphasizing that he alone knew of Déroulède's plans for 23 February and that he followed the leadership of his friend out of loyalty to the nation and the movement:

At a time when certain intellectuals have shown a marked tendency toward anarchy . . . which is a sure sign of decadency . . . disorder and disruption are the natural results for the nation. . . . But our Ligueurs . . . are directly opposed to those who have preached disorder. They know that obedience is not to be confused with servitude.[19]

Thus, Habert claimed that when the streets threatened anarchy, it was Déroulède who called upon the Ligue to restore order. Obviously the fault lay within the parliamentary system, "that illegitimate son in whose veins runs the blood of the Royalist Assembly of 1871."

Habert's statement was brief and called on recent events to justify the action at Reuilly. Déroulède, in contrast, used the occasion to review the development of the Ligue des Patriotes since 1882. As he had done in December, with the cry of "the Republic in danger," Déroulède enunciated the ideological foundations for his past actions. Once again, the deed preceded the creed: "Our attempt of 23 February, which one calls the affair of the place de la Nation, is not confined only to that time and place. It dates from much earlier, and its applications are much broader."

To Déroulède, the corruption of the parliamentary regime had been long apparent. Gambetta's promise of a strong presidency and the restoration of Alsace-Lorraine had proven false. Boulangism, too, had failed, and had ushered in a decade of parliamentary decadence and decay—a process that was only accelerated by the Dreyfus Affair:

As for myself I have doubted neither the reality of the crime which was committed in 1894 nor the justice of the sentence which was pronounced. But, if it is possible to have two opinions concerning the treason of Dreyfus, there can be but one opinion about the treason of the government.

For Déroulède, then, what others called the perils of cosmopolitans, anarchists, Jews, Protestants, or capitalists was instead the result of the weakness and corruption of the parliamentary system. The affair of la place de la Nation was a response to thirty years of governmental decay for which the president of the Ligue believed he had found the cause. Good government, asserted Déroulède, ought to guarantee three essential elements: social progress within order, prosperity and stability, and equality before the law. Within this model, social progress can develop only under governmental stability. Lacking the full confidence of its people, the France of 1899 was bankrupt and without a future. Specifically, the instability of the regime had caused "ethical" capital to hide, which created an atmosphere of speculation. "We must arrive at this unfortunate conclusion. The supremacy of money has in all ways dominated our national sovereignty and democracy." Déroulède thus saw his coup as a rejection of mediocrity and corruption, as a popular revolution which rallied the army and the people.

Déroulède turned to the jury and asked that it acquit Habert and himself— not because of their actions, but for the reasons behind those actions. After twenty minutes, the verdict of not guilty was pronounced. "That," declared the leader of the Ligue, "is a condemnation of parliamentarianism and of President Loubet."

The period of calm which had persisted since late February was over. By virtue of foul play or sincere persuasion, a jury had acquitted the nationalists' most important spokesman.[20] If the government had hoped to act firmly, it had failed. The outcome of the trial put Déroulède back into national focus and gave new hopes to other leaders and groups on the Right. Coincidentally, on the same day as a the acquittal, the Court of Appeals announced its recommendation that the Dreyfus trial be reopened. Although the nationalists had missed the opportunity provided in February, and the government in March to May, both sides again were faced with a set of circumstances which called for decisive actions.

Responding to the nationalists' call to celebrate the acquittal of Déroulède and Habert, more than five thousand people jammed the Manège St. Paul on 31 May 1899. Overcome with joy, the crowd listened to speeches by orators who represented a "Who's Who" of the French Right.[21] As they had some six months earlier, the Parisian crowds repeated the rumor that Déroulède was once again the "master of the situation."[22] Overnight, he reemerged as the most popular anti-Dreyfusard leader, a fact annoying to a considerable degree to the master of Fort Chabrol and his partners.[23] Within three days of Déroulède's acquittal, the Ligue des Patriotes proudly announced receipt of more than twenty-five hundred membership applications.[24]

The five days that followed the end of the trial of Déroulède and Habert totally reversed the Left's sense of euphoria and victory which had resulted from the most recent decision in the Dreyfus Affair. Clemenceau spoke gravely of the possibility of civil war, while Jaurés predicted the triumph of reaction.[25]

The leader of the Ligue, however, did not choose to capitalize on the situation. Though exhilarated, Déroulède was exhausted from his trial and left Paris on 3 June for Langely, while the excited royalists sent word to the duke to ready himself again at the border.[26] Déroulède was determined not to repeat his mistakes of February 1899. Although no doubt impressed by the reception that had greeted him, the deputy from Angoulême remained cautious; he was not yet emotionally caught up in the charged atmosphere of anticipation. Déroulède decided that in the future, his actions would be well planned and timed to produce a maximum effect. After all, it was only on 3 June that the Court of Appeals had reversed the decision of 1894 and announced that Dreyfus was to be released from prison in order to appear before a military court in Rennes. The future looked, as a result, even more promising than the present. Moreover, the Ligue was in financial difficulty, and Déroulède needed to build up his capital before proceeding further.[27]

The excitement that followed Déroulède's acquittal was climaxed by the demonstrations at Auteuil on 4 June. That President Loubet had his top hat crushed by the stroke of a cane belonging to a Baron de Christiani was not so important as the fact that the incident toppled Dupuy's government a week later.[28] Déroulède's absence from Paris cleared him of any suspicion in the caning, although several members of the Ligue were arrested for taking part in the nationalist demonstration that ensued.[29] The episode apparently had been provoked by orders from Guérin who, feeling threatened by Dérou-

lède's popularity, was determined to create a national disturbance.[30] The
result was not only the important resignation of Dupuy on 12 June but also
the resumption of daily police surveillance of Déroulède, Guérin, Buffet,
Habert, and others. For the next month, these men were followed day and
night while they were in Paris.[31]

Despite Guérin's initiative, the nationalists looked to Déroulède for leadership in the new and critical situation. The Ligue sensed that Dupuy's
government might not withstand the shock of the series of events which
occurred between 31 May and 4 June, and thus decided to provoke as many
"spontaneous" nationalist demonstrations as possible. Conscious of increased police vigilance, Déroulède did not want the Ligue officially to
sponsor meetings and claim responsibility for street disorders; instead, he
thought that popular manifestations of antigovernment sentiment would be
more effective.[32] Word was passed among *ligueurs* that they were to appear
on the infield grass at Longchamps on 11 June when Loubet was scheduled
to make his second appearance of the racing season. The *ligueurs* were to
react spontaneously to the crowd's cheers for the army and against the
president of the Republic.[33] However, the plans were withdrawn quickly on
the eve of the demonstrations when it was learned that more than thirty
socialist and republican groups were planning to show their support for
Loubet.[34]

Déroulède clearly was not yet prepared for the kind of confrontation
which the situation offered. He was behaving much more cautiously than he
had several months earlier and was sufficiently certain of Dupuy's fate that
he did not think it necessary to send the Ligue into the field. If a governmental crisis was at hand, Déroulède felt no more ready to exploit the situation
on 12 June than he had a week earlier. Again, he preferred to bide his time.

For the moment, the great outpouring of popular support which greeted
Loubet at Longchamps signified that the pendulum was beginning to swing
the other way. The problem for all parties was whether a strong government
could be formed to succeed Dupuy, restore internal order, and surmount the
difficulties that were sure to arise during the new Dreyfus trial. As a result of
this uncertain political situation, the Republic was faced with the necessity
of defending itself and liquidating the problems that had dominated the
events of the past two years. An aggressive posture on the part of the next
government could put the nationalists on the defensive. In that situation,
they would either disintegrate from inactivity or gamble on taking an
imprudent initiative. The great question in mid-June was, could a strong
and forceful government be found which would tackle these problems?

President Loubet, aware of the need to form a staunchly republican government, called first on Poincaré, who declined, and then on René Waldeck-Rousseau to be prime minister. After five days of negotiation, from 17 to 22 June, Waldeck-Rousseau formed a cabinet composed of moderate republicans who were for the most part in agreement with the decision to grant Dreyfus a new trial. The cabinet also included General Gallifet and Alexandre Millerand as ministers of war and commerce, respectively. An arch enemy of Boulanger, Gallifet was most willing to be called out of retirement to join Waldeck-Rousseau. His appointment gave the government a strong minister of war as well as an official who had not previously been involved in the Dreyfus Affair. Millerand's acceptance caused a great crisis of conscience within socialist ranks, but little effort was expended to defeat the government on the issue of socialist participation; few expected the coalition to work.[35]

In a sense, Waldeck-Rousseau's investiture made it easier for the opponents of revision to focus their energies. In the past, the government had been a creature neither of the Dreyfusards nor of the anti-Dreyfusards, but rather a third party whose confidence and cooperation were still to be won. With the formation of the new cabinet, the government and the Dreyfusards were one and the same. Although some greeted the ministry with cries of *"C'est le 16 Mai Dreyfusard,"*[36] Déroulède saw it as symbolic of the nation's continuing division between the "French party and the cosmopolitan party."[37] Thus, the government of *défense républicaine* was, for the nationalists, the "Ministère Dreyfus." Waldeck-Rousseau's policy was to act decisively with the aim of restoring public confidence in the government.[38]

The issue that most demanded wisdom of action and also most threatened the maintenance of public order was, of course, the new trial for Dreyfus at Rennes, scheduled to begin on 7 August. Prior to June of 1899, the affair had evoked periods of excitement interspersed with weeks of calm; in contrast, the summer of 1899 was characterized by intense and continuous political activity that focused solely on the affair. The opportunities for nationalist agitation in the past seemed negligible in comparison with the circumstances offered in July and August. As in the past, however, Déroulède's role as a nationalist leader was not yet clearly defined.

While Waldeck-Rousseau formed his government, the deputy from Angoulême returned to his electoral home and remained there until the Chamber had given its vote of confidence.[39] Déroulède, determined to do nothing that would attract police attention, pondered the possibilities for action, including nationalist demonstrations in Paris on 14 July and in

Rennes in early August.[40] The preparation of a coup with the cooperation of the army was yet another possibility.[41] Many of those who had ridiculed the episode at Reuilly were once more convinced that without Déroulède the nationalist movement had little success.[42] Anti-Semitism remained the greatest single obstacle to unity on the Right. Clearly, Déroulède began to see the need to appeal to those sentiments in order to attract those still loyal to Guérin and to keep his own house in order.[43]

After a delay that was indicative of considerable reflection, Déroulède decided on a course of acion. On the one hand, he would seek to elaborate his ideas by speaking often and vigorously in public; in this way, he would serve as an obvious rallying point for all anti-Dreyfusard opinion. On the other hand, he intended to maintain his control over the Ligue, preserving its independence from others, and holding it ready for political action. As the first step in this process, Déroulède spoke in Angoulême before an estimated ten thousand local supporters, presenting himself for what he called "a vote of confidence."[44]

For the greater part of the summer of 1899, Déroulède maintained his public posture as political critic. Within a day of his Angoulême speech, he introduced a resolution urging a revision of the constitution of 1875.[45] Although his motion was defeated by a vote of 397 to 90, the effect created by his maneuver provoked one of the stormiest sessions of the year. Without realizing it, Déroulède spoke his last words to the legislature: "Il faut donner un maître à cette chambre."[46] A week later, he addressed a large crowd at the Pavillon Bleu in St. Cloud, where he delimited the change in emphasis among the Ligue"s goals. Alsace-Lorraine had not been forgotten, but first France had to be saved.[47]

To many, Déroulède's promise to save France meant that he was planning to repeat the events of 23 February.[48] His closest supporters, however, were fearful that the government would use any pretext to arrest their leader and thus urged him to avoid making compromising appearances at demonstrations, which exposure might prove to be either unsuccessful or dangerous.[49] The appointment of Louis Lépine as prefect of police deepened the fears of Déroulède's supporters. To the nationalists, Lépine's return to Paris from Algeria as a replacement for the weak-willed Charles Blanc was a sign that Waldeck-Rousseau meant to deal firmly with them.[50] As a result, the Ligue abruptly canceled one meeting[51] and curtailed its plans for demonstrating on 14 July, a day on which many expected that Déroulède would act.[52] Instead, Déroulède merely appeared at the statue of Strasbourg and, surrounded by armed bodyguards, spoke briefly to some four hundred *ligueurs*, urging them to remain ready but calm.[53]

Two days later, after the Ligue's failure to demonstrate at Longchamps, Déroulède spoke to a private audience, making the most important declaration of the formation of a Parti républicain plébiscitaire. Reiterating his condemnation of the parliamentary regime, the deputy from Angoulême evoked his Jacobin heritage by calling for a system of government responsive to the will of the people, based on the principles of universal suffrage and plebiscite. Most importantly, however, he continued:

In 1666 Colbert demanded that gentlemen furnish proof of a certain number of quarters of nobility in order to be enrolled in the *livre d'or* of the aristocracy. Let us also demand a certain number of quarters of nationality to permit our countrymen the title of citizen and elector . . . I am neither for a government of *curés* or for a government against the *curés*, but I am less again for a government of Jews and Protestants. . . . My friend Drumont, whose passions I do not completely share, would agree with my statement: *La France aux Français.*[54]

Dedicating the new party to the fight against parliamentary sovereignty, Déroulède proposed that membership be restricted to third-generation Frenchmen. Then he urged his followers: "Prepare yourselves . . . I shall call you to the revolution of honor and order against disorder and dishonesty, the revolution of the soul of France against the spirit of the foreigner."[55]

In addition to the fact that Déroulède's speech included a veritable call to arms, its dominant message was overwhelmingly racist—indeed, anti-Semitic.[56] For a man who many had begun to call a *philosémite*, and who had maintained his political distance from Guérin and Drumont since 1897, the cry of "La France aux Francais" seemed a remarkable change.[57] Yet anti-Semitism and nationalism had been edging closer together at least since August 1898; in a sense, Déroulède's announcement only verified the merging of the two. The pressure of both the reopening of the affair and the sentiment of the *ligueurs* pushed the Ligue des Patriotes to this position. Something new had been created—a movement dedicated to a nation of Frenchmen, defined racially, proclaiming plebiscite to be democracy. Déroulède's appearance on 16 July proved to be the climax of his public addresses in 1898-1899. He had spoken thirty-six times before crowds of a thousand to ten thousand people, a remarkable feat for a man of fifty-three.

Finally, on 19 July he called together his most trusted lieutenants—Barillier, Galli, and Le Menuet—to inform them of his hopes and plans. Though tired, Déroulède was elated by the reception he had received during his recent speech. He thought the moment was near when the Ligue would be prepared to act. There was some talk of absorbing Guérin's organization, although the possibility for such a merger was still slim. The president of the

Ligue des Patriotes urged his subordinates to begin an intense campaign of propaganda aimed at discrediting the forthcoming trial at Rennes, which was three weeks away.[58] He also announced that several days earlier he had received a visit from the Duc de Ramel, a royalist deputy, who had offered him the financial support of his party. In contrast with his attitude in February 1899, Déroulède had declined, saying that for the moment the Ligue had sufficient funds.[59] Although this was not true, his polite refusal implied that the door was still open for future cooperation with the Orléanists. That Déroulède and Habert may even have seen the Duc d'Orléans in mid-July indicates further the possible *rapprochement* between the two groups.[60] Above all, Déroulède stressed that the Ligue must be ready for any action that might be necessary after the trial at Rennes began.

The president of the Ligue stated his intentions of going to Rennes at an unspecified date and, in the meantime, of remaining out of the police's view.[61] The double announcement that the Ligue was to be readied for action and that Déroulède would remain out of sight was a most welcome one to his collaborators.[62] On the one hand, they had been urging caution on their *maître* for more than a month;[63] on the other hand, they had been hard pressed to respond to their militant members' demands for action.[64] Since the middle of June, in fact, the Ligue had not been officially convened for any action or demonstration. Rather, Déroulède had continually urged his *ligueurs* to remain calm and transmitted his orders only by word of mouth.[65]

In the weeks that followed, just as in the month prior to 23 February, Déroulède's whereabouts were known only to a few people other than the police. Residing at his suburban home in Croissy, the nationalist leader met with his friends, several politicians, and with at least a few representatives of general staff. Evidence of these conferences seems to support the notion that Déroulède intended to act in concert with the army. Since his plot was nipped in the bud, it is impossible to be certain. There is, however, sufficient documentation to suggest that the possibility was being carefully considered.[66] He was also given assurances of loyalty by his long-time allies, including the Ligue de la Patrie française, the Jeunesse antisémite, the Blanquists, and the Rochefortists.

As a result of this renewed support, Déroulède began to reorganize the Ligue itself. By 23 July, he decided that its militants would be divided into three groups in the city of Paris.[67] Each of these brigades, as they were called, was to be commanded by Ballière, Barillier, and Foursin, respectively.[68] Although it had not been decided exactly how and when any future action would take place, the brigades were given specific locations in Paris to which they were to report on Déroulède's orders.[69] It was also agreed that at some date, perhaps when Mercier was to testify, Déroulède would make an appearance at the trial. His presence would thus be coordinated with demonstrations to be held simultaneously in Rennes and Paris.[70] It was indicated that Déroulède had the support not only of the Bonapartists but also of Commander Marchand and Generals Mercier and Négrier.[71] It is not surprising, then, that he was reported to have said: "We have the necessary men."[72]

Whereas Déroulède remained generally out of public view after 16 July, the man whom he still considered to be guilty had returned to France to discover that there was in fact a Dreyfus Affair. In early June, Esterhazy had admitted that he had been the author of the *bordereau;* Picquart was released from prison after almost a year of confinement; and national attention was directed to Rennes, and there it remained fixed for the next two months. The Waldeck-Rousseau government was determined to see that Dreyfus received a fair judicial review in an atmosphere of order. In early July, Waldeck-Rousseau, as the minister of the interior—a position he held concurrently with that of prime minister—initiated extensive plans to assure the security of those present at Rennes: troops carefully placed throughout the city, buildings continually searched for bombs, streets closed to traffic, police assigned to guard the more important figures who were to testify. Finally, the Sûreté established a system of communications to enable the minister of the interior to keep up with the most minute details of the trial.[73] Clearly, the government was taking no chances. Waldeck-Rousseau wanted a definitive decision on Dreyfus, one which would terminate the two years of intense agitation that had gripped France.[74]

During the first week of July 1899, Waldeck-Rousseau met with his prefect of police, Lépine, and asked him to determine if the events at Reuilly and Auteuil had been the result of a concerted nationalist-royalist-anti-Semitic effort. In response, Lépine sent the prime minister the reports and testimony that the police had been gathering since 1898.[75] The police had collected material on Déroulède's July speeches and attempts to reorganize the Ligue. Both dossiers reached Waldeck-Rousseau's desk by 8 August, the day after the trial at Rennes began.[76] The prime minister was uncertain about what he should do. Waldeck-Rousseau was aware of and alarmed by reports that indicated the creation of Déroulède's three battalions as well as by the nationalists' intention to create disturbances simultaneously in Paris and Rennes; however, he knew that there was not enough evidence to convict Déroulède of potential conspiracy.[77] Thus, he had either to arrest Déroulède and other anti-revisionist leaders or take the chance that they might not act. Given the nature of the republican defense cabinet, Waldeck-Rousseau was obliged to act first. The problem was to find grounds on which the leaders of the Ligue des Patriotes, anti-Semites, and royalists could be convicted. Rather than indict on the basis of what the nationalists had not yet done, the government had to return to the evidence collected, particularly with regard to the events of 23 February.

Having made this preliminary decision, the prime minister undertook the task of convincing the rest of his cabinet, the president himself, and ultimately the Commission d'instruction, of the wisdom of his decision. Loubet's reluctance was overcome only after the arrests were made on 11 August,[78] but the cabinet gave its support on 10 August as a result of Waldeck-Rousseau's presentation, which overemphasized the royalists' potential danger.[79] A month later, the president of the High Court, Senator Berenger, wrote to the minister of the interior, stating that he found little evidence of the guilt of Déroulède and others who had been charged with conspiracy.[80] Waldeck-Rousseau was apparently in no mood to back down and commissioned a police official named Hennion to prepare a report establishing that a conspiracy did in fact exist among Déroulède, Guérin, and Buffet. The report was a conbination of truth and fabrication; though written in late September 1899, it was predated 4 August.[81] Waldeck-Rousseau perceived his duty to be the restoration and preservation of order and public confidence: "We had to choose between two attitudes—to act or to leave things alone. Between our duty and weakness, we have chosen duty rather than the easier way."[82] The Dreyfus trial had to proceed without the disruption that Waldeck-Rousseau correctly suspected the nationalists were planning. Believing them to be dangerous if left to their own devices and predicting that they would disintegrate under a strong shock, the prime minister decided to act.

On 11 August 1899, at approximately 6:30 A.M., Paul Déroulède was arrested at his residence at Croissy, where he had been staying in relative seclusion for several weeks. At the same time, thirty-four others, including members of the Ligue des Patriotes and royalist and anti-Semitic organizations, were detained. Marcel Habert and the Duc de Lur-Saluces went into hiding, while Jules Guérin locked the doors on Fort Chabrol and prepared to defend himself. Those arrested were charged with "conspiracy aiming at the overthrow of the government."[83] At the announcement of the arrests, prices at the Bourse fell briefly; but generally, as Waldeck-Rousseau had predicted, the reaction was one of calm and relief.[84]

On 14 August, Paul Déroulède was permitted to write to some members of his family. His youngest sister, Jeanne, had been with him at the time of his arrest, but his older sister, Marie Heurtey, knew little of the events that had just taken place:

Here I am, a prisoner of the state again, but this time under the fantastic indictment of plotting with the Royalists. Mr. Waldeck-Rousseau has forgotten that his friend and admirer, Ranc, is the author of a new detective work entitled the novel of a conspiracy.[85]

While the notion of a nationalist-royalist plot either in February or August 1899 was fantastic, the changed attitude of the government produced in each case a different outcome. That Déroulède would have been any more successful in August than he had been in February is doubtful, but what is certain is that the threat he posed as the dominant nationalist leader provoked the government to take a stand or be discredited. In acting with strength and vigor, Waldeck-Rousseau assured a relatively peaceful conclusion of the Dreyfus trial at Rennes. Ironically, however, he had chosen to perpetrate a similar miscarriage of justice by use of the Hennion report to indict Déroulède, Guérin, and Buffet. The arrests of 11 August shattered the power of the Ligue in Paris and, consequently, throughout France. For Déroulède and others, the only hope remaining was that their forthcoming trial before the Senate might serve as a platform from which they could again rouse public opinion and recapture their prestige and power. Yet by the fall of 1899 the mood of France was considerably changed. Waldeck-Rousseau had been correct in surmising that the nation, demanding order and calm, would welcome an end to the Ligue's domination of the streets. He was equally correct in comprehending that the destruction of the Right was the necessary prerequisite for dealing with the Left. It is in this context that "Millerandism" gains meaning and significance and establishes that Waldeck-Rousseau, while operating from bourgeois assumptions was willing to follow paths that his liberal European colleagues a generation later would fear to tread.

NOTES—CHAPTER 9

[1] Charles Tilly and E. Shorter, *Strikes in France*, pp. 321-323.
[2] Pierre Sorlin, *Waldeck-Rousseau*, pp. 320-329.
[3] On 1 March 1899.
[4] APP B/A 108, 25 March 1899.
[5] APP B/A 1,104, 26 March 1899.
[6] APP B/A 1,338, 26 March 1899.

[7] APP B/A 1,103, 13 April 1899.

[8] In obvious reference to the Freemasons.

[9] APP B/A 1,108, report of February 1899.

[10] APP B/A 1,103, May 1899, entitled "Guérin man of political action."

[11] Ibid.

[12] APP B/A 968, 4 March 1899.

[13] APP B/A 968, 4 March 1899.

[14] APP B/A 1,103, 8 March 1899.

[15] APP B/A 1,104, 2 May 1899.

[16] APP B/A 968, 13 May 1899.

[17] APP B/A 1,103, 24 May 1899.

[18] APP B/A 1,103, 26 May 1899.

[19] *Le Drapeau*, 4-11 June 1899. All subsequent quotations from the trial are from this source.

[20] APP B/A 1,338, 30 May 1899, suggesting that the jurors were bribed.

[21] APP B/A 108, 1 June 1899.

[22] APP B/A 1,034, 2 June 1899; AN F[7] 12,456, 3 June 1899.

[23] *La Libre Parole*, 1 June 1899; APP B/A 1,034, 3 June 1899.

[24] AN F[7] 12,451, 3 June 1899.

[25] Sorlin, *Waldeck-Rousseau*, p. 399.

[26] APP B/A 1,034, and B/A 368, 3 June 1899.

[27] APP B/A 1,338 and B/A 1,034, 5 June 1899.

[28] Sorlin, *Waldeck-Rousseau*, p. 399.

[29] AN F[7] 12,870, 5 June 1899.

[30] AN F[7] 12,458, 5 June 1899.

[31] APP B/A 1,034, 9 June 1899.

[32] AN F[7] 12,458, 8 June 1899.

[33] Ibid.

[34] AN F[7] 12,458, 11 June 1899.

[35] Sorlin, *Waldeck-Rousseau*, pp. 399-403.

[36] *La Libre Parole*, 3 June 1899.

[37] *Le Drapeau*, 25 June 1899.

[38] Sorlin, p. 405.

[39] AN F[7] 12,458, 17 June 1899.

[40] APP B/A 1,034, 19 June 1899.

[41] AN F[7] 12,870, 20 June 1899.

[42] APP B/A 1,034, 21 June 1899.

[43] APP B/A 1,034, 22 June 1899.

[44] *Le Matin Charentais*, 19 June 1899.

[45] *Le Drapeau*, 2 July 1899.

[46] APP B/A 1,034, 27 June 1899, telegram.

[47] *Le Drapeau*, 9 July 1899; APP B/A 1,338, 3 July 1899.

[48] BIMS 4,578, manuscript notes of Waldeck-Rousseau referring to Déroulède's speeches in July of 1899: "We had good reason to think that a new attempt was in preparation."

[49] APP B/A 1,034, 24 June and 2 July 1899.

[50] APP B/A 1,034, 24 June 1899; and APP B/A 1,338, 13 July 1899.

[51] AN F[7] 12,458, 24 June 1899.

[52] APP B/A 1,338, 13 July 1899.

[53] AN F[7] 12,870, 17 July 1899.

[54] *Le Drapeau*, 30 July 1899.

[55] Ibid.

56 APP B/A 1,034, 17 July 1899.

57 APP B/A 1,034, 27 June 1899.

58 AN F⁷ 12,451, 19 July 1899.

59 AN F⁷ 12,449, 19 July 1899.

60 AN F⁷ 12,458, report of visitors received by the Duc d'Orléans between 1896 and 1900.

61 AN F⁷ 12,870, 19 July 1899.

62 APP B/A 1,338, 27 July 1899.

63 AN F⁷ 12,464, 3 July 1899.

64 APP B/A 1,338, 19 July 1899.

65 APP B/A 1,338, 25 June 1899.

66 BIMS 4,578, August 1899, manuscript notes; AN F⁷ 12,454, 25 July; 12,449, 26 July; 12,464, 5 August, all 1899.

67 APP B/A 1,338 and B/A 1,034, 23 July 1899.

68 AN F⁷ 12,464, 28 July 1899.

69 AN F⁷ 12,449, 6 August 1899. These details were reported but one day before the commencement of the Rennes trial.

70 AN F⁷ 12,870, 28 July 1899. The demonstration in Rennes was to be led by the Jeunesse antisémite.

71 AN F⁷ 12,449, 28 July 1899.

72 Ibid.

73 AN F⁷ 12,464. This entire carton is devoted to the trial at Rennes.

74 Abel Combarieu, *Sept ans à l'Elysée*, p. 35.

75 Sorlin, *Waldeck-Rousseau*, p. 415.

76 AN F⁷ 12,449, 8 August 1899.

77 BIMS 4,578, manuscript notes of Waldeck-Rousseau; AN F⁷ 12,874, 27 September 1899, Waldeck-Rousseau to Berenger.

78 BIMS 4,578, manuscript note of Waldeck-Rousseau.

79 Sorlin, *Waldeck-Rousseau*, p. 415.

80 AN F⁷ 12,462, 24 September 1899.

81 Sorlin, *Waldeck-Rousseau*, p. 416; AN F⁷ 12,462, Waldeck-Rousseau to Berenger, 2 October 1899. Even with the Hennion report available, it is impossible to prove that a conspiracy existed prior to 23 February 1899. As noted earlier, Waldeck-Rousseau himself became convinced that there were in fact several plans, although he did not come to this conclusion until 1901.

82 BIMS 4,578, manuscript notes of Waldeck-Rousseau.

83 AN F⁷ 12,449, 11 August 1899.

84 AN F⁷ 12,466, 12 August 1899; AN F⁷ 12,449, 13 August 1899, telegram Reinach to Lazare.

85 BIMS 4,578, 14 August 1899, telegram, Déroulède to Mme. Heurtey.

CONCLUSIONS
Toward a New Right

IRONICALLY, THE FIRST victory of the nationalists came less than a year after Déroulède's arrest, trial, and banishment. Paradoxically, though not inexplicably, the victory was electoral rather than revolutionary. Following the banishment of Déroulède, Habert, Guérin, and Buffet, the sole remaining organization on the Right was the Ligue de la Patrie française. Working with the remnants of the Ligue des Patriotes, led by Galli, the nationalists were able to capture more than one-third of the total vote in the municipal elections.[1] At the expense of conservatives and radicals, the nationalists emerged as the largest party in Paris.

The year 1900 was the beginning of what has been called the nationalist revival in France.[2] Coinciding with the last fourteen years of Déroulède's life, the era was one in which France moved increasingly toward the Right and, after 1905, toward acceptance of the necessity of military preparations against Germany. The presence of more than one hundred thousand Parisians at Déroulède's funeral in 1914 on the eve of the war was no less symbolic of the popularity of nationalism than it was of the man who had embodied its spirit for more than forty years.[3] At that moment there was no mention of the ridicule of 23 February 1899. Like many others Déroulède was more respected in death than he had been for the greater part of his life. Yet the nationalist electoral victory of 1900 and the largest public funeral since the death of Victor Hugo attested to the impact and failure of the founder and president of the Ligue des Patriotes.

Just three days before the verdict at Rennes, Waldeck-Rousseau constituted the Senate as the High Court to be convened on 18 September. Of the sixty-one nationalists, royalists, and anti-Semites arrested, only seventeen were indicted, and three of these—Habert, Lur-Saluces, and Guérin—were not yet under arrest. Habert finally surrendered in December, but Lur-Saluces was not brought to trial until 1901. Déroulède and Habert already had been acquitted for "l'affaire de Reuilly," and the defendants could be charged only with general conspiracy. Indicted with Déroulède and Habert were Ballière and Barillier of the Ligue des Patriotes; Buffet, Baron Vaux, de Chevilly, de Frenchencourt, de Sabran-Pontevès, Lur-Saluces, Godefroy of the royalists; and Guérin, Dubuc, Cailly and Brunet of the Ligue antisémitique. In the course of the procedure charges were dropped against all but Déroulède, Guérin, Buffet, and finally Habert, who insisted that he join his leader in whatever fate and history demanded.

Déroulède called the charges against him fantastic, but the Ligue showed less indignation and surprise. With the exception of a brief but violent confrontation between nationalists and "anarchists" on 20 August, there were no demonstrations organized to protest Déroulède's detention. Clearly, with the sudden shift in initiative from the nationalists to the government, those who had been disposed to follow the lead of Déroulède in the past were just as ready to respect the policy of Waldeck-Rousseau.

In the month between his arrest and the decision at Rennes, the president of the Ligue des Patriotes maintained control of his organization by means of a series of coded letters and occasional visits by subordinates to his cell.[4] Urging his followers to remain calm and thus avoid any action that might compromise his position, Déroulède placed his immediate trust in the decision at Rennes.[5] Like his colleagues he hoped vainly that a verdict of guilty might spark a popular movement that would "open our prison doors."[6] Realistically, however, he knew that if his case reached the High Court, he was finished as a political figure.[7] Thus, despite his small hope that the Dreyfus Affair might still save him, Déroulède ordered the Ligue to destroy its files and membership lists and to seek out sympathetic senators with an eye to forming a pro-nationalist bloc in the High Court.[8]

Although this tactic was to be the core of Déroulède's defense, the public reaction to the trial was minimal. After two years of intense activity, a calm atmosphere had settled over Paris. The Dreyfus Affair had come to an end, the leagues were disintegrating, and the public turned its attention to more mundane aspects of life. In short, the crisis was over. The trial of Déroulède, Guérin, and Buffet was simply anticlimactic. Had it taken place a year earlier, Déroulède might have counted on the Ligue to inflame public opinion and thus alter his judicial destiny, but by November 1899 the old fires had burned low. The Ligue itself was already a shadow.[9] Its militant leaders were imprisoned or hiding. Without Déroulède's active leadership, its few important members remaining in Paris were in constant conflict over future action and policy.[10] Consequently, it was decided that the Ligue would initiate no anti-government demonstrations during the trial.[11] It was difficult to recall that a Ligue bearing the same name had contributed to the fall of the Brisson government just a year earlier.

With the exception of Rochefort's *L'Intransigeant*, the Parisian press reacted to the Haute Cour proceedings with a yawn: "One wonders when the lawyers of the accused will begin to discuss anything important."[12] Having grown to hate Guérin, Rochefort decided to support Déroulède as fully as possible, clinging to the hope that a mass demonstration in favor of Déroulède could bring about a change of government and thus halt the trial.[13] Nevertheless, it droned on through forty-four sessions over a period of more than two months, failing to excite the population.

During this lengthy legal procedure, Déroulède spoke on no more than half a dozen occasions.[14] He was among the first group of defendants to testify, taking the stand between 20 and 23 November. At some length he justified his actions of the past two years with the same arguments that he had used in his trial of May 1899. Admitting that he had sought to overturn the parliamentary system, Déroulède proclaimed his faith in republicanism and his hatred of the royalists.[15] He did not testify again until a month later. On 20 December Marcel Habert returned to Paris and presented himself to the police. Though he was not tried until late January 1900, he appeared at the Haute Cour the next day to testify. During the previous week Déroulède had appealed to the judges to be allowed to comment on Habert's courageous act. When he was refused permission, Déroulède grew furious, saying: "I spit my disdain in your faces." Immediately condemned to two years of imprisonment for contempt, the angry defendant replied, "The more I am attacked by you, the more I am honored by France."[16]

Although the ex-deputy from the Charente had not lost his talent for invective, it appears that no one was listening.[17] On 4 January 1900 the Senate voted to acquit all defendants except Déroulède, Guérin, and Buffet. Guérin was sentenced to ten years' imprisonment, and Déroulède and Buffet were to be banished for the same period of time.

The decision came as a surprise to neither Déroulède nor his colleagues in the Ligue. Since late November the leadership, notably Galli and Méry, had been making plans for the Ligue's future in the event of Déroulède's conviction.[18] They decided that the Ligue could be most effective as an electoral organization. Therefore, rather than arrange a series of demonstrations to greet the president's departure from France, they concentrated their efforts on preparations for the municipal elections of 1900.[19] For these elections the committees of the Ligue des Patriotes aligned with those of the Ligue de la Patrie française. The victory that this nationalist coalition produced was due to the efforts and spirit of Lemaître's group rather than to the impact of the Ligue, already in the process of disintegration.[20] While Déroulède's domination over the nationalists can be said to have for a time infused the public mind with his ideals, his political-action organization was crippled by his absence.

Following the trial, Déroulède left Paris for St. Sébastien where, along with Habert, he spent his years of exile. After his outburst in 1901 which led to duels with Buffet and Jaurès, he turned away from active politics and resumed writing. He produced several more volumes of poetry and completed a two-volume memoir of the war of 1870-1871. In 1905 he was amnestied and returned to find that he was in great demand as a public speaker, but not as a politician.[21] Though sponsored in the Académie française by Barrès, he was rejected, which deeply disappointed him.[22]

The Ligue des Patriotes continued to function for a time after Déroulède's departure for St. Sèbastien. By 1902 it was one of fifty organizations that identified themselves as nationalist.[23] Barrès edited *Le Drapeau* for a few years, but soon it, too, became one more limping survivor of a more vigorous past. In 1908 the Ligue des Patriotes was evaluated by the prefecture of police:

If the Ligue des Patriotes did not continue to celebrate yearly anniversaries of the great battles of 1870-1871, it would have no reason to exist. . . . Since his return from St. Sébastien, Déroulède has remained outside of any political-patriotic agitation. One can really now speak of the "ex-Ligue" because its most ardent supporters have long since left its inert organization. It is this which has permitted l'Action française to rally to itself a certain number of these ex-*ligueurs*, particularly those prone to action and agitation.[24]

Not unlike the cavalry of the American West a generation earlier, René Waldeck-Rousseau, prime minister of France, in the fall of 1899 had decided to head 'em off at the pass.[25] The arrest, trial, and subsequent exile of royalist, nationalist, and anti-Semitic leaders of the street leagues were due as much to the fact that there were yet bigger fry on the government's political agenda as to the threat that the new Right posed to the stability of the regime. The strike movement, particularly in Paris in 1898, was indeed a prelude to an increasingly militant series of working-class manifestations which would not only ring in the new century but continue to grow in size and intensity throughout most of the prewar era.[26] The convening of the Senate as the High Court of Justice to try Paul Déroulède, for a generation the apostle of *revanche*, and others for conspiracy was the last act in liquidating the Dreyfus Affair prior to facing what many considered to be an even more serious problem: the "social question."

For the first time in almost a generation, however, Waldeck-Rousseau, the embodiment of bourgeois virtue and respectability, terminated what had been the Opportunist political formula of "no enemies to the right".[27] Indeed, in political terms the affair represented the final legacy of a generation of republican efforts whose energies had been devoted to the avoidance of responding to change. Like the driver of a car low on petrol, the Opportunists preferred abandonment along the roadside to filling the tank. Between 1881 and 1896, with the French economy in a state of stagnation, if not depression, no one noticed the gauge, but in the boom that followed, too much began to change to allow for such a prosaic solution.[28] France was a part of the modern world, and the rapidity of change was becoming more apparent to those who chose to notice. Until the termination of the Dreyfus Affair it was the government, above all, which was blind to the changes swirling about.

Yet such an accusation is unfair. Those who dominated France in 1899 were men whose political consciousness had been formed a generation earlier. Of all those who fell victim to Waldeck-Rousseau's initiatives, Paul Déroulède exemplified the man of 1870-1871.

Then the poet-patriot of France, as he came to be known, was but a youthful follower of Léon Gambetta. Following the dictum "think of it always, speak of it never," Paul Déroulède adhered to the kind of nationalism which was still recognizably Jacobin. By his association with Gambetta, the Adams, and Arthur Ranc, he was a man of the republican Left. Though Déroulède was far from being a systematic or powerful thinker, his concept of France resonated with the traditional themes of Jacobin nationalism. A strong and independent France, politically, socially, and internationally, was the necessary requisite of his nationalism. In 1870-1871 French pride and cohesion had been shattered not just by defeat, but by the Treaty of Frankfort. The "impotent" constitution of 1875 had added insult to injury. Both had to be revised for France to regain her place among nations, among men.[29] *Revanche* and revision became the themes of the young poet's nationalist longings.

Revenge will come, perhaps slowly,
Perhaps with fragility, yet a strength that
    is sure.
For bitterness is already born and force
    will follow
And cowards only the battle will ignore.[30]

Thus armed, Paul Déroulède, poet, revanchist, Gambettist, entered the ranks of what was to become an unofficial, yet loyal, opposition to the politics and person of Jules Ferry. Anti-Opportunism was the trademark of his nationalism in the 1880s. The conjuncture in 1881-1882 of the origins of the depression, the launching of modern French imperialism, and the political dominance of Ferry and the Opportunists with the founding of the Ligue des Patriotes by Paul Déroulède is not without significance. Opportunist policies of social and fiscal conservatism, parliamentary shilly-shallying, and international caution were all greeted by the Ligue des Patriotes as signs of weakness or corrupt manipulation. The Ligue was both nationalist and anti-Opportunist. Given the economic context of stagnation and depression, the calls for *revanche* and revision which the Ligue and Déroulède soon attached to Boulanger's rising star were the slogans of a nationalism whose inspiration was if not 1792, at least 4 September.

Recent work by American historians of France has underlined the essentially reformist and parliamentary nature of the Boulangist movement.[31] The history of the Ligue des Patriotes in the first decade of its existence further substantiates this interpretation. In addition, history offers compelling evidence for maintaining that those in France who called themselves nationalists were drawn to Boulangism precisely because the movement represented their interests in real political terms. Déroulède and the Ligue were anti-Opportunist and so were the Boulangists.

In short, if one looks to the Boulangist episode as the setting in which one nationalism was exchanged for another, or as the place where nationalism slipped quietly over the line separating Left from Right, one will see shadow, not substance. Déroulède and Boulanger, the Ligue des Patriotes and the Comité national, stood well within the context of anti-Opportunist republican revisionism.

The much-heralded counterattack by the minister of the interior, Constans, in 1889 was in reality a spirited defense of status quo politics. The exorcism of Boulangism in the early 1890s was thus the crowning achievement of French conservative liberalism—a triumph whose tenure, however, was short-lived. The Republic that was saved in 1889 was Ferry's republic, and the France of 1896 proved to be a society whose contours were in the process of change.

The last years of the nineteenth century, then, gave rise to three factors whose combined impact significantly altered the political, social, and ideological equilibrium of the Republic of the Opportunists. Economic recovery and industrial growth, concomitant socialist and working-class activity, and the events that made up the Dreyfus Affair produced a new France, one in which the responses and formulas of the 1880s became increasingly anachronistic. Opportunism, though, in the guise of the Méline tariff and the clause "there is no Dreyfus Affair," continued. For some, like Paul Déroulède, the weakness of such a regime, revealed in the scandals of the late 1880s and early 1890s, whcn combined with continued failure to compete with—not to mention obtain revenge from—Germany, illustrated even more strongly the need for change.

Yet such change was not forthcoming. Indeed, the Dreyfus Affair, especially from October 1898 to January 1899, produced governmental paralysis, even as the trade unions' demands for wage increases coincided with domestic and international crises.[32] The subsequent counterattack by the Dreyfusards, especially after Henry's suicide, and the damage inflicted on the honor and integrity of the army ensured a particular dynamic whereby those like Déroulède who had stood for *revanche* and revision and for a version of the Jacobin nation now opposed not just political ineptitude of the government but increasingly the fundamental tenets of the republican regime as well.

The reorganization of the Ligue des Patriotes in the fall of 1898 represented Déroulède's response to the new forces operating on French society. Its reincarnation as a street league violently opposed to the denigration of the instrument of the nation's safety and future, the army, and to the ineffective political and constitutional framework of the regime was the first of three significant steps in the transformation of French nationalism. Déroulède and the Ligue had joined the ranks of a new opposition—one that spoke now not from the Left but from the Right. Déroulède's loyalties, his steadfast belief in the interrelatedness of the issues of *revanche* and revision with the Dreyfus Affair, formed the milieu in which the Ligue's primary political attack from the Right, the abortive *coup d'état* of 23 February 1899, took place. Despite the abject, indeed embarrassing, failure of that moment, for Déroulède and the Ligue the war was not over. The forces of social and economic change had not yet displayed their effects on the soldiers of the Ligue who had taken their battle to the streets.

Convention has it that much of Déroulède's success, if one may use such a term, was due to the unswerving loyalty of his *ligueurs*. It is clear that this remained true as long as the Ligue continued to articulate the concerns of its members accurately. Déroulède's nationalism and antigovernmental stance maintained the political balance between *le maître* and *ligueur*. Yet in the ideological wars that surrounded the affair there loomed the twin specters of imperialism and anti-Semitism—neither of which was appealing to the traditional nationalism of Déroulède but both of which had begun to exercise a powerful appeal on the imaginations of those who belonged to the Ligue.

Thus, while Déroulède scrupulously avoided any political connection with his anti-Semitic rivals, those who belonged to his Ligue were equally attracted by the anti-Semites' appeal. With a membership drawn, by 1899, largely from the Parisian lower middle class, itself buffeted by the gale winds of industrial expansion and socialist militancy, the Ligue's social composition was of a different order from what it had been a decade earlier. Living in precisely the *quartiers* and *arrondissements* of Paris which were undergoing substantial social change as a result of altered industrial and demographic patterns, the members of the Ligue des Patriotes could find considerable solace in an ideology that linked their plight to that of the nation.[33] Modern French anti-Semitism, born of racist doctrines of the 1860s and nurtured on the economic distress of depression and inflation of the eighties and nineties, was subsequently bloated by the diet of the Dreyfus Affair. Although its older leaders, Drumont for example, were past their prime, new ones, like Jules Guérin, posed a serious and popular threat to Déroulède's pretensions as the leader of the anti-Dreyfusard movement.

It is quite clear in retrospect that the social composition of the Ligue des Patriotes was a critical element in Déroulède's decision in July of 1899 to make implicit and incorporate the slogans of popular and racist anti-Semitism. For the Ligue the ideology of nationalism now included the exclusivity of racial anti-Semitism. "France for the French," the words that Déroulède employed as a battle cry as he attempted to militarize the Ligue in a last-ditch effort to stop the momentum of Dreyfus's revision, became his concession to the social and economic needs of his followers.

Similarly, the same Déroulède who had so vociferously opposed the new imperialism of Ferry eighteen years earlier was by 1899 one of the loudest trumpets supporting French forces at Fashoda. The failure of Commander Marchand resulted in his canonization by the Ligue in the spring of 1899. Then, only weeks before the arrest of Déroulède and the disintegration of the

Ligue des Patriotes, the last two steps, social and ideological, in the transformation of the nationalism of the nationalists had taken place.

Speaking now from the Right, flirting with Orléanists over a possible
alliance, and unalterably opposed to the parliamentary Republic that not
only continued to conciliate on matters of *revanche* and revision but was as
well about to grant a new trial to a proven traitor, a Jew, Paul Déroulède
embraced the doctrines of anti-Semitism and imperialism. The new nationalism of the French Right embodied by Déroulède and the Ligue bore little
resemblance—with the exception of the Alsace-Lorraine issue—to the
nationalism that both had represented a decade earlier.

New social, economic, political, and ideological forces had, in the caldron
of the Dreyfus Affair, made their presence known. The result was not so
much, then, a "new" nationalism but rather a new Right, and indeed a new
France.

Yet it is true that men like Déroulède were "nationalists" to the extent that
their political consciousness had been forged a generation earlier, to the
extent that they articulated, in sometimes hyperactive ways, the desire not
just for a restored France but for a nation seeking to fulfill some kind of
historic destiny, however vaguely they interpreted that mission. Too, there
had been reference to the greatness that once was, now in a state of disarray,
but still hoped for in the future. That kind of thinking is not unique to
French nationalists; it is present, it would seem, in much of French thinking
from Rousseau to Camus. But its replacement by ideas of decline and
decadence and the use of biological metaphors of disease and survival signal
a retreat from the universal and historic, from searching for truths that
transcend the movement, to a preoccupation with the particular and the
exclusive. Simply put, by the end of the nineteenth century those who called
themselves nationalists had bowed to a louder appeal of authoritarianism,
racism, and fear whose *etiquette* may have been identified as "nationalist" by
their contemporaries, but whose actions and political ideology were not of
that stripe.

Why, then, should one not hesitate simply to apply the word "new" to the
changed content of the "old" nationalists' ideological baggage and political
actions? Why does it not suffice to perceive a simple and basic shift of
nationalism from the liberal and parliamentary to the conservative and
authoritarian, from, in other words, the Left to the Right?

As has been shown, this *glissement* is surely a pattern that one can not only
perceive but that one can account for as well. Yet the description is only a
political one, and it has been argued that this change was but part of a larger

alteration involving both the sociological and ideological factors as well. When these perspectives are added, it becomes clear that there is more "new" than there is "nationalist" to the new nationalists. Further, the presence of something new on the Right forces us to reconsider more closely the nature of that historical category as well.

It is this latter point that this study at least in part has sought to clarify. What began as an inquiry into the transformation of nationalism in late nineteenth-century France has in fact resulted in the questioning of the relationship of nationalism to the Right as well as the nature of that phenomenon itself. This seeming shift in emphasis, however, ought not lead one to put forth the corollary, namely that if the nationalists became something else, then nationalism itself disappeared from the French stage. The work of Eugen Weber, among others, shows importantly how it was that many who in 1899 or even 1906 would have never mouthed a nationalist phrase were by 1910 full card-carrying members.[34] Indeed, even an elderly Paul Déroulède, whose funeral in 1914 supposedly rivaled that of Hugo, can be thought of as a returning to the fold—this after six years in exile and eight more in eclipse. No, nationalism surely was not displaced; rather it was generalized. And by 1914 there were few, if any, who denied it at least lip service.

But by 1899 there did appear, first in the guise of the Ligue des Patriotes and subsequently in the *camelots* of Action française, a new force on the Right, one committed to violent, direct action, ringing with the slogans of anti-Semitism and preying on the fears of the new lower middle class. This new Right, unlike the conservative liberalism of mid-century, surely unconcerned with the aristocratic niceties of a whole variety of neoroyalisms, had little in the past on which to draw. Rather it was, it is argued, something new, pointing toward the twentieth century.

The appearance in France after 1881 of an increasingly virulent and racist anti-Semitism whose ideological assumptions were advanced first by Gobineau and subsequently by Drumont is a phenomenon of great historical significance.[35] The ideological formulation of anti-Semitism, moreover, was matched by its alarming popular appeal, itself due to the reinforcing dynamic of an important social factor: the migration of eastern-European Jews to precisely those *quartiers* in Paris in which the lower middle class was experiencing the kind of social dislocation which makes radical politics and movements possible.[36] Hannah Arendt has pointed out with considerable insight that, in fact, for France, the convergence of anti-Semitism with the Dreyfus Affair represented the crisis of the modern nation a generation before its time.[37]

That French social structure in the 1930s exhibited less disintegration than that of Germany and Italy at the same time or that French politics came close to chaos before rather than after the Great War ought not blind the historian to the fact that within the French experience there were men and movements called nationalist, whose ideas and actions were better understood to represent a radical, even counterrevolutionary force on the Right. Their eclipse and failure notwithstanding, the men of the Ligue des Patriotes were the first of something whose nature it is crucial to comprehend.

That this occurred at the end of the nineteenth century in France is no accident. The formation of the new Right was part of the evolving historical dynamic which in fact characterized France in that era. The conjuncture of industrial prosperity, urbanization, growing working-class consciousness and militancy, and imperialism, resulted in a society that was increasingly in a state of tension with liberal political and conservative social ideals.

That the emergence of a new Right in France reflects the tensions between politics and society, that in its most fundamental sense it is a reaction to, not modernization, but the increasingly modern features of that society, forces us to revise our understanding of that society itself.

The Third Republic was more than a political regime whose founding between 1870 and 1875 stamped, à la Tocqueville, its enduring features. The social basis of that regime, surely, changed over time, and it was that change, most profoundly a social and economic one, which can in some sense be held responsible for subsequent political alterations. That the Opportunists held on for dear life for as long as they could ought not to be surprising. But their clinging to power and the political games that they invented to do so, which games would be continued by the radicals after 1905, ought not be taken as the necessarily dominant features of French historical reality. For France between 1870 and 1900 that reality was not a static one. France was not the same in 1900 as she had been a generation earlier. The history of the Ligue des Patriotes and the relationship of nationalism to the Right speaks eloquently to this point. Waldeck-Rousseau not only understood this development but acted on it as well. By 1900 the hostility of the extreme Right was directed against the most salient features of modern society: capitalism, socialism, industrialism, egalitarianism, in a word, change itself. Increasingly its ideal became one that resided in the past: in Gambetta, Louis XIV, or the soil of France. The enemy became not just the present but the future, and the relationship of hostility to fear more pronounced. The replacement of traditional French nationalism by a combination of anti-Semitic, racist, and imperialistic doctrines is vivid testimony to these changes. Paul Déroulède, grand *naïf* though he was, articulated through the Ligue des Patriotes the concerns of his generation. And like his rival, Waldeck, he acted on them.[38] It is with some justification that one may say that, indeed, he embodied the spirit, if not the form, of French fascism, before the fact, as defined by Raoul Girardet: "Romanticisme de l'action d'abord, . . . et plus précisement de l'action révolutionnaire."

NOTES—CONCLUSIONS

[1] AN F[7] 12,720, March 1900; Watson, p. 68.

[2] See Weber, *Nationalist Revival*, and Watson.

[3] *Le Matin*, 4 February 1914.

[4] AN F[7] 12,451, 9 September 1899; AD 47,031, 18 September 1899, Thiébaud to Déroulède. Thiébaud was in Brussels and announced that he had come upon a new formula for invisible ink.

[5] AN F[7] 12,451 and APP B/A 1,108, 9 September 1899.

[6] AN F[7] 12,453, 7 September 1899.

[7] AN F[7] 12,453, Lépine to Waldeck-Rousseau, 7 September 1899.

[8] AN F[7] 12,451, 31 August and 13 September 1899.

[9] APP B/A 1,338, 20 October 1899.

[10] APP B/A 1,338, 8 November 1899.

[11] APP B/A 1,338, 10 November 1899.

[12] *Le Matin*, 16 November 1899.

[13] APP B/A 1,338, 31 October 1899. Rochefort's dislike of Guérin was also responsible for the rumor that he had been in the employ of the police during the Chabrol fiasco. AN F[7] 12,458, 14 November 1899.

[14] The stenographic record of the trial is preserved in three sources: the archives of the Senate; the archives of the Prefecture of Police, APP B/A 1,344-1,350, 1899; and *L'Eclair*, 9 November 1899-6 January 1900. *L'Eclair* was the only Parisian daily to publish a record of the complete proceedings.

[15] *L'Eclair*, 20-23 November 1899.

[16] *L'Eclair*, 22 December 1899.

[17] AN F[7] 12,453, prefectural reports, November 1899-April 1900.

[18] APP B/A 1,338, 24 November 1899.

[19] APP B/A 1,338, 26 November 1899; AN F[7] 12,458, 11 December 1899.

[20] AN F[7] 12,719, general reports, January-April 1900.

[21] Déroulède was defeated in his attempt in 1906 to regain his old Chamber seat.

[22] AD 35,017, 17 December 1906, Barrès to Déroulède.

[23] AN F[7] 12,720, reports, 1901-1902.

[24] APP B/A 1,033, 4 December 1908.

[25] Sorlin, *Waldeck-Rousseau*, pp. 320-329.

[26] Tilly and Shorter, pp. 321-323.

[27] Zeldin, pp. 642-646.

[28] Mitchell, pp. 721, 763.

[29] Tint, pp. 37-50.

[30] Paul Déroulède, "Vive la France!" from *Chants du soldat*, p. 3.

[31] Especially Seager, *Boulanger*; Doty, *Barrès*; and Patrick Hutton, "The Impact of the Boulangist Crisis."

[32] Brown, pp. 54-60.

[33] See the author's "The Ligue des Patriotes: The Radical Right and the Dreyfus Affair," *French Historical Studies*, Fall 1974.

[34] Weber, *Revival*; Girardet, *Nationalisme*; and Watson.

[35] Brynes and Pierre Sorlin, *La Croix et les Juifs*.

[36] Chevalier and Roblin.

[37] Hannah Arendt, *The Origins of Totalitarianism*.

[38] Raoul Girardet, "Notes sur l'esprit d'un fascisme francaise," p. 532. See also the judgments of Soucy and Doty on one of Déroulède's companions, Barrès. They disagree on the influence of anti-Semitism and the degree to which Barrès, the Boulangist, was also a socialist. What is clear, however, is that Barrès' career is parallel to that of Déroulède though the novelist did not have the Ligue of the poet! For a discussion of the relationship of Déroulède to fascism and the historiography of the debate concerning the French Right, see the author's discussion, "Rémond, Nationalism and the Right," in *Proceedings of the Western Society for French Historical Studies*, vol. 4 (1977).

SELECTED BIBLIOGRAPHY

1. ARCHIVAL SOURCES

a. Déroulède archives, Langely (Gurat), France; referred to as AD

The Déroulède archive is at present under the care of Déroulède's great-grandnephew, M. Yves Barbet-Massin. The archive consists of approximately sixty thousand pieces. The first fifty thousand are arranged in dossiers containing three hundred letters each. They are almost exclusively letters received by Paul Déroulède from the late 1860s to 1914. They are in six alphabetical series, according to place of receipt. They are numbered consecutively from one to fifty thousand, a feat accomplished by Jeanne Déroulède. The remaining ten thousand pieces consist of Déroulède's manuscripts and notebooks, plus some important financial records of the Ligue des Patriotes in the 1880s. In 1979 Déroulède's papers were given to the Archives Nationales. They are now classed as follows: Archives Nationales, Archives privées, 401 AP.

b. Archives de la Préfecture de Police; referred to as APP

Series B/A

Number	Subject	Years
105-108	Daily Reports	1897-1900
1,032-1,034	Déroulède, Paul	1875-1899
62	Comités Bonapartistes	1870-1889
70	Prince Victor	1894-1899
1,137-1,140	Ligue des Patriotes	1882-1909
905	Presidential Demonstrations	23 February 1899
1,072	Félix Faure, Death of	1899
1,334-1,337	Ligue de la Patrie Française	1899-1902
906	Buffet, André	
1,103-1,106	Guérin, Jules	
316	Fort Chabrol	

169

1,107-1,108	Ligue Antisémitique de France	1889-1900
1,088	Galli, Henri	
947	Bartillier, Edouard	
1,042	Richard, Pierre	
935	Archdeacon, E.	
906	Dillon, C de	
1,245-1,254	Rochefort, Henri	
1,553	25 October 1898	
1,344-1,350	Haute Cour de Justice	1889; 1899; 1902
201	Socialists	1885-1892

Series E/Z

27,33	Castellane, Comte Boniface	
43	Déroulède, Paul	

c. Archives nationales; referred to as AN series F7 (Minister of the Interior)

12,445	Déroulède, Paul	1889
12,449	Ligue des Patriotes	1888-1898
12,450	"	1882-1889
12,451	"	1882-1907
12,452	Ligue des Patriotes	1899
12,453	Haute Cour de Justice	1897-1902
12,454	Nationalists	1899-1905
12,455	"	1899-1905
12,456	"	By department
12,457	"	"
12,458	"	Paris
12,462	Ligue des Patriotes and Ligue Antisémitique	
12,464-12,466	Dreyfus Affair	1894-1906
12,717	Coup d'Etat	23 February 1899
12,720	Nationalists	
12,870	Ligue des Patriotes	1898-1906
12,871	"	1900-1903
12,872	"	1901-1906
12,873	"	1902-1925
12,874-12,876	Déroulède, Buffet	1899-1904
12,877	Ligue des Patriotes	1900-1905
12,926	Habert, Buffet, Lur-Saluces	
12,721	Nationalists	1898-1910

12,719	Action Libérale	
12,459	Ligue Antisémitique	
12,460	"	1890-1907
12,461	"	1890-1907
12,882	"	1897-1901
12,883	Ligue Antisémitique	1901-1903
12,853	Jeunesse Royaliste	
12,861	Royalists	1900-1901
12,539	Felix Faure, Death of	1899
12,540	Emile Loubet, Election of	1899
12,867	Imperialists	1899-1912

    d. Bibliothèque de l'Institut,

       papers of Waldeck-Rousseau; referred to as BIMS (Cartons MS 4,560 to 4,620)

4,576	Papers relative to the Dreyfus Affair
4,577	Papers relative to 1898-1899
4,578	Papers relative to 1899
4,579	" " " "
4,580	Papers relative to 1900
4,600	Papers relative to the police question
4,609	Papers relative to administrative questions

    e. Bibliothèque nationale,

      cabinet des manuscripts; referred to as BN-NAF

      N. A. F. letter by Lucien Millevoye, January 1898

2. GOVERNMENT DOCUMENTS

    Archives du Sènat. *Procès Buffet-Déroulède en Haute Cour*, 18 September 1899 to 23 February 1900.

    Journal officiel de la République française. Débats parlementaires (Chambre des Députés). Sessions ordinaires et sessions extraordinaires de 1892, 1893, 1898, 1899. Referred to as *JO*.

    Préfecture de la Seine, Service de la statistique municipale. *Résultats statistiques du dénombrement de 1896 pour la ville de Paris et le Département de la Seine*, Paris, 1896.

3. NEWSPAPERS

    a. Parisian dailies

      L'Eclair

      L'Intransigeant

      La Libre Parole

      La Patrie

b. Parisian weeklies
   L'Antijuif, 1897-1899.
   Le Drapeau, 1886-1899.
c. Parisian dailies, consulted irregularly
   L'Aurore
   Droits de l'Homme
   L'Echo de Paris
   Le Figaro
   Le Gaulois
   Gazette de France
   Le Journal du Peuple
   La Liberté
   Le Matin
   Le Parti Ouvrier
   Le Petite Bleu
   Le Petite Caporal
   La Petite République
   Le Peuple Francais
   La Reforme
   Le Siècle
   Le Soir
   Le Soleil
   Le Temps
   Le Grelot, 1887 only
d. Provincial newspapers
   Le Matin Charentais

4. WORKS OF PAUL DÉROULÈDE, LISTED CHRONOLOGICALLY;
   PUBLISHER: CALMANN LÉVY, PARIS, EXCEPT WHERE INDI-
   CATED

Déroulède, Paul. *Claude*. 1866.
————. *Juan Strenner*. 1869.
————. *Chants du soldat*. 1872.
————. *Nouveaux chants du soldat*. 1875.
————. *L'Hetman*. 1877.
————. *Pro Patria*, 1879.
————. *La Moabite*. 1881.
————. *Marches et sonneries*, 1881.
————. *Chants patriotiques*, Librarie Delagrave, 1882.
————. *De l'éducation militaire*. 1882.
————. *La Défense nationale*. 1883.
————. *Monsieur le Hulan et les trois couleurs*. Flammarion, 1884.

_____. *Le Premier Grenadier de France.* 1886.

_____. *Le Livre de la Ligue des Patriotes.* George Hurtel, 1887.

_____. *Refrains militaires.* 1889.

_____. *Histoire d'amour.* 1890.

_____. *Désarmement?* E. Dentu, 1891.

_____. *Chants du paysan.* 1894.

_____. *Messire du Guesclin.* 1896.

_____. *Poésies militaires.* 1896.

_____. *La Mort de Hoche.* 1897.

_____. *La Plus Belle Fille du monde.* 1898.

_____. *1870—Feuilles de route.* 1907.

_____. *1870-1871—Nouvelles feuilles de route.* Félix Juvien, 1907.

_____. *Homage à Jeanne d'Arc.* Bloud, 1909.

_____. *Pages françaises.* Bloud, 1909.

_____. *La Patrie, la nation, l'état.* Bloud, 1909.

_____. *Les Parlementaires.* Bloud, 1909.

_____. *L'Alsace-Lorraine et la fête nationale.* Bloud, 1910.

_____. *Qui vive? France "Quand Même!"* Bloud, 1910.

_____. *Corneille et oeuvre.* Bloud, 1911.

5. WORKS ON PAUL DÉROULÈDE AND THE LIGUE DES PATRIOTES

Collier, André. *Les Poésies patriotiques de Paul Déroulède.* Paris: Calmann Lévy, n.d.

Canu, A. H. *La Ligue des Patriotes, son but et son oeuvre.* Paris: Nouvelle Librarie Parisienne, 1886.

Chenu, le Bâtonnier, ed. *La Ligue des Patriotes.* Paris: Plon, 1916.

Claritie, Jules. *Paul Déroulède.* Paris: Félix Juvien, 1883.

Cornilleau, Robert. *Types et silhouettes.* Paris: Bloud, n.d.

Delabonne, Lé. *Déroulède en exile.* Paris: Calmann Lévy, 1900.

Ducray, Camile. *Paul Déroulède.* Paris: Librarie Ambert, 1914.

Falateuf, Oscar. *Cour d'assise de la Seine, Plaidoirie de Falateuf, 29 Mai 1899.* Paris: Macon, Protat Frères, 1899.

Gaffre, L'Abbé. *Le Patriotisme, son incarnation nationale, Paul Déroulède.* Paris: Plon, 1900.

Galli, Henri. *Paul Déroulède.* Paris: Plon, 1900.

Herscher, Sébastien. *Paul Déroulède, patriot chrétien.* Paris: Bloud, 1915.

Lemaître, Jules. *Les Contemporains.* 9th ed. Paris: Fayard, n.d.

Ligue des Patriotes. *L'Almanach du Drapeau.* Paris: Le Drapeau, 1900.

Marat, Léon. *Le Parti de la guerre et la Ligue des Patriotes.* Paris: Calmann Lévy, 1887.

Matter, Florent. *Paul Déroulède.* Paris: E. Sansot, 1909.

Perret, L. *Guerre 1914-1916: Les Mots parlent, le grand voix de Paul Déroulède.*
    Lyon: Bloud, 1916.
Petit, Alexandre. *Paul Déroulède.* Paris: P. Lethielleux, 1947.
Plat, Armand. *Paul Déroulède: Héros national.* Paris: Jean D'Halluin, 1965.
Tharaud, Jean, and Tharaud, Jérome. *La Vie et la morte de Paul Déroulède.* Paris:
    Plon, 1933.

6. CONTEMPORARY ACCOUNTS, MEMOIRS

Barrès, Maurice. *Mes cahiers.* Vol. 3, 1902-1904. Paris: Plon, 1904.
————. *Scènes et doctrines du nationalism.* Paris: Plon, 1925.
Bertrand, Alphonse. *La Chambre des Députés.* 1898-1902. Paris, 1903.
————. *Le Sénat de 1894: Biographies des trois cents sénateurs.* Paris, 1894.
Brisson, Henri. *Souvenirs: L'affaire Dreyfus.* Paris: Plon, 1908.
Burchard, N. *1896-1901: Petites memoires du temps de la Ligue.* Paris, n.d.
Combarieu, Abel. *Sept ans a l'Elysée avec le Président Emile Loubet.* Paris:
    Fayard, 1932.
France, Jean. *Trente ans à la rue des Saussaires: Ligues et complots.* Paris: Félix
    Juvien, 1931.
Freycinet, C de. *Souvenirs 1878-1893.* Paris: Plon, 1913.
Gall, Louis le. *Félix Faure a l'Elysée.* Paris: Armand Colin, 1956.
Lépine, Louis. *Mes souvenirs.* Paris: Bloud, 1929.

7. SECONDARY WORKS

Arendt, Hannah. *The Origins of Totalitarianism.* New York: Meridian Books,
    1964.
Ashley, S. A. "The Failure of Gambetta's Grand Ministry." *French Historical
    Studies,* vol. 9, no. 1 (Spring 1975): 105-24.
Baurdrel, Philippe. *Histoire des Juifs en France.* Paris: Gallimard, 1972.
Bordeaux, Henri. *La Vie au théâtre.* 4th ed. Paris: Plon, 1919.
Brogan, Dennis W. *The Development of Modern France.* Rev. ed. 2 vols. New
    York: Harper and Row, 1966.
————. *French Personalities and Problems.* New York: Harper and Row, 1946.
Brombert, Victor. *The Intellectual Hero: Studies in the French Novel.* Chicago:
    University of Chicago Press, 1964.
Brown, Marvin. *The Comte du Chambord: The Third Republic's Uncompromis-
    ing King.* Durham: Duke University Press, 1969.
Brown, Roger G. *Fashoda Reconsidered.* Baltimore: Johns Hopkins University
    Press, 1970.
Buthman, William. *The Rise of Integral Nationalism in France.* New York:
    Columbia University Press, 1939.

Byrnes, Robert. *Anti-Semitism in Modern France.* New Brunswick: Rutgers University Press, 1950.

Capéron, Louis. *L'Anticléricalisme et l'affaire Dreyfus.* Toulouse, 1948.

Carroll, E. M. *French Public Opinion 1870-1914.* New York: Columbia University Press, 1931.

Chapman, Guy. *The Dreyfus Case.* London: Reynal & Company, 1955.

_____. *The Third Republic of France: The First Phase.* London: Reynal & Company, 1962.

Chastenet, Jacques. *Histoire de la Troisième République.* 7 vols. Paris: Hachette, 1952-1960.

Cheval, René. *Romain Rolland: L'Allemagne et la guerre.* Paris: Presses universitaires de France, 1968.

Chevalier, Louis. *La Formation de la population Parisienne au XIX siècle.* Paris: Presses universitaires de France, 1950.

Clément, Marcel. *Enquête sur le nationalisme.* Paris: Armand Colin, 1957.

Clough, S. *France: A History of National Economics.* New York: Octagon Books, 1964.

Collins, Irene. *The Government and the Newspaper Press in France.* London: Longmans, 1959.

Combe, Paul. *Niveau de vie et progrès technique depuis 1860.* Paris: Presses universitaires de France, 1955.

Contamine, Henry. *La Revanche: 1871-1914.* Paris: Hachette, 1957.

Cornilleau, Robert. *De Waldeck-Rousseau â Poincaré.* Paris: Plon, 1926.

Curtis, Michael. *Three Against the Republic.* Princeton: Princeton University Press, 1959.

Dansette, Adrien. *Le Boulangisme.* Paris: Fayard, 1946.

Digeon, Claude. *La Crise allemand de la pensée francaise.* Paris: Presses universitaires de France, 1959.

Doty, C. Stewart. *From Cultural Rebellion to Counterrevolution: The Politics of Maurice Barrès.* Athens, Ohio: Ohio University Press, 1976.

_____. "Parliamentary Boulangism After 1889." *The Historian* 5 (October, 1971): 250-269.

Duveau, Georges. *La Vie ouvrière sous le Second Empire.* Paris: Gallimard, 1947.

Englund, Stephen. "The Grand Ideal: The Ligue des Patriotes, 1887-1888." M.A. thesis, Colgate University, 1967.

Fisher, H. A. L. "French Nationalism." *Hibbert Journal* 15 (January 1915): 217-229.

Foner, Thomas F. *Jules Ferry and The Renaissance of French Imperialism.* New York, 1966.

Garçon, Maurice. *Histoire de la justice sous la Troisième République.* 3 vols. Paris: Hachette, 1957.

Girardet, Raoul. "L'Idéologie nationaliste." *Revue francaise de science politique* 15 (June 1965): 423-445.

――――. *Le Nationalisme francais.* Paris: Armand Colin, 1966.

――――. "Notes sur l'esprit d'un fascisme français." *Revue francaise de science politique* 5 (July 1955): 529-546.

――――. "Pour une introduction à l'histoire du nationalisme français." *Revue francaise de science politique* 8 (June 1958): 505-528.

――――. *La Société militaire dans la France contemporaine.* Paris: Armand Colin, 1953.

Goldberg, Harvey. *The Life of Jean Jaurès.* Madison: University of Wisconsin Press, 1962.

――――. *The Life of Jean Jaurès.* Madison: University of Wisconsin Press, 1965.

Golob, E. O. *The Méline Tariff.* New York: Columbia University Press, 1945.

Gutkind, G. A. *Urban Developments in Western Europe: France and Belgium.* Glencoe, Ill.: Free Press, 1970.

Halasz, Nicholas. *Captain Dreyfus: The Story of Mass Hysteria.* New York: Grove Press, 1955.

Hutton, Patrick. "The Impact of the Boulangist Crisis upon the Guesdist Party at Bordeaux. *French Historical Studies,* vol. 7, no. 2 (Fall 1971): 226-244

――――. "Popular Boulangism and the Advent of Mass Politics in France." *Journal of Contemporary History,* vol. 11, no. 1 (January 1976): 85-106

Johnson, Douglas. *France and the Dreyfus Affair.* London: Walker and Company, 1962.

Kemp, Tom. *Economic Factors in French History.* London: St. Martin's Press, 1972.

Kessner, Thomas. *The Golden Door.* New York: Oxford University Press, 1977.

Kuznitz, Simon. "Jewish Emigration from Russia," *Perspectives in American History,* vol. 3, 1974.

Lalou, René. *Histoire de la littérature francaise contemporaine.* Paris: Fayard, 1923.

Lefranc, Georges. *Le Mouvement syndical sous la Troisième République.* Paris: Presses universitaires de France, 1967.

Ligou, Daniel. *Histoire du socialisme en France 1810-1961.* Paris: Presses universitaires de France, 1962.

Marrus, Michael. *The Politics of Assimilation.* London: Oxford University Press, 1971.

McManners, John C. *Church and State in France, 1870-1914.* New York: Harper and Row, 1973.

Miquel, Pierre. *L'Affaire Dreyfus.* Paris: Presses universitaires de France, 1964.

Mitchell, B. R., ed. *European Historical Statistics, 1750-1950.* New York: Columbia University Press, 1975.

Muret, Charlotte. *French Royalist Doctrine Since the Revolution.* New York: Knopf, 1933.

Néré, Jacques. *Le Boulangisme et la presse*. Paris: Presses universitaires de France, 1963.

Olivier, Albert. *La Commune*. Paris: Gallimard, 1939.

Ollivier, L. "Les Déroulèdes sous l'ancien régime." *Souvenirs et mémoires*, Vol. 4. Paris, 1900.

Osgood, Samuel. *French Royalism under the Third and Fourth Republics*. The Hague: Martinus Nijhoff, 1960.

Poliakov, Léon. *Histoire de l'antisémitisme*. 3 vols. Paris: Hachette, 1968-1972.

Pulzer, Peter. *The Origins of Political Anti-Semitism in Germany and Austria*. New York: John Wiley, 1969.

Reinach, Joseph. *Histoire de l'affaire Dreyfus*. 7 vols. Paris: Charpentier et Fasquelle, 1903-1911.

Rémond, René. *The Right in France: From 1815 to DeGaulle*. Philadelphia: University of Pennsylvania Press, 1968.

Roblin, Michel. *Les Juifs de Paris*. Paris: Picard, 1952.

Rothney, John. *Bonapartism after Sedan*. Ithaca: Cornell University Press, 1969.

Rougerie, Jacques. "Remarques sur l'histoire des salaires à Paris au XIX siècle." *Le Mouvement sociale*, no. 70 (April-June 1968).

Sacrey, Françisque. *Trente ans du théâtre*. Vol. 7. Paris, 1900.

Scott, Joan. *The Glassworkers of Carmaux*. Cambridge, Mass.: Harvard University Press, 1975.

Seager, Frederich. "The Alsace-Lorraine Question in France, 1870-1914." In *From Ancien Régime to Popular Front*, edited by Charles K. Warner. New York: Columbia University Press, 1969.

Sedgwick, Alexander. *The Ralliement in French Politics*. Cambridge, Mass.: Harvard University Press, 1965.

Seignobos, Charles. *L'Evolution de la Troisième République*. Paris: Hachette, 1921.

Shapiro, David, ed. *The Right in France, 1890-1919*. St. Anthony's Papers, no. 13. London: 1962.

Silvera, Alain. *Daniel Halery: A Gentleman Commoner in the Third Republic*. Ithaca: Cornell University Press, 1966.

Soltan, Roger. *French Political Thought in the Nineteenth Century*. New Haven: Yale University Press, 1931.

Sorlin, Pierre. *La Croix et les juifs*. Paris: Grasset. 1967.

————. *Waldeck-Rousseau*. Paris: Armand Colin, 1966.

Soucy, Robert. *Fascism in France: The Case of Maurice Barrès*. Berkeley: University of California Press, 1972.

————. "The Nature of French Fascism." *Journal of Contemporary History* 1 (1966): 27-56.

Sternhell, Zeev. "Barrès et la gauche: du Boulangisme à *la Cocarde*." *Le Mouvement social*, no. 75 (April-June 1971), pp. 77-130.

Swart, Koenraad. *The Sense of Decadence in Nineteenth Century France.* The Hague: Martinus Nijhoff, 1964.

Szajkowski, Zosa. "The Growth of the Jewish Population in France," *Jewish Social Studies*, vol. 3, no. 3 (October 1946).

_____. *Poverty and Social Welfare among French Jews 1800-1880.* New York, 1954.

Tannenbaum, Edward. *The Action Francaise.* New York: John Wiley Sons, 1962.

Thomas, Marcel. *L'Affaire sans Dreyfus.* Paris: Fayard, 1961.

Tilly, Charles, and Shorter, E. *Strikes in France.* New York: Cambridge University Press, 1975.

Tint, Herbert. *The Decline of French Patriotism 1870-1914.* London: Weidenfeld & Nicholson, 1964.

Villiers, Marjorie. *Charles Péguy.* New York: Harper and Row, 1964.

Weber, Eugen. *L'Action française.* Palo Alto, Calif.: Stanford University Press, 1962.

_____. *The Nationalist Revival in France 1905-1914.* Los Angeles: University of California Press, 1959.

_____. "The French Right." In *European Right*, edited by Eugen Weber and Hans Rogger. Berkeley, California: University of California Press, 1966.

Williams, Roger. *Henri Rochefort: Prince of the Gutter Press.* New York: Scribners, 1967.

Wohl, Robert. *French Communism in the Making.* Palo Alto: Calif.: Stanford University Press, 1966.

Zeldin, Theodore. *France 1848-1945: Love, Ambition, and Politics.* Vol. 1. New York: Cambridge University Press, 1974.

Index

179